D1681236

Reforming Principal Preparation at the State Level

Providing an in-depth look at the processes, pitfalls, and successes that can emerge from major education reform efforts at the state level, this volume covers the full policy change cycle in the development and transformation of Illinois principal preparation programs. Offering perspectives from the major stakeholder groups involved in transforming Illinois principal preparation—school districts, universities, state education agencies, teacher unions, and professional associations—this book documents the three policy stages: policy formation, implementation, and improvement. As a national award-winning leader in principal preparation policy and practice, Illinois serves as a model for effective policy reform. Grounded in a strong theoretical framework, this volume provides candid observations and lessons learned for researchers, scholars, higher education faculty, distirct officials, and policymakers.

Erika Hunt is Senior Researcher and Policy Analyst for the Center for the Study of Education Policy at Illinois State University, USA.

Alicia Haller is Project Director at the DuPage Regional Office of Education, USA.

Lisa Hood is Senior Researcher and Policy Analyst for the Center for the Study of Educational Policy at Illinois State University, USA.

Maureen Kincaid is Professor of Education at North Central College, USA.

Routledge Research in Education Policy and Politics

The Routledge Research in Education Policy and Politics series aims to enhance our understanding of key challenges and facilitate on-going academic debate within the influential and growing field of Education Policy and Politics.

Books in the series include:

Education and the Production of Space
Political Pedagogy, Geography, and Urban Revolution
Derek R. Ford

Pedagogy in Poverty
Twenty Years of Curriculum Reform in South Africa
Ursula Hoadley

The PISA Effect on Global Educational Governance
Louis Volante

Academies and Free Schools in England
A History and Philosophy of the Gove Act
Adrian Hilton

Risk Society and School Educational Policy
Grant Rodwell

Neoliberalism and Market Forces in Education
Lessons from Sweden
Magnus Dahlstedt and Andreas Fejes

Reforming Principal Preparation at the State Level
Perspectives on Policy Reform from Illinois
Edited by Erika Hunt, Alicia Haller, Lisa Hood, and Maureen Kincaid

For more information about this series, please visit: www.routledge.com/Routledge-Research-in-Education-Policy-and-Politics/book-series/RREPP

Reforming Principal Preparation at the State Level

Perspectives on Policy Reform from Illinois

Edited by Erika Hunt, Alicia Haller, Lisa Hood, and Maureen Kincaid

Foreword by Arne Duncan, former US Secretary of Education

Routledge
Taylor & Francis Group
NEW YORK AND LONDON

First published 2019
by Routledge
711 Third Avenue, New York, NY 10017

and by Routledge
2 Park Square, Milton Park, Abingdon, Oxon, OX14 4RN

Routledge is an imprint of the Taylor & Francis Group, an informa business

© 2019 Taylor & Francis

The right of Erika Hunt, Alicia Haller, Lisa Hood, and Maureen Kincaid to be identified as editors of this work has been asserted by them in accordance with sections 77 and 78 of the Copyright, Designs and Patents Act 1988.

All rights reserved. No part of this book may be reprinted or reproduced or utilised in any form or by any electronic, mechanical, or other means, now known or hereafter invented, including photocopying and recording, or in any information storage or retrieval system, without permission in writing from the publishers.

Trademark notice: Product or corporate names may be trademarks or registered trademarks, and are used only for identification and explanation without intent to infringe.

Library of Congress Cataloguing-in-Publication Data
A catalog record for this book has been requested

ISBN: 978-1-138-29922-1 (hbk)
ISBN: 978-1-351-09809-8 (ebk)

Typeset in Sabon
by Apex CoVantage, LLC

Contents

Illustrations	vii
Foreword	viii
THE HONORABLE ARNE DUNCAN, US SECRETARY OF EDUCATION (2009–2015)	

SECTION 1
Policy Formation: Theory in Action — 1

1 Setting the Stage for State Policy Change Involving Principal Preparation in Illinois: The What and How — 3
   ALICIA HALLER, ERIKA HUNT, AND DEBRA BARON

2 Applying the Advocacy Coalition Framework to the Policy Change Process in Illinois — 28
   ALICIA HALLER, ERIKA HUNT, AND DEBRA BARON

3 Policy Transfer from Local to Statewide: Scaling Evidence-Based Principal Preparation Practices in Illinois — 62
   DIANE RUTLEDGE AND STEVE TOZER

4 Durable Levers for State Policy Change: Independent Policy Entrepreneurs — 89
   LYNNE HAEFFELE AND JIM APPLEGATE

SECTION 2
Policy Implementation: From Theory to Practice — 123

5 The Role of Policy Networks to Support Policy Diffusion through Implementation: A Multi-case Study of Four Universities Working Together — 125
   LISA HOOD, ERIKA HUNT, ALICIA HALLER, AND DEBRA BARON

6 Modeling Innovation into Principal Preparation: The Illinois Partnerships Advancing Rigorous Training (IL-PART) Project 150
KATHY BLACK, MAUREEN KINCAID, KATHLEEN KING, PAMELA BONSU, MELISSA BROWN-SIMS, AND MATTHEW CLIFFORD

SECTION 3
Policy Improvement and Sustainment 185

7 Monitoring Implementation: Findings and Implications from a Statewide Study 187
BRADFORD R. WHITE, AMBER STITZIEL PAREJA, HOLLY HART, MICHELLE HANH HUYNH, BRENDA K. KLOSTERMANN, AND JANET K. HOLT

8 Designing a Continuous Improvement Process to Monitor Program Effectiveness for Illinois Principal Preparation Programs 212
JOSEPH PACHA, LISA HOOD, AND KRISTINE SERVAIS

9 Statewide Collaborations for Improvement: Lessons Learned from the State of Illinois 231
MICHELLE D. YOUNG AND MARCY A. REEDY

Notes on Contributors 244
Index 256

Illustrations

Tables

1.1	Nine-Point Template for Judging the Quality of School Leadership Programs	6
1.2	Program Approval Process Overview for Principal Endorsement	14
1.3	Principal Preparation Timeline for Illinois	16
2.1	Forums to Discuss Principal Preparation Prior to Passage of Public Act 096-0903	41
4.1	Number of Type 75 Certificates Compared with Principal Vacancies	103
4.2	Supply and Demand of Administrative Positions in Illinois, 2008 ISBE Supply and Demand Report	103
4.3	Crosswalk of PSEL Standards, ISLLC Standards, and SREB Critical Success Factors	107
8.1	Logic Model—Principal Preparation Program Continuous Improvement and Review Process	217
8.2	Leadership Program Data Collection Matrix	222

Figures

2.1	Diagram of the Advocacy Coalition Framework	30
6.1	IL-PART Graduate Hires: By Position	160
6.2	Status of Certification Attainment by Internship Type	161
7.1	District Partner Responses	190
7.2	Enrollments in Initial Year of Implementation, in 2014–2015, and Needed for Sustainability ($n = 16$)	191
7.3	Course Coverage of Instructional Leadership, School Improvement, Data Literacy and Analysis, and Organizational Management, by Institution	193
7.4	Course Coverage of Special Education, Early Childhood Education, and English Language Learners, by Institution	194
7.5	Graduate Data Collected by Principal Preparation Programs	195
8.1	Principal Preparation Program Continuous Improvement Process (PPP CIP) Diagram	219

Foreword

During my time as US Secretary of Education, I was lucky enough to travel the country and explore what's working and what's not in our nation's schools. Despite the well-reported challenges facing educators today, I remain optimistic. I've been fortunate to visit and explore nearly every type of school: high performing, low performing, and everything in between. Those of us who have worked in district administration know what works: great principals and great teachers. We've seen what's possible, and a solid body of research supports this claim. The challenge is in translating those findings into effective practices that systemically improve preparation programs so that we have great teachers and leaders in every school.

While research has demonstrated a strong correlation between family income and student outcomes, we have also seen schools that have beaten those odds. They have succeeded in transcending negative projections for low-income students and provided us with evidence that a child's level of academic performance does not have to be limited by their zip code. For every school that has a 65 percent dropout rate, there is another school serving a similar population, producing a 95 percent graduation rate, with 95 percent of graduates going on to college. So what is the difference? Previous research has suggested teacher quality is the key. In fact, there is little doubt that instructional quality is the number one school-level factor influencing student performance.[1] However, an exclusive focus on the individual classroom ignores the need for scaling best practices and supporting positive elements of a school-wide learning environment. The principal acts as a "multiplier of effective teaching practice"[2] that can transform a school from having isolated pockets of excellence in a few classrooms to one that demonstrates school-wide success. This comes as no surprise. In education, as in nearly every other industry, leadership matters tremendously.

Simply put, there are no good schools in our country without great principals. This is not just a cliché. Great schools with ineffective principals simply don't exist. There are also no documented cases of troubled schools being turned around without the intervention of a powerful school leader.[3] Many other factors may contribute to such turnarounds, but leadership is the catalyst. Additionally, I found during my time in Chicago that quite the opposite is true as well: that ineffective leaders can negatively impact a school. Districts cannot afford to rest on their laurels. They may find themselves in a situation where a great principal has built a successful school slowly over 8, 10, or 12-plus years, but without a highly competent principal as successor, that school can decline dramatically in as little as six months. If at the end of the day our nation's 95,000 schools each had a great principal, we would have nothing but high-performing schools.

Great principals attract and nurture great teachers and others who contribute time and talent to the school. Contrary to popular belief, most leaders are not born to lead. They are developed intentionally and authentically, over time. Therefore, equipping principals with the knowledge, skills, and abilities necessary to take excellence to scale is essential to school success. Efforts to improve their preparation represents an excellent return on investment. But building a strong program that consistently produces great principals isn't easy. I've always said the best ideas rarely come from Washington. In fact, the best ideas for improving schools are almost always generated by the excellent principals, teachers, and others working at the local level. The challenge for policymakers is how to elevate the voice of great educators so that their practices and ideas are translated into policies that address the delicate balance between the need for standardization and the flexibility necessary to bring best practices to scale. This book describes the collaborative efforts in Illinois, by a diverse set of educators and other stakeholders, to develop innovative state and local policies aimed at creating rigorous principal preparation programs that produce school leaders capable of transforming schools.

Like many books before it, this policy change story could have been told from the point of view of policymakers who drafted the legislation or by researchers who provide a descriptive history through document analysis. However, those approaches often ignore or misrepresent the importance and complexity of ongoing relationships, discussions, strategies, levers of change, and negotiations that take place over time and result in meaningful change. The reform efforts in Illinois involved a multitude of educators and other stakeholders. Therefore, the editors felt it essential to tell the story from a wide variety of perspectives by those who were deeply engaged in the change process. The reach of those involved in the process was vast and included my involvement as CEO of the Chicago Public Schools. Collectively, the stakeholders involved left their mark on principal preparation in Illinois. The innovative state policy that culminated from those efforts has been recognized nationally, by the Council of Chief State School Officers, the Education Commission of the States, the National Conference of State Legislators, the National Governors Association, and the US Department of Education.

Individual actors involved in the policy change process may have differing views on the impact of the reforms on the education system in the long run. However, this book shines a light on the wide variety of motivations, actions, intentions, and strategies employed by those involved in the improvement efforts and describes how a disparate group of stakeholders came together around a common goal: to ensure all schools in Illinois are led by well-trained, effective principals who create the conditions necessary to improved outcomes for each and every student.

This book captures the complexity, nuisances, missed opportunities, and challenges that were ultimately part of the path to success. Real change is never simple or easy, and it is often messy. Efforts began in 2005 and continue today as part of an ongoing improvement process. Credit for the success of this effort belongs to all of the stakeholders, representing a wide variety of organizations, who contributed their time and talent to ensure aspiring leaders are provided with rigorous and relevant training that prepares them to take on the challenges of twenty-first-century schools. Their engagement has proven to be both a catalyst for change and the key to its sustainability. There is a lot that can be learned from what transpired in Illinois. The lessons learned in this book can be used to inform principal preparation improvement efforts by other policymakers, practitioners, and researchers across the country.

The Honorable Arne Duncan
US Secretary of Education (2009–2015)

Notes

1. L. Darling-Hammond. "Teacher Quality and Student Achievement." *Education Policy Analysis* 8, no. 1 (2000).
2. P. Manna. *Developing Excellent School Principals to Advance Teaching and Learning: Considerations for State Policy*. New York: The Wallace Foundation, p. 40, 2015.
3. K. Leithwood, K. Seashore-Louis, S. Anderson, and K. Wahlstrom. *How Leadership Influences Student Learning*. New York: The Wallace Foundation, 2004.

Section 1
Policy Formation
Theory in Action

1 Setting the Stage for State Policy Change Involving Principal Preparation in Illinois
The What and How

Alicia Haller, Erika Hunt, and Debra Baron

This chapter is intended to provide an overview of the policy change process that resulted in dramatic improvements to principal preparation in Illinois. The chapter explores how a broad group of stakeholders was engaged for more than a decade in this effort. Further, the chapter provides descriptions of both *how* the change process occurred and ultimately *what* changes were included in the new state policy.

The chapter was developed by reviewing various documents dating back to the beginning of the reform effort in 2000, which included committee and task force meeting minutes, final reports, and other artifacts from various collaborations. In addition, the summary incorporates reflections from twenty interviews with key individuals who were deeply involved in the reform efforts. The chapter includes accounts of how the policy change process progressed through the regular interactions of advocacy coalitions that operated within the education policy arena.

Background

Since 2000, Illinois has been working at the forefront of innovation and improvement in principal quality. Policymakers and practitioners worked together to pursue an ambitious goal to strengthen principal preparation. This was a vital goal, as research has demonstrated the powerful impact principals had on school improvement and student learning (Bryk et al. 2010; Grissom, Kalogrides, and Loeb 2015; Leithwood et al. 2010; Moore 1995; Spillane 2009; Waters, Marzano, and McNulty 2003).

In fact, empirical research found that principals play a vital role in three main areas: (1) recruiting, developing, and retaining effective teachers; (2) creating a school-wide culture of learning; and (3) implementing a continuous improvement plan aimed at increasing student achievement (Branch, Hanushek, and Rivkin 2013; Clifford, Behrstock-Sherratt, and Fetters 2012; Clotfelter, Ladd, and Vigdor 2007; Darling-Hammond et al. 2007; Marzano, Waters, and McNulty 2005; Murphy et al. 2006; Seashore-Lewis et al. 2010).

Research established that principals are second only to teacher quality in terms of influence on student achievement, and the impact of leadership is greatest in schools with the greatest need (Branch, Hanushek, and Rivkin 2013; Clifford, Behrstock-Sherratt, and Fetters 2012; Clotfelter, Ladd, and Vigdor 2007; Darling-Hammond et al. 2007; Marzano, Waters, and McNulty 2005; Murphy et al. 2006; Louis et al. 2010).

While it has been widely accepted that instructional quality is the single most important school-based factor leading to student achievement, researchers have also found that effective school leadership is crucial to scaling quality instruction and other practices school-wide (Darling-Hammond 2000; Bryk et al. 2010). This idea was reiterated in a recent report that described the school principal as a "powerful multiplier of effective teaching and leadership practices in schools" (Manna 2015, 7).

The principal's role in scaling was found to be essential to improvement efforts. Studies provided evidence of this multiplying effect, as they found that the principal's influence accounts for about one-quarter of school-level variation in student achievement (Leithwood et al. 2004; Waters, Marzano, and McNulty 2003). Additionally, a meta-analysis revealed that increasing leadership effectiveness by one standard deviation could lead to a ten-percentile point gain in student achievement (Waters, Marzano, and McNulty 2003).

Policy Change Process: How Change Occurred

The change process that took place in Illinois involving improvements to principal preparation occurred over time, taking more than a decade to culminate in a revised statute and regulations. The initial phase of policy change, involving problem identification, was informed primarily by research and practice. Highlighting the need for improvement, scholars had long criticized principal preparation programs for providing programs that did not adequately prepare leaders for the realities of modern schools.

Critics argued that traditional preparation programs—those that relied primarily on coursework as the main mechanism of knowledge transmission—failed to link theory with practice, did not reflect the complexities and demands of schools, and largely ignored research on effective leadership development (Copland 1999; Elmore 2000; Institute for Educational Leadership 2000; McCarthy 1999; Murphy and Vriesenga 2004). For that reason, principal preparation programs in Illinois began exploring their own practices and sought to improve their programs even before 2000.

It is impossible to pinpoint with accuracy the exact moment at which various Illinois stakeholders began their efforts to improve principal preparation. Isolated or scattered efforts at individual universities or within specific districts may have a much longer history with improvement efforts. However, through a project funded by the Wallace Foundation, a statewide coordinated effort began in 2000.

A grant awarded to the Center for the Study of Education Policy (CSEP) at Illinois State University allowed the organization to launch the Illinois State Action for Education Leadership Project (IL-SAELP), which engaged several preparation programs in voluntary improvement efforts through regular meetings held throughout Illinois. Recognizing the need for additional structure and broader stakeholder engagement, in 2001 CSEP created the Illinois Consortium for Education Leadership to serve as the first IL-SAELP advisory body.

The group of thirty-five members included representatives from state agencies, statewide professional associations, business leaders, districts, and universities. To provide a baseline of data from which to operate, over the course of three years IL-SAELP staff conducted research regarding the condition of school leadership preparation and development in Illinois. In its culminating report (Illinois Consortium for Education Leadership 2004), the Consortium outlined an action plan for improvements by state agencies, as well as for individual programs.

Shortly thereafter, in 2005, a scathing report by former president of Teachers College at Columbia University, Arthur Levine, proved to be a national catalyst for increased attention to the preparation of school leaders. The Levine Report, as it became known, scrutinized university principal preparation programs based on a four-year study of leadership programs at schools of education across the country.

The study found that the majority of principal preparation programs suffered from curricular disarray, low admissions and graduation standards, weak faculty with no experience in schools, inadequate clinical instruction, inappropriate degree structures, and a lack of research-based elements. Levine described the work of education leadership programs as "a race to the bottom" that existed as "a competition among school leadership programs to produce more degrees faster, easier, and more cheaply" (Levine 2005, 24).

None of the over 500 schools or departments of education offering degree-granting graduate programs leading to principal credentials included in the study was found to be considered exemplary, and only a very small number were considered strong programs. The release of the Levine Report depicted the dismal condition of principal preparation across the country and increased a sense of urgency for faculty to improve their training programs. The report included nine criteria for judging principal preparation programs (see Table 1.1).

Table 1.1 Nine-Point Template for Judging the Quality of School Leadership Programs

Purpose	The program's purpose is explicit, focusing on the education of practicing school leaders; goals reflect the needs of today's leaders, schools, and children; and the definition of success is tied to student learning in the schools administered by the program graduates.
Curricular Coherence	The curriculum mirrors program purposes and goals. The curriculum is rigorous, coherent, and organized to teach the skills and knowledge needed by leaders at specific types of schools and at the various stages of their careers.
Curricular Balance	The curriculum integrates the theory and practice of administration, balancing study in university classrooms and work in schools with successful practitioners.
Faculty Composition	The faculty includes academics and practitioners who are expert in school leadership, up to date in their field, intellectually productive, and firmly rooted in both the academy and the schools. The faculty's size and fields of expertise are aligned with the curriculum and student enrollment as a whole.
Admissions	Admissions criteria are designed to recruit students with the capacity and motivation to become successful school leaders.
Degrees	Graduation standards are high and the degrees awarded are appropriate to the profession.
Research	Research carried out in the program is of high quality, driven by practice, and useful to practitioners and/or policymakers.
Finances	Resources are adequate to support the program.
Assessment	The program engages in continuing self-assessment and improvement of its performance.

Source: Levine (2005, 13).

In response to the Levine Report, in August 2005 the Illinois Board of Higher Education (IBHE) awarded CSEP a grant to convene the Commission on School Leader Preparation in Illinois Colleges and Universities. This marked a critical shift in the efforts to improve leadership preparation in Illinois, as it was the first time a group of stakeholders was convened by a state agency. The twenty-six-member Commission comprised representatives from numerous education stakeholder groups and undertook a comprehensive analysis of the state of affairs in Illinois educational administration programs at both public and private institutions.

The Commission met several times and brought in national experts, including Arthur Levine. In addition, the Commission was presented with findings from accreditation reviews conducted by the National Council for Accreditation of Teacher Education (NCATE). In a final report presented to IBHE in August 2006 (Commission on School Leader Preparation in Illinois Colleges and Universities 2006), the Commission included a summary of data utilized in their analysis and a list of recommendations. The Commission's culminating report has been described as the Illinois Levine Report, as its findings regarding local program quality mirrored the national findings in the original Levine Report.

Because the Commission was funded and commissioned by IBHE, ownership and support for its work was mainly found in the arena of higher education. Further, the Commission report focused primarily on conceptual recommendations aimed at institutions of higher education and did not include an action plan for how the state could develop comprehensive policy changes. While IBHE's role in convening the group was a substantial shift in terms of increasing the political will for change, the Commission lacked the full force of the regulatory power involving educator licensure that was the purview of the Illinois State Board of Education (ISBE).

In 2006, ISBE came under the direction of a new state superintendent. The new state superintendent developed a close working relationship with the executive director of IBHE, and collaboratively called for a legislatively commissioned task force charged specifically with developing strategies for the implementation of the Commission's recommendations. Bringing the combined political capital of the two regulatory agencies together made the topic of leadership preparation a real priority in the state.

The Illinois School Leader Task Force was convened in 2007 after the Illinois General Assembly unanimously passed resolutions supporting its creation (HJR66 and SJR56). ISBE, IBHE, and the Office of the Governor jointly appointed the twenty-eight members, representing public and private universities, public school districts, teacher unions, professional associations, both chambers of the state legislature, ISBE, and IBHE. Staffing for the Task Force was provided by CSEP, IBHE, and ISBE. The design of the Task Force as a co-commissioned effort by both education agencies set the course for the future success of this work.

Agenda setting for the Illinois School Leader Task Force was the responsibility of the chair, with input from the members. The Task Force began with a tension between two matters of fact: (1) strong principals can have a significant impact on student learning, and (2) learning outcomes in Illinois schools as a whole were unsatisfactory. Therefore, the Task Force organized its work around one question: how to prepare principals who could routinely improve student learning in Illinois schools.

The Task Force met in person six times between 2007 and 2008. Members reviewed existing and emerging research and data on principal preparation practices and outcomes. Despite the variety of perspectives and roles represented, the Task Force arrived at a consensus and developed three overarching recommendations involving (1) state policy, (2) university/district partnerships, and (3) principal preparation and assessment. Specifically, the Task Force recommended that the state should:

1. Enact rigorous standards for certification that provide a comprehensive approach to leadership development by aligning formal preparation programs with early career mentoring, ongoing professional development, and master principal designation;
2. Require universities to formally engage school district(s) in the design, delivery, and assessment of principal preparation programs;
3. Design an approval and oversight system to ensure programs demonstrate that they develop and rigorously assess the aspiring principals' competencies most likely to improve student learning in PK-12 schools.

The final report by the Illinois School Leader Task Force detailed the proposed systemic changes that aligned to the overarching recommendations (Illinois School Leader Task Force 2008). In response to the report, the General Assembly directed ISBE and IBHE to work collaboratively with Task Force members and other stakeholders in the development of new requirements for a standards-based program design and a state approval process and oversight/reporting system. That directive led to the establishment of the Illinois School Leader Redesign Committees, convened by ISBE and IBHE.

The committees were charged with developing action plans in five key areas of improvement: (1) school leadership standards; (2) leadership certification and endorsements; (3) school/university partnerships and selection criteria; (4) residencies and internships; and (5) assessments of candidates and graduates. Each committee included a member of the Task Force, and representation from both higher education and K-12 public school districts. Membership totaled fifty representatives from public and private colleges and universities, school districts, regional offices of education, teachers' unions, professional associations, and research organizations.

From 2008 to 2009, four Redesign Committee meetings were held in various locations around the state in an effort to encourage participation from all geographic regions. In addition, the Redesign Committees all met on the same days and in the same location so that different committees could share the directions they were taking as they were building the model. This was an essential design structure, which was complicated due to the overlapping nature of the focus areas of each committee.

Further, subject matter experts representing the fields of early childhood, special education, and English Language Learners were also invited to sessions to react to proposed policy changes and provide insight on developing recommendations. A website was created to share research and policy initiatives and to house materials from these meetings (see www.education.ilstu.edu/isl).

The culmination of the work of the Redesign Committees resulted in a draft of recommendations for policy changes involving principal preparation. ISBE and IBHE then cohosted eight dissemination meetings around the state between 2009 and 2010 to further understanding by the field regarding the proposed changes. This represented a clear effort by the state to provide timely information to all school districts and universities regarding the proposed policy changes and timeline for implementation. The dissemination meetings also provided the agencies an opportunity to gain input from those in the field regarding how the proposed changes might impact their work and other administrative positions and licenses.

One of the major areas of concern expressed at those meetings involved the proposed phasing out of the old general administrative certificate. Over eight hundred constituents participated in one or more of the dissemination meetings. Presentations were also made at several professional association conferences and a legislative briefing was conducted at the capitol to assist legislators in understanding the policy changes. During the dissemination meetings, the state agencies encouraged participants to provide feedback, which resulted in some modifications to the recommendations made by the redesign teams.

At the same time that the Illinois School Leader Task Force work was being completed, the state was also increasing efforts to better align early learning with the K-12 structure. Representatives from the McCormick Foundation expressed interested in convening a statewide committee to explore the role of school principals in aligning the two systems. They approached CSEP to take on that role, based on the organization's work with the School Leader Task Force.

The Leadership to Integrate the Learning Continuum (LINC) Advisory Group was then convened in 2008 by CSEP. The fifty-member LINC Advisory Group included members of the Illinois General Assembly, representatives from ISBE, IBHE, the Illinois Department of Human Services, the Illinois Department of Children and Family Services, the Illinois Community College Board, the teachers' unions, early care and education organizations, and K-12 school administrators.

The LINC Advisory Group released a report (Leadership to Integrate the Learning Continuum 2008) that outlined strategies for educators to better bridge identified gaps in the coordination between early childhood care and education and K-12 schools in an effort to create a seamless learning continuum. Included in the report was a recommendation that "the Illinois State Board of Education should broaden its principal endorsement to PreK-12." That recommendation was embraced by ISBE and IBHE and was ultimately reflected in policy changes to the state's new licensure system, which included internship experiences in PreK settings.

On May 25, 2010, close to the end of legislative session, the recommendations of the ISBE- and IBHE-convened Redesign Committees were ready to be proposed in legislation. Prior to the introduction of the bill, much work occurred behind the scenes to build support for the legislation, including conference calls with all of the key stakeholder groups.

During one of these calls, a representative from the Chicago Public Schools (CPS) expressed concern that the district would not support the legislation unless a provision was added to allow not-for-profit organizations to prepare principals. CPS had a strong partnership with New Leaders, a national nonprofit organization that provided principal preparation and development services to large urban districts around the country.

According to committee minutes this topic was discussed during Task Force and Redesign Committee meetings but was not included as part of the final recommendations. During previous discussions, some stakeholders had expressed concern about allowing alternative routes to licensure. The consensus was that an expedited route to a Principal Endorsement would undermine the importance of the framework that had been agreed upon by the stakeholders that was designed to ensure candidates would be able to demonstrate leadership competencies to improve schools. But in order for the legislation to have adequate political will, it was necessary to establish consensus on the recommendations with CPS.

In order to do so, an important distinction was made between *alternative programs* (nontraditional programs that provide expedited routes to licensure), which all agreed should not be allowed, and *alternative providers* (programs provided by nonprofit organizations that must meet the same rigorous standards and criteria for program approval as university programs), which were deemed allowable in the final draft of the bill. Additionally, to prevent opposition from institutions of higher education, the new statute made clear that nonprofit organizations approved as principal preparation programs would only be granted the authority to entitled principal endorsement but would not grant masters or other degrees.

In May 2010, SB 226 was finally introduced by Representative Mike Smith. He had been involved in these efforts for quite some time, as he had previously served as one of the legislative representatives on the IL-SAELP Executive Committee. The legislation passed the Illinois House of Representatives (98–11–01) on May 26, 2010. The bill then went to the Senate. Senator Deana Demuzio, another legislative representative who had served on the IL-SAELP Executive Committee, sponsored the bill in the Senate, where it passed (55–0–0) on May 27, 2010. The legislation was signed into law by Governor Pat Quinn as Public Act 096-0903 on June 1, 2010.

Shortly after the legislation was signed, ISBE staff began drafting the rules and regulations that would institutionalize the new statute into the

Illinois School Code. Development of the rules and regulations proved to be more challenging than anticipated. A conceptual draft of the rules was put together and shared with a representative group of stakeholders from higher education, professional organizations, school districts, and teachers' unions at a meeting convened by ISBE on July 21, 2010.

To assist, ISBE enlisted the assistance of Dr. Joe Murphy, a respected professor and researcher from Vanderbilt University. Dr. Murphy had previously led the development of the Interstate School Leaders Licensure Consortium's (ISLLC) Standards, which provided guidance to school districts and preparation programs around the country. Stakeholders offered opinions, some supporting a state-mandated minimum number of hours for the internship, while others advocated for a competency-based internship model designed to provide candidates with authentic leadership experiences that could be evaluated through performance-based assessments.

The Internship Redesign Committee had developed a competency-based performance assessment rubric, but it only included three broad competency areas, and many felt that the rubric was not comprehensive. ISBE staff believed the competency-based internship model (instead of the former hour-based requirements) would provide a better structure to support candidate development. However, they were unsure whether or not there was enough time to fully articulate all the competencies that should be included in the rules. No consensus was reached at that meeting, although a variety of suggestions and recommendations were made.

After the meeting, ISBE staff determined that rather than recommending a specific number or range of hours for the internship, it was more important to define the knowledge and skills that candidates needed and for a candidate to demonstrate competency through authentic internship experiences. ISBE staff ultimately included internship requirements that incorporated thirteen critical success factors and thirty-six corresponding leadership activities developed by the Southern Regional Education Board. This requirement moved the internship in a performance-based direction rather than the former structure that required a specific number of hours of practicum experience.

The rules for PA 096-0903 were released by ISBE in October 2010 and the public comment period lasted sixty days. A summary and analysis of the statements gathered during the public comment period was presented at the ISBE board meeting on December 15, 2010. According to staff, 140 public comments had been received: 46 percent from Illinois colleges, 21 percent from current or retired district administrators and teachers, 13.6 percent from Illinois education associations and groups representing students, 7 percent from Illinois nonpublic schools, and the remainder from other state agencies, other states, education programs outside of Illinois, and writers indicating no affiliation.

According to the Board report:

> writers expressed hopes that a redesigned program for principals would lead to increased academic success for each child in school, thereby working to eliminate achievement gaps. Commenters commended the rules' emphasis on partnerships, the broadening of endorsements to cover prekindergarten through grade 12, and the requirement for candidates to incorporate work with teachers of English language learners (ELLs) and students with disabilities. . . . Many writers described the proposed rules as being overly prescriptive, as micromanaging on the part of the State Board, as mandating expenditures at the university and school-levels, and showing programmatic biases against candidates in some parts of the state. One writer stated that the rules would shrink the pool of applicants for the principalship to such an extent that small districts will have little or no chance to hire one.

Based on the public comments, ISBE staff did make some minor changes to the rules that were approved by its governing body. However, some felt that the changes made by ISBE did not go far enough, and that led to further consternation with the rules process.

Traditionally, the final step in the approval process involves a vote on the proposed rules by the Joint Committee on Administrative Rules (JCAR), a bipartisan legislative oversight committee created by the Illinois General Assembly in 1977. It is authorized to conduct systematic reviews of administrative rules promulgated by state agencies. JCAR is made up of twelve legislators proportioned equally between the House and Senate and consisting of an equal number of Democrats and Republicans.

Recognizing that the continuing commitment of stakeholders would be instrumental in gaining final approval for the rules from JCAR, Advance Illinois, a statewide advocacy group, endeavored to support the fidelity of intent behind PA 096-0903 as it moved through the rulemaking process. Advance Illinois convened a Principal Preparation Steering Committee (PPSC) focused on supporting the proposed policy changes.

The PPSC made numerous trips to Springfield to talk with legislators serving on JCAR about the importance of the proposed policy changes and how they were designed to respond to the identified need to raise the rigor of principal preparation in Illinois. This group included public and private university leadership and the executive director of a professional association representing numerous districts throughout the state.

Further, a presentation was provided to the State Educator Preparation and Licensure Board (SEPLB) to educate them on the proposed changes in principal preparation and provide the rationale for ISBE's policy approach. SEPLB was established by statute to serve as an independent board for reviewing new and existing educator preparation programs and making recommendations to ISBE. As an independent body to ISBE, it was important for members of SEPLB to be well informed and supportive of the new changes.

While the principal preparation rules and regulations had been submitted to JCAR in January 2011 and the Principal Preparation Steering Committee had been meeting with its members, on March 26, 2011, ISBE received a letter from JCAR citing concerns raised by representatives from the Illinois Council of Professors of Educational Administration (ICPEA) that the new rules would create a crippling burden on some programs. Legislators on JCAR cited concerns over the new rules but demanded no specific changes.

For a three-month period, negotiation meetings were held between ISBE, various stakeholders, and JCAR legislators. Concessions were made by ISBE that included the following: (1) the maximum percentage of coursework allowed to be taught by adjunct faculty was increased from the initial 50 percent to 80 percent; (2) the number of candidates that mentor principals were allowed to supervise was increased from two to three candidates; and (3) an additional requirement was added stipulating the two representatives from institutions of higher education that were to be placed on the Principal Preparation Program Review Board (PPPRB) had to include one from a public institution and one from a nonpublic institution.

In April 2011, JCAR met and unanimously voted to approve the rules for Public Act 096-0903, with additional revisions and recommendations:

- Elimination of the requirement that a candidate must have four years of teaching prior to entry into a principal endorsement program;
- Elimination of the requirement that two out-of-state individuals be appointed to the PPPRB;
- Recommendation that ISBE move swiftly on legislative changes to the Teacher Leadership Endorsement;
- Recommendation that ISBE move swiftly to propose rules that allowed candidates trained out of state to provide evidence that they have completed a comparable program in another state or that they hold a comparable certificate issued by another state.

Following these changes, the rules went back to ISBE for reconsideration by their board, and the amended rules were passed in June 2011.

While the process for approving the rules and regulations took longer than anticipated, the state statute passed by the General Assembly included specific deadlines involving principal preparation. According to the statute, by September 1, 2012, institutions of higher education could no longer admit new candidates to the old General Administrative (Type 75) programs. Beginning September 1, 2012, candidates could only be accepted to Principal Endorsement programs that had been approved under the new regulations. Further, by June 1, 2014, all programs for the preparation of principals were to have been approved under new program rules or cease operations. Table 1.2 outlines the major activities leading to the enactment of PA 096-0903.

Table 1.2 Program Approval Process Overview for Principal Endorsement

Applications for approval can be submitted by two types of organizations:	Universities	Nonprofits

The following review process outlines the steps and options for applicants:

IBHE—All programs must have operational approval from IBHE. (This will be an additional step for all nonprofits.)

	Approved	Not Approved
Principal Preparation Program Review Panel (PPPRP)—Scores full application and supporting materials using the same scoring guide with enhancements. Responds with written recommendations to the program. From this step, programs have the following options:	Proceed with the process by having their application and the Panel's recommendation sent to the ISEPLB.	Rescind their application and make revisions based on PPPRP recommendations. Then resubmit to either the PPPRP or to the ISEPLB at a later date. (Programs will be allowed to submit a narrative in response to the panel's recommendation.)
The Principal Preparation Program Review Panel (PPPRP) shall acknowledge receipt of the request for approval within thirty days after receipt. Based upon its review, the Panel may:	Issue a recommendation to the IL State Educator Preparation and Licensure Board (ISEPLB) that the principal preparation program be approved; a copy of that recommendation and notification of the ISEPLB's meeting to consider the Panel's recommendation shall be provided to the applicant; or	Issue a recommendation to the ISEPLB that the principal preparation program be denied approval, including the reasons for the recommended denial; a copy of that recommendation and notification of the ISEPLB's meeting to consider the Panel's recommendation shall be provided to the applicant.
IL State Educator Preparation and Licensure Board (ISEPLB) Approval—Scores full application and supporting materials using a scoring guide with enhancements and recommendations from the Principal Review Panel. ISEPLB will approve or reject applications.		

With the regulations finally in place, universities worked diligently to redesign their programs, and the Illinois State Superintendent appointed members to a new Principal Preparation Program Review Panel (PPPRP). In an effort to support the redesign efforts, ISBE had established in the rules a requirement that a PPPRP be established for the purpose of (1) examining program applications, (2) providing feedback to the program regarding whether or not they provided adequate evidence that the redesigned program met the new requirements, and (3) making recommendations for approval to the Illinois State Educator Preparation and Licensure Board (ISEPLB).

Recognizing the extent of substantive changes that were required by the new statute, ISBE envisioned the Review Panel as an initial mechanism for programs to receive constructive feedback on their applications that could inform program revisions prior to the final application being formally submitted for approval by ISEPLB. Unlike ISEPLB, which makes recommendations to ISBE for approval or nonapproval, the PPPRP was only designed to give constructive feedback to the programs.

The PPPRP was made up of stakeholders with expertise regarding school leadership and its impact. This included two teachers, four principals, two superintendents, two university representatives (one public and one private), one member from a school district in a city with a population exceeding 500,000, and one representative from the Illinois business community. In January 2012, ISBE provided a comprehensive training for the new members of PPPRP and ISEPLB that involved an overview of the new program structure, rules and regulations, review of the application scoring rubric, and guidance on indicators of program quality. The optional and required elements of the approval process are outlined in Table 1.3.

Illinois Principal Preparation Policy: Changes Made 2000–2015

Through the work of numerous statewide committees and consortia; funding support from several foundations; and leadership at the state, regional, and institutional levels, the goal of improving principal preparation program requirements had come to fruition in Illinois. There were multiple lessons learned and numerous recommendations that emerged from various collaborations over more than a decade that prompted the passage in 2010 of Illinois Public Act 096-0903.

The statute represented a substantial overhaul of leadership preparation requirements and included the following key elements:

Table 1.3 Principal Preparation Timeline for Illinois

Year	Month	Activity	Detail
2005	August	Commission on School Leader Preparation convened by IBHE	Comprising leaders from K-12 schools, colleges and universities, business and professional education organizations, ISBE, and IBHE
2006	August	Report presented to IBHE	*School Leader Preparation: A Blueprint for Change* Included three major goals: • Recruit strategically • Focus preparation programs • Improve statewide assessment and coordination
2007	July	House Joint Resolution 66	Resolved that ISBE, IBHE, and the Office of the Governor shall jointly appoint a task force to recommend a sequence of strategic steps to implement improvements in school leader preparations in Illinois based on, but not limited to, the measures detailed in *Blueprint for Change*.
2007–2008	October–January	Illinois School Leader Task Force convened	Recommended *three primary instruments* for improving leadership: 1. *State policies* that set high standards for school leadership certification and align principal preparation, early career development, and distinguish principal recognition with those standards; 2. *Formal partnerships* between school districts, institutions of higher education, and other qualified partners to support principal preparation and development; 3. *Refocused principal preparation programs* committed to developing to rigorously assessing in aspiring principals the capacities that are most likely to improve student learning in PreK-12 schools.
2008	May	Two-day conference sponsored by ISBE and ISHE for the Illinois School Leader Task Force Report	Stakeholders in higher education, professional organizations, and members of the Illinois School Leader Task Force attended to disseminate the Illinois School Leader Task Force Report.

2008	August	Two-day conference for open discussions on the recommendations set forth by the Task Force report and to develop school leader redesign teams	
2008	September	One-day meeting sponsored by ISBE and IBHE to convene the five School Leadership Redesign Teams	• School Leader Redesign Team members consisted of fifty representatives of public and private institutions of higher education, the IPA, IFT, IEA, Illinois School Board Association, regional offices of education, ICPEA, IASA, the Illinois School Leader Task Force, and ISBE and IBHE staff members. • Five School Leader Redesign Teams researched and redrafted recommendations in alignment with the *School Leader Team Charges.*
2008	October	One-day meeting sponsored by ISBE and IBHE to convene the five School Leadership Redesign Teams	• School Leader Redesign Team members consisted of fifty representatives of public and private institutions of higher education, the IPA, IFT, IEA, Illinois School Board Association, regional offices of education, ICPEA, IASA, the Illinois School Leader Task Force, and ISBE and IBHE staff members. • Five School Leader Redesign Teams researched and redrafted recommendations in alignment with the School Leader Team Charges.
2008	November	One-day meeting sponsored by ISBE and IBHE to convene the five School Leadership Redesign Teams	
2009	January	Invited representatives for parents, special education, early childhood education, English Language Learners from around the state of Illinois, as well as additional ISBE and IBHE staff to attend the 4th School Leader Redesign Team Meeting	

(Continued)

Table 1.3 (Continued)

Year	Month	Activity	Detail
2009	February	Brought together participants from the May and August conferences to present draft recommended changes from School Leader Redesign Teams and Special Interest Representatives	
2009	March	Leadership to integrate the Learning Continuum released its report, *Building a Seamless Learning Continuum, The Role of Leadership in Bridging the Gaps Between Early Childhood and K-12 Education Systems*. Presented final draft Recommended Changes to the School Leader Advisory Council.	Recommended that the new principal endorsement span from PreK-Grade 12.
2009	April	Presented changes to the Illinois Certification Board and the Illinois State Board of Education Informed Illinois Board of Higher Education of New Principal Preparation Model	
2010	June	Legislation signed into law	
2010	Fall	Rules released for public comment	
2011		ISBE rules passed by Joint Committee on Administrative Rules (JCAR)	
2012		By September 1, institution or not-for-profit entities may admit new candidates only to principal preparation programs that have been approved under new rules	
2014		By September 1, institution or not-for-profit entities may admit new candidates only to principal preparation programs that have been approved under new rules	

1. Terminated programs leading to a General Administrative (Type 75) certificate that had prepared a wide variety of administrative positions but had proven insufficient to meet the increasing demands of the principalship;
2. Established a targeted PK-12 Principal Endorsement designed specifically to prepare principals capable of addressing the challenges faced by today's schools;
3. Mandated formal partnerships be established between principal preparation programs and districts that required school district officials be involved in the design, delivery, and continuous improvement of the principal preparation programs;
4. Mandated rigorous selection criteria requiring aspiring candidates to submit a portfolio that includes evidence of positive impact on student growth, previous leadership experiences, and exemplary interpersonal skills that must also be evidenced through participation in face-to-face interviews;
5. Established minimum qualifications and training requirements for mentor principals and faculty supervisors, including at least two years of experience as a successful school principal and/or superintendent as evidenced by positive student growth data, and successfully completing state-mandated training and assessments on teacher evaluation and mentoring principal interns;
6. Established a PK-12 grade span focus that required coursework and internship experiences be aligned to local and national performance standards and provide development across the PK-12 grade span and with specific student subgroups (special education, English Language Learners, gifted students, and early childhood);
7. Mandated a yearlong, performance-based internship designed to provide the candidates with authentic leadership experiences intended to increase proficiency in areas shown to improve student learning;
8. Mandated competency-based assessments of candidate performance aligned to the Interstate School Leadership Licensure Consortium (ISLLC) Standards and Southern Regional Education Board (SREB) thirteen critical success factors and thirty-six leadership tasks;
9. Mandated collaborative supervision and support of candidates by trained and qualified faculty supervisors and mentor principals, requiring both the faculty supervisor and mentor principal be involved in assessing the candidate's performance during the internship;
10. Mandated candidates pass an eight-hour exam administered by the state, prior to being awarded a PK-12 Principal Endorsement.

These key elements represent a major paradigm shift for principal preparation programs, moving them from a focus on "candidate as consumer" to "district as consumer." In other words, these changes require programs to move beyond the focus on a single program outcome—graduates securing administrative positions—to the actual impact the principal candidate ultimately has on school improvement and student outcomes. However, these accomplishments did not happen overnight. In reality, stakeholders and policymakers throughout Illinois had been engaged in improvement efforts for more than ten years. But the work was not over.

In fall 2013, during the initial implementation phase of the newly approved principal preparation programs, feedback was provided to ISBE from faculty members from various institutions of higher education and some district administrators. A number of unintended consequences were identified by stakeholders in specific areas of the rules and regulations that proved challenging to some programs. That feedback led the state to make several small changes to the rules, which were approved by the ISBE Board on March 12, 2014.

Those changes included:

- The licenses required to serve as a mentor principal supervising principal interns was expanded to include endorsements for superintendent, assistant superintendent, and special education director, provided they are assigned to the location where the internship will take place, and that they possessed at least two years of experience relevant to the role of principal;
- The number of years of experience as a principal required to serve as a mentor principal was reduced from three to two. However, mentor principals must provide evidence of two years of successful experience as a principal, demonstrated by student growth data in at least two of the previous five years and by formal evaluations or letters of recommendation;
- The qualifications for faculty supervisors were expanded to include possession of a current and valid license that is comparable to the Illinois general administrative license or Principal Endorsement issued by the state in which the internship site is located;
- Deadlines for the successful completion of training and assessments qualifying candidates to conduct teacher evaluations and the successful completion of the administered principal content exam were redefined as "prior to licensure" instead of before entering the internship;
- The maximum number of aspiring candidates completing internships to be supervised by a single mentor principal was increased from two to no more than five.

In addition to the changes that ISBE made to the rules and regulations, a statutory amendment was introduced during the spring 2014 legislative session to allow a greater amount of time to transition educators to the new system. In that case, the statute revisions provided that until June 30, 2019, those endorsed in a school support personnel area (i.e., school counselor, school psychologist, speech language pathologist, school nurse, school social worker, and school-based marriage and family counselor) could qualify for admission to the new Principal Endorsement programs.

The language of the original statute established a criterion of a minimum requirement of four years of teaching experience to be eligible to apply to new principal preparation programs. This essentially barred other school support personnel without teaching experience from securing a Principal Endorsement in Illinois. The revised legislation, which provided a phase-in period that included reduced teaching experience requirements, passed both houses of the Illinois General Assembly on May 28, 2014, and was signed by Governor Quinn as Public Act 098-0872 on August 11, 2014.

Conclusion

In hindsight, the long and messy process that policymakers in Illinois followed to bring new principal preparation regulations to fruition may seem like a daunting experience. Yet the experiences are characteristic of the complex work involved in the policy change process. The following chapter applies the Advocacy Coalition Framework to provide a more nuanced analysis of the process of interaction and negotiations that occurred among stakeholders involved with this work in Illinois.

Bibliography

Branch, Gregory F., Eric A. Hanushek, and Steven G. Rivkin. "School Leaders Matter." *Education Next* 13, no. 1 (2013): 62–69.

Bryk, Anthony S., Penny Bender Sebring, Elaine Allensworth, John Q. Easton, and Stuart Luppescu. *Organizing Schools for Improvement: Lessons from Chicago*. Chicago: University of Chicago Press, 2010.

Clifford, Matthew, Ellen Behrstock-Sherratt, and Jenni Fetters. *The Ripple Effect: A Synthesis of Research on Principal Influence to Inform Performance Evaluation Design. A Quality School Leadership Issue Brief*. Chicago, IL: American Institutes for Research, 2012.

Clotfelter, Charles T., Helen F. Ladd, and Jacob L. Vigdor. "Teacher Credentials and Student Achievement: Longitudinal Analysis with Student Fixed Effects." *Economics of Education Review* 26, no. 6 (2007): 673–682.

Commission on School Leader Preparation in Illinois Colleges and Universities. *School Leader Preparation: A Blueprint for Change*. Springfield, IL: Illinois Board of Higher Education, 2006.

Copland, Michael. "Problem-based Learning, Problem-framing Ability and the Principal Selves of Prospective School Principals." Doctoral dissertation, Stanford University, 1999.

Darling-Hammond, Linda. "Teacher Quality and Student Achievement." *Education Policy Analysis Archives* 8 (2000): 1.

Darling-Hammond, Linda, Michelle LaPointe, Debra Meyerson, Margaret Terry Orr, and Carol Cohen. *Preparing School Leaders for a Changing World: Lessons from Exemplary Leadership Development Programs*. School Leadership Study. Final Report. Stanford, CA: Stanford Educational Leadership Institute, 2007.

Elmore, Richard F. *Building a New Structure for School Leadership*. Washington, D.C.: Albert Shanker Institute, 2000.

Grissom, Jason A., Demetra Kalogrides, and Susanna Loeb. "Using Student Test Scores to Measure Principal Performance." *Educational Evaluation and Policy Analysis* 37, no. 1 (2015): 3–28.

Illinois Consortium for Education Leadership. *Leadership for Learning: Strengthening Policies on Education Leadership on Behalf of Illinois Schools*. Normal, IL: Center for the Study of Education Policy at Illinois State University, 2004.

Illinois School Leader Task Force. *Illinois School Leader Task Force Report to the Illinois General Assembly*. Springfield, IL: Illinois State Board of Education and Illinois Board of Higher Education, 2008.

Institute for Educational Leadership. "Leadership for Student Learning: Reinventing the Principalship." School Leadership for the 21st Century Initiative: A Report of the Task Force on the Principalship. Institute for Educational Leadership, Washington, DC, 2000.

Leadership to Integrate the Learning Continuum (LINC). *Building a Seamless Learning Continuum: The Role of Leadership in Bridging the Gaps Between Early Childhood and K-12 Education Systems*. Normal, IL: Center for the Study of Education Policy, Illinois State University, 2008.

Leithwood, Kenneth, Karen Seashore Louis, Stephen Anderson, and Kyla Wahlstrom, K. *Review of Research: How Leadership Influences Student Learning*. New York: The Wallace Foundation, 2004.

Leithwood, Kenneth, Sarah Patten, and Doris Jantzi. "Testing a Conception of How School Leadership Influences Student Learning." *Educational Administration Quarterly* 46, no. 5 (2010): 671–706.

Levine, Arthur. *Educating School Leaders*. New York: Teachers College, Education School Project, 2005.

Louis, Karen Seashore, Kenneth Leithwood, Kyla L. Wahlstrom, Stephen E. Anderson, Michael Michlin, and Blair Mascall. "Learning from Leadership: Investigating the Links to Improved Student Learning." *Center for Applied Research and Educational Improvement/University of Minnesota and Ontario Institute for Studies in Education/University of Toronto* 42 (2010): 50.

Manna, Paul. *Developing Excellent School Principals to Advance Teaching and Learning: Considerations for State Policy*. New York: Wallace Foundation, 2015.

Marzano, Robert J., Timothy Waters, and Brian A. McNulty. *School Leadership That Works: From Research to Results*. Alexandria, VA: ASCD, 2005.

McCarthy, Martha. "The Evolution of Educational Leadership Preparation Programs." In *Handbook on Research on Educational Administration*, edited by Joseph Murphy and Karen Lewis, 119–139. New York: Longman, 1999.

Moore, Mark Harrison. *Creating Public Value: Strategic Management in Government*. Cambridge, MA: Harvard University Press, 1995.

Murphy, Joseph, Stephen N. Elliott, Ellen Goldring, and Andrew C. Porter. *Learning-Centered Leadership: A Conceptual Foundation*. Nashville, TN: Learning Sciences Institute, Vanderbilt University, 2006.

Murphy, Joseph, and Michael P. Vriesenga. *Research on Preparation Programs in Educational Administration: An Analysis*. Charlottesville, VA: University Council for Educational Administration, 2004.

Spillane, James P. "Managing to Lead: Reframing School Leadership and Management." *Phi Delta Kappan* 91, no. 3 (2009): 70–73.

Waters, Tim, Robert J. Marzano, and Brian McNulty. *Balanced Leadership: What 30 Years of Research Tells Us about the Effect of Leadership on Student Achievement*. Aurora, CO: Mid-Continent Regional Educational Lab, 2003.

Vignettes

Keeping an End Goal in Mind

Christopher Koch

As the Illinois School Leader Task Force convened to address a need to better train and retain high-quality principals, the Illinois State Board of Education's role was to provide historical data and context. Later, we were tasked with facilitating discussions among stakeholders.

There was a strong base of research pointing to the importance and impact of the principal role on teacher retention and overall school effectiveness. Knowledge and skill levels of principals in Illinois were far-ranging, leaving skepticism about all principals being well prepared to do the job. Jason Leahy, leader of the Illinois Principals Association, was routinely advocating for and providing meaningful professional development opportunities, sometimes with the help of state funding and other times without. Nevertheless, there was a recognition from many constituents, that a more systematic approach was needed to prepare principals with the knowledge and skills to effectively do all aspects of the job.

It was important for the Illinois Board of Higher Education (IBHE), with the jurisdiction of most higher education functions and the Illinois State Board of Education (ISBE), with higher education teacher and principal preparation program approval responsibilities, to work together. Judy Erwin, executive director of the IBHE, made this collaborative work effective. Illinois partners (e.g., higher education, the Illinois Principals Association, unions, and others) approached this work sensibly. They engaged one another, continually coming back to the guiding question: "What are the skills and knowledge principals need to do their work successfully?" Steve Tozer, a faculty member at the University of Illinois at Chicago, had spoken to me and members of the ISBE on numerous occasions, presenting a compelling case for how to reach scale with school improvement through well-prepared principals. In fact, his institutions' principal preparation program was demonstrating success with their model in Chicago.

Through the collaborative work done by all constituents, we found the best way to make policy was to get all the stakeholders impacted by the proposed policy around the same table to work out the details. The aspirational and the practical elements, and everything in between, needed to be worked through from all perspectives to identify potential challenges and solutions. This happened with the principal preparation redesign initiative in Illinois.

It is important to remember from a historical context what the political environment was at the time. States were pursuing federal "Race to the Top" funds and the US Department of Education, under Secretary Arne Duncan's leadership, were pushing states to revamp teacher evaluation and to hold teachers accountable for their work through student test results. We had inspired leadership in several areas of the state including Audrey Soglin, who led the Illinois Education Association with a practical, intelligent, forward-thinking approach.

The state had adopted the Danielson framework for teacher evaluation, but the unions rightly wanted to make sure the principals were trained on the framework first. How could we ask teachers to use data about student performance to create learning interventions when the people supervising them didn't necessarily have a similar skill set? While many of us knew the research showing that teacher retention was greatly impacted by principal leadership, the union members and leadership were living with those realities daily.

Working Together to Prepare Illinois School Leaders

Judy Erwin

The publication of Dr. Arthur Levine's national study on school leadership programs sparked the Illinois Board of Higher Education (IBHE) to turn the spotlight on Illinois. With their establishment of the Commission on School Leadership (the Commission) in 2006, the IBHE examined higher education principal preparation programs to identify issues raised in the Levine study. The Commission's work resulted in the report, *School Leader Preparation: A Blueprint for Change*.

A joint task force was convened by IBHE and the Illinois State Board of Education (ISBE): the Illinois School Leader Task Force (Task Force), charged with reviewing Illinois' programs and making reform recommendations to ISBE, IBHE, and the Illinois General Assembly (ILGA).

Given that government agencies, like all organizations, naturally repel change, ISBE and IBHE asked an independent expert to facilitate the work of the Task Force. While the Task Force included a large group of stakeholders and sometimes seemed unwieldy, it permitted the variant opinions to be represented.

Aware of the interagency work on school leadership, the Illinois General Assembly passed a legislative resolution in 2009 (Senate Joint Resolution 66) charging ISBE, IBHE, and the Task Force to prepare legislative recommendations to restructure school leader preparation and licensure. The resolution kept pressure on the Task Force to develop actionable legislative recommendations. Legislation to restructure principal preparation and licensure was introduced, debated, and ultimately passed and signed into law in 2010, as Illinois Public Act 096-0903.

It is unlikely this work would have been successful without several key elements. First, the leadership of ISBE and IBHE were 100 percent supportive of the work of the Task Force and the ultimate goal of reforming Illinois' school leadership programs. This effort allowed a united front in facing schools of education, individual colleges and universities and various interest groups in working through the process.

Second, the decision to utilize an outside expert to facilitate the work of the Task Force helped to avoid turf battles between agencies and interest groups, as well as bringing greater independence in presenting and debating research, data, and case studies.

Third, the appointment of a large membership to the Task Force allowed every constituency involved in school leadership training to be a part of the process. While sometimes a little messy, it was essential that the process considered all viewpoints. It avoided any claims that stakeholders were not heard.

Finally, the Illinois General Assembly's supportive resolution served as an impetus to the Task Force to complete and defend the work to the state's elected representatives. Since legislators hold the power of the purse, stakeholders were less likely to ignore their mandate.

The strong collaboration of the state agencies and the Task Force was and is unusual for one of the country's most political states. And because of it, the implementation of the new principal preparation and licensure requirements in Illinois was framed in cooperation.

"Working Together to Prepare Illinois School Leaders" became our theme. We always started our meetings with that mantra, and logos and carefully selected verbiage were displayed on the screen and in discussions. The shared leadership and strong collaboration of ISBE and IBHE prevented wedge issues from developing.

State agency collaboration, the use of independent expertise, and the willingness to include all stakeholders remains the gold standard in how to develop and get difficult education policy reforms approved in Illinois.

Perspectives from Philanthropy: The "What and How" of Leadership in the Learning Continuum

Sara R. Slaughter and Cornelia Grumman

K-12 issues are front and center when examining the "what and how" of the Illinois principal preparation reform story, but it is crucial not to overlook other elements of this strategic policy reform process. Specifically, this change process heeded the importance of the years preceding kindergarten. With all principal preparation programs now incorporating early learning into their curricula, the internship experiences, and their assessments, Illinois is positioned as a national leader in preparing principals to lead across an education continuum, beginning with early childhood classrooms and teachers.

Early childhood advocates often say that there is a gap between what we know and what we do. Most often this references the gap between the high benefits of early childhood and the relatively low investments of public funds. That gap between what we know and what we do also exists when it comes to leadership. Anecdotally, we knew that although the number of schools with preschool classrooms was increasing, there were few principals with early childhood teaching degrees or experiences.

In 2008, the Robert R. McCormick Foundation funded the Center for the Study of Education Policy (CSEP) at Illinois State University to convene the Leadership to Integrate the Learning Continuum (LINC). This statewide committee, which examined the role of leadership in aligning early childhood and K-12 systems, recommended that the Illinois State Board of Education (ISBE) extend its principal endorsement to P-12.

The recommendation was integrated into Illinois's legislation to create the new Principal Endorsement and as a result, Illinois became the first—and still the only state—to include early childhood content, experiences, and assessments specifically in its principal licensure programs.

Of course, change takes time and many elements need to be in place for change to take root. One of those elements is being able to point to a successful program that embodies the desired changes, which shows legislators that change is within reach: it can be done. So, the Robert R. McCormick Foundation turned to Steve Tozer, professor at University of Illinois at Chicago (UIC). Professor Tozer was known for his successful principal preparation program: in 2010, the Chicago Public Schools recognized UIC for having its graduates leading nine of the twenty-five highest gaining elementary schools on a value-added Illinois Standards Achievement Test (ISAT) results. But that wasn't all: Professor Tozer is also a former kindergarten teacher with an early childhood degree from the Erikson Institute. The McCormick Foundation supported his work in bolstering the early education curricula in the UIC principal preparation program.

With the requirement to integrate early learning content into programs as well as the model programs, Illinois had critical elements of policy reform in place. Nonetheless, challenges remain. A 2016 statewide task force (Illinois School Leader Advisory Council [ISLAC]) found that many principal preparation programs in Illinois were struggling to find early childhood internship opportunities for candidates, especially if their partnering school districts did not have an early childhood program. To address this, ISLAC recommended helping "school districts to access regional or neighborhood partnership 'hubs' to optimize and equalize resources for training . . . including opportunities for principal candidates to access high-quality experiences during their internship." The W. Clement and Jessie V. Stone Foundation is supporting CSEP's efforts to develop and pilot these regional hubs.

The Illinois journey isn't over. Nonetheless, Illinois is a pioneer in bridging two areas that correlate to good student outcomes: quality leaders and quality early childhood education. According to a 2015 New America survey, "even though a majority of elementary principals are now responsible for pre-K classrooms, only about 20 percent of those principals feel well-versed in early childhood education." While Illinois has implementation hurdles, its design for change can serve as a model for others to create a learning continuum to produce excellence for all.

2 Applying the Advocacy Coalition Framework to the Policy Change Process in Illinois

Alicia Haller, Erika Hunt, and Debra Baron

This chapter will examine the policy change process through the interaction and engagement of stakeholders involved. To do so, we explored primary documents from various improvement efforts and included data gathered from interviews with twenty key actors that were identified in the documents as instrumental to the effort. The voices of these stakeholders and their reflections on the levers of change are included in the analysis of these data through the application of the Advocacy Coalition Framework (ACF).

Developed by Paul Sabatier and colleagues (Jenkins-Smith, Nohrstedt et al. 2014; Nowlin 2011; Sabatier 1988; Sabatier and Jenkins-Smith 1999; Sabatier and Weible 2007; Weible and Sabatier 2006; Weible, Sabatier, and McQueen 2009), the ACF provides a more nuanced exploration of factors that promoted or inhibited certain approaches involved in the policy change process. This chapter provides a case study of the Illinois policy change process, through the ACF theoretical lens, focusing on the struggle between various advocacy coalitions involved.

Advocacy Coalition Framework

The principal preparation redesign efforts in Illinois align well with the concepts of policy change, advocacy coalitions, and policy-oriented learning described in the AFC framework. This analysis complements the previous historical description of events by providing detailed descriptions of influences on the policy formation process. In this case study, the unit of analysis is the arena in which actors and organizations interacted around improvement efforts in the area of leadership development. That arena is referred to as the *policy subsystem* in the ACF.

According to ACF scholars, within any policy subsystem various actors are drawn together around a broad common goal. Policy subsystems are somewhat stable entities, as actors rarely shift their support from the broad common goal. However, conflict often arises among actors when subsystems organize around policy *approaches* to the broad common goal. In those cases, actors align themselves with an advocacy coalition that represents their policy beliefs.

Within any policy subsystem, it is common to find two or more *advocacy coalitions* have formed. Advocacy coalitions comprise a set of actors, including any individual or organization that regularly attempts to influence a given policy subsystem. Individuals and organizations coalesce into advocacy coalitions through the expression of specific beliefs and values related to the policy subsystem.

In that sense, an individual advocacy coalition has the potential to influence a given policy subsystem over time through at least three methods: (1) collaboration in a professional learning environment to promote the dissemination of research and best practices related to the policy subsystem; (2) conflict with other advocacy coalitions around specific approaches to policy; and (3) by complementing the efforts of other advocacy coalitions in sync with their policy beliefs that may or may not operate exclusively within a single policy subsystem.

Ultimately, the extent of influence by any advocacy coalition varies greatly from one policy subsystem to another. Examining the role of advocacy coalitions highlights many of the nonrational aspects of policy change, as policies and programs reflect the implicit beliefs of one or more coalitions. Illinois' new principal preparation program policy is an ideal case to examine through this framework, as the ACF requires researchers to explore change over a period of a decade or more, in order to provide a long-term perspective of the process influencing a policy subsystem (Sabatier and Weible 2014). The relationships between the general conceptual categories that constitute the ACF are depicted in Figure 2.1 from Weible, Sabatier, and McQueen (2009).

The *policy subsystem* in this analysis includes those stakeholders involved directly or indirectly with principal preparation programs in Illinois and is depicted by the box on the right. For the purpose of illustration, only two competing *advocacy coalitions* are indicated representing opposing beliefs regarding proposed changes, but in a given situation there could be more.

While the composition of coalitions can remain somewhat stable, there may be fluidity based on the specific issue(s) being considered. Additionally, the ACF established that efforts by two or more coalitions can generally be mediated by *policy brokers* who are very involved in the subsystem and frequently interact with opposing coalitions.

In the Illinois case, policy brokers included staff at the CSEP and representatives from IBHE and ISBE. Policy brokers may not necessarily be completely neutral parties in terms of their beliefs involving policy change. Nevertheless, opposing factions view them as working toward improvements through consensus between coalitions. Equally important to note, advocacy coalitions form around high-level, deeply held beliefs, such as "all schools deserve well-trained, effective leaders." However, actors within a coalition also hold their own beliefs and have differing levels of access to resources and/or existing relationships.

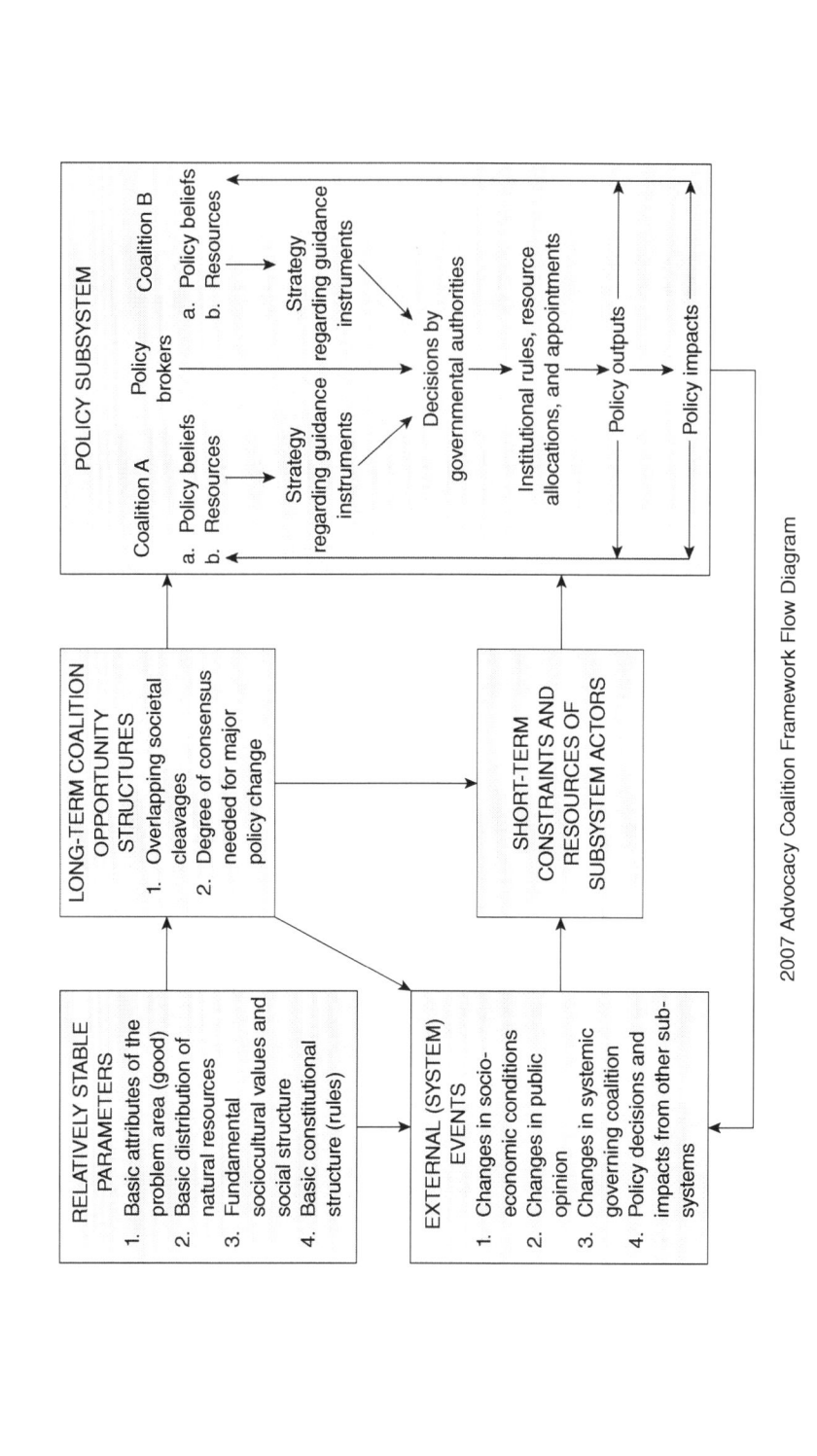

Figure 2.1 Diagram of the Advocacy Coalition Framework
Source: Weible, Sabatier, and McQueen (2009).

Therefore, actors within an advocacy coalition may differ in terms of preferred strategies aimed at influencing policy decisions made by governing authorities. For that reason, advocacy coalitions are not generally completely stable factions over time. By exploring a policy change process over a decade or more, the natural fluidity of actors within advocacy coalitions can be viewed from a long-term perspective and the sources of influence identified. The ACF demonstrates how various communications and/or decisions loop back to further influence the subsystem as well as potentially impacting external subsystems.

Depicted in the upper left corner of Figure 2.1 is a category of variables that shape a policy subsystem: *relatively stable parameters*. These variables are considered relatively stable and include institutions and social, economic, and cultural environments both within and external to the policy subsystem (the Illinois School Code, state funding for education, university principal preparation programs policies, etc.).

The nature of these relatively stable parameters affects the extent of impact likely to be influenced by organizations involved in advocacy coalitions, such as professional associations, interest groups, or findings from statewide committees and/or conferences. The stable conditions within which a policy subsystem and/or advocacy coalition provide opportunities or barriers to minor, incremental, and major policy changes. But they do not operate in isolation. *External subsystem events*, shown on the lower left side of the diagram, are stimuli that can also influence policy change.

In this case, unsatisfactory student achievement and failing schools in Illinois (as demonstrated by the assessment system put in place by the national No Child Left Behind [NCLB] legislation) provided a window of opportunity for those seeking improvements to principal preparation. NCLB, in combination with the growing body of evidence on the important role of the principal in school improvement efforts and the dreadful state of principal preparation in the United States, serve as external stimuli for policy change.

Principal preparation, which had previously been understood as the purview of universities, began to be examined more closely by school districts. External stimuli influenced an increase in district engagement in reform efforts aimed at improving principal preparation. As districts began to view their role in the equation as consumers of preparation programs, they also began to advocate for necessary improvements.

In addition to influencing the policy subsystem directly, stable environmental factors can also influence external subsystem events by helping to shape public opinion or advocating for changes in other policy subsystems (teacher preparation, or principal performance evaluation, etc.). They can also influence the *short-term constraints and resources of subsystem actors* (loss of funding, leadership turnover, etc.) and the *long-term structures* (the state's educator licensure system, etc.) that impact policy change activities.

These short-term conditions and long-term structures can provide opportunities for coalitions to act upon or exploit a power imbalance (Sabatier and Weible 2014). In a sense, external events and/or short-term factors can act as a catalyst to mobilize or provide the energy needed to ignite and sustain forward movement of the policy change process, if policy structures exist and can be influenced to support a necessary policy change.

The ACF approach to examining policy change provides an excellent foundation for examining the Illinois policy formation process as it attempts to inform understanding about the factors which contribute to change by considering the policy-oriented beliefs of the actors involved. The ACF breaks down actors' belief systems into three levels: deep core beliefs, policy core beliefs, and secondary beliefs that align to specific details involving change (Sabatier and Jenkins-Smith 1999).

Deep core beliefs are very stable ideals held by almost all of the actors in a subsystem and serve to foster cohesion among diverse interests. One state official explained a deep core belief of the actors involved with the principal preparation policy changes as

> at the beginning of each meeting/conference/event we always stated that this work was about doing what was in the best interest of our students—that became our mantra. This helped in taking individuals out of an institutional mentality and aligning them with a greater goal, that of raising the quality of education across the state.

That deep core belief was reiterated in language found in official and unofficial documents, as well as interviews with key actors involved in the reform efforts.

According to the ACF, *policy core beliefs* differ from deep core beliefs in that they are more likely to be shaped by the position one has in relation to the subsystem and are not as universally shared by all of the actors in the subsystem. In fact, conflicts that arise from competing policy core beliefs are frequently the genesis for the formation of the advocacy coalitions.

Conflicts related to *secondary beliefs*, while important to how the subsystem functions, are generally more easily negotiated because they result in only minor changes to the advocacy coalition. For that reason, this analysis focuses primarily at the policy core belief level.

The formation of advocacy coalitions within a specific policy subsystem results from four distinct pathways: (1) significant external disruption(s); (2) a significant internal event; (3) policy-oriented learning resulting from new research or some other form of knowledge discovery; and/or (4) the absence of another mechanism to resolve a perceived need to challenge the status quo (Sabatier and Weible 2014). In this case study, all four of these pathways played a key role during the decade (2000–2010) leading to the passage of Illinois Public Act 096-0903.

A chronological description of the policy change process was outlined in Chapter 1. Rather than reiterate, the following section describes the alignment of the sources of influence that led to the formation of advocacy coalitions involved in principal preparation reform in Illinois. The sources of influence involved are presented in no particular order, as some events occurred sequentially, simultaneously, or during somewhat overlapping time periods, while others represent unique conditions that were present at various times or throughout the change process.

ACF Applied to the Leadership Development Policy Subsystem in Illinois

As far back as 2000, individuals from very different backgrounds and from a variety of organizations came together voluntarily to discuss the state of principal preparation in Illinois and share improvement strategies and emerging best practices. Actors involved represented public and private universities, professional associations, teachers' unions, public school districts, regional offices of education, education research organizations, and state education agencies.

Through multi-year funding from the Wallace Foundation, efforts began to intentionally engage a large group of stakeholders from across the state that included a wide range of perspectives. The initial effort established a culture focused not on individual opinions or organizational agendas but on a common purpose that drew all the participants together. In fact, there was no evidence found in any of the group's early documents that suggested that changes to state regulations were the ultimate outcome envisioned by those initially involved in the early principal preparation program improvement efforts.

Rather, the group was forged around the simple, shared *deep core belief* that all schools deserved well-trained, highly effective principals capable of improving school and student outcomes, and that more could be done to improve principal preparation and development. This point was highlighted by one faculty member from a public university who claimed that due to the disparate views of the stakeholders involved, he did not think the redesign efforts would ever have gotten past advancing the statewide dialogue and raising awareness around the need for improvements to principal preparation and induction support.

However, regardless of differences of opinion, stakeholders remained committed to the shared goal of improving principal preparation as a means to improve school and student outcomes. As one former superintendent claimed, even when those involved changed roles within their organization or shifted to a new organization, they often continued to come to the meetings and engage in the work "because they understood the importance of leadership development."

This was echoed by another school administrator who stated that the commitment stemmed from the desire of a "variety of key stakeholders to improve the pool of principal talent by giving teacher leaders the instruction and experiences they need to be effective principals." Maintaining commitment by participants was achieved by consistently reinforcing a focus on the common purpose. One state official indicated that was an effective strategy, arguing,

> despite contentious issues, people really tried to hammer out positive and effective means to accomplish our goals. Individuals from many different sectors worked side by side for a common cause, and they were all dedicated and passionate about the work.

Significant Internal Event(s) within the Policy Subsystem

Two significant internal events transpired that caused advocacy coalitions to form within the leadership development policy subsystem. The first occurred in 2007 after a new state superintendent was appointed to lead ISBE. The new state superintendent began collaborating with the head of IBHE, and both agreed that previous efforts to improve principal preparation lacked the benefit of a legislatively commissioned task force charged specifically with developing policy strategies. They proposed that the charge of the task force be to develop practical guidelines for the implementation of the previous commission's recommendations.

Thus, bringing the combined influence of two regulatory agencies together to work on this issue resulted in leadership preparation becoming a real priority for the state. As a result, the Illinois School Leader Task Force was convened in 2007 after the Illinois General Assembly unanimously passed a resolution supporting its creation.

Despite a great deal of previous collaboration among actors in the policy subsystem and their common deeply held core beliefs, efforts to bring about meaningful policy change were not always harmonious. Indications of the ongoing tension between changes that could potentially be mandated by the state versus those that would be merely recommended were indicated in the final report from the Illinois School Leader Task force (2008).

According to the ACF, this demonstrates the point at which actors involved in the policy change process begin to coalesce into separate advocacy coalitions. As previously indicated, the ACF promotes the notion that actors within a policy subsystem typically find strong consensus in deep core beliefs, however, two or more advocacy coalitions are likely to form when there is a difference of opinion involving specific policy *strategies* aimed at addressing the main goal of the group.

In Illinois, previous reports from various consortia and committees involved over the years had been consistent in defining the root cause of the problem through research and practice and in developing action plans calling for further exploration of the subject. These early efforts were important in terms of raising awareness around the need for improvements to principal preparation. However, the previous coalitions and committees stopped short of outlining specific policy strategies.

It was not until the Illinois School Leader Task Force was convened, with the express purpose of making policy recommendations to the General Assembly, that conflict among various actors was clearly identifiable. The shift away from the broader goal(s) aligned to the deep core beliefs of the actors to a more specific focus on policy beliefs highlighted a schism within the subsystem. In this case, the shift away from *what* the group ultimately wanted to accomplish, to the more specific policy requirements defining *how* to achieve the goal, resulted in conflict between some actors and resulted in the formation of two main advocacy coalitions.

This conflict occurred despite the fact that many of the actors were involved in improvement efforts since the initial IL-SAELP work. Among the members appointed to the Task Force, there was a distinction between those that believed all improvement strategies should be codified only as recommendations and those that believed that replicable research-based best practices should be made mandatory for all programs. The schism was created not by a shift in core belief but rather the shift in focus on how best to operationalize policy beliefs into state regulations.

External Disruption(s)

In addition to the influence from seminal reports such as *Educating School Leaders* (Levine 2005) and *School Leader Preparation: A Blueprint for Change* (CSLPICU 2006) that exposed the dismal state of principal preparation nationally and within Illinois, there were other sources of external influence on the policy change process. The efforts in Illinois to improve principal preparation and development from 2000 to 2014 coincided with the explosion of the accountability movement that was occurring nationally.

Federal mandates, such as 2001's No Child Left Behind Act (NCLB), ushered in a new level of standards-based reform, and high-stakes testing swept the country. Numerous stakeholders commented that NCLB created a sense of urgency with regard to the significant number of low-performing schools throughout the state. As one faculty member put it, NCLB was a wake-up call that drove home the "failure of Illinois schools to produce significant gains in student achievement."

The US Department of Education's Race to the Top (RTTT) grant program also provided incentives for state officials to embrace policy reform efforts aimed at school improvement. One former superintendent recalled that the federal expectations for those receiving grant funding through NCLB and RTTT were substantial levers that spurred involvement by state education officials in efforts to improve school leader preparation and development.

Another former superintendent confirmed, "the potential for the state to receive federal RTTT funds also helped to move legislation through the process." An example of the mechanism used to influence policy can be found within the scoring criteria of RTTT. Six criteria were used in scoring. The highest weighted criterion, accounting for almost 30 percent of the total points, involved strategies to ensure schools employed highly qualified teachers and leaders. As states competed for a portion of over $4 billion in grant funds, policymakers prioritized reform efforts aimed at improving the quality of the educator pipeline.

As one Illinois education official asserted, there was tremendous "support for change nationally spurred on by NCLB and Race to the Top." In addition to policy changes made to principal preparation, several other pieces of legislation passed. For example, Illinois Public Act 096-0861 (Performance Evaluation Reform Act [PERA]) ushered in a performance-based principal evaluation system that was required statewide. While it is hard to determine the extent to which the focus on accountability influenced the direction of the policy process involving principal preparation, responses from many of the key actors involved in the state's reform efforts indicated they were acutely aware of the external environment within which their reform efforts were occurring.

Policy-Oriented Learning across Advocacy Coalitions

While external forces were certainly at play in Illinois, additional work that moved efforts forward aligned to what the ACF describes as policy-oriented learning. Researchers defined this as "enduring alternations of thought or behavioral intentions that result from experience and which are concerned with the attainment or revision of the precepts of the belief system of individuals or of collectives" (Sabatier and Jenkins-Smith 1993, 198). That type of cross-advocacy coalition learning is often the intent of professional meetings, conferences, and/or the dissemination of research and policy briefs.

These mechanisms are often designed in such a way to convince minority advocacy coalitions to alter their position. Policy-oriented learning can result from formal or informal communications between actors and/or organizations that hold competing views and/or through the efforts of policy brokers. According to the ACF, competing policy beliefs are the result of two conditions: (1) differences in understanding the causal relationship with regard to the policy issue and (2) differences in preferred policy responses to the problem.

In Illinois, CSEP provided actors involved in the policy subsystem with numerous learning opportunities that brought a variety of people together to identify and disseminate findings on research-based best practices, share lessons learned, and provide information on demonstration sites operating within Illinois. Many innovative and effective university preparation and school district partnership strategies were presented at IL-SAELP and other statewide meetings. Additionally, CSEP provided opportunities for actors to connect with various national networks and other state agencies to explore bold and effective models operating elsewhere.

Through intentional policy-oriented learning opportunities, actors within advocacy coalitions in Illinois engaged in a critical analysis of existing research, empirical evidence, and policy comparisons in an effort to examine alternative strategies for improving principal quality. The policy-oriented learning that occurred over more than a decade reflected the iterative nature of the policy change process. That does not mean that policy-oriented learning resolved all conflicts between opposing advocacy coalitions. The ACF asserts that the extent of threats to an advocacy coalition's policy belief will determine the level of conflict between coalitions.

It is important to consider and attempt to understand the level of conflict involved among opposing coalitions, as the effectiveness of cross-coalition learning is influenced by the extent of conflict within the policy subsystem. The ACF established that cross-coalition or policy-oriented learning could have a powerful mediating effect on members of opposing coalitions in certain situations. For example, ACF scholars claim that policy-oriented learning is most effective when there is only an intermediate level of conflict:

> At low levels of conflict, there is little cross-coalition learning as coalition actors attend to other subsystem affairs. At high levels of conflict . . . coalition actors defend their positions and reject information that undermines their belief systems. At intermediate levels of conflict, opposing coalitions are threatened just enough to attend to the issue and remain receptive enough to new information to increase the likelihood of cross-coalition learning.
> (Sabatier and Weible 2014, 199)

Therefore, if policy-oriented learning is required to bring about change, actors must attend to the level of conflict between coalitions, aiming to strike a balance.

When examining a variety of data dating back to 2000, it appears that the advocacy coalitions in Illinois experienced at least an intermediate level of conflict that encouraged member participation in the improvement efforts. A number of actors involved described the culminating conflict prior to the final policy changes as either an opportunity for improvement through substantive research-based approaches or an unreasonable threat to current practices that ignored local context and capacity. Because the early efforts had primarily focused on program improvement, rather than regulatory change, the conflict between opposing coalitions was less intense and allowed for a greater level of policy-oriented learning to occur.

Researchers applying the ACF also found that issues "for which accepted quantitative data and theory exist are more conducive to policy-oriented learning across belief systems than those in which data and theory are generally qualitative, quite subjective, or altogether lacking" (Sabatier and Weible 2014, 200). Many of the participants who chose to become involved with IL-SAELP and/or other statewide leadership development improvement efforts did so in reaction to both national pressure for reform and pressing conditions within Illinois, with many focused on quantitative evidence to support their positions.

For example, research conducted by Levine (2005), Fry, Bottoms, and O'Neill (2005), Murphy et al. (2006), and Waters, Marzano, and McNulty (2003) served as a catalyst for educators and policymakers in Illinois seeking to identify root causes of the problem. Quantitative data on school and student outcomes indicated that our schools were performing poorly overall.

Few, if any, actors within the policy subsystem disputed the fact that too many of Illinois' schools were failing and school leaders were ill-prepared to lead meaningful change in those buildings. In fact, a teachers' union representative described the condition in Illinois as one in which it was becoming increasingly apparent both inside and outside of education "that school leaders were inadequately prepared for the current job of principal. I think NCLB made that more transparent."

The growing research base linking principal leadership to school improvement and increased student achievement, combined with increasing public acceptance of quantitative date indicating how poorly many of our schools were performing, created a sense of urgency for improving systems of support for school leaders. According to a state education official,

> It seemed to be the right time and place. There was support to make change and the realization that principals needed to be leaders rather than managers was important to this change. Kids were not being helped, and teachers needed support. Strong leaders were essential for change to happen and to support learning.

Another state education official noted, "The results coming out from the work of researchers such as Leithwood and Levine were disturbing and raised questions as to how Illinois programs fared in contrast." While much of the research on principal quality was qualitative in nature, the growing accountability movement ushered in a flood of quantitative research that demonstrated the severity of the problem.

Many respondents, including district administrators, faculty members, deans, professional association representatives, and state education officials, reported the vital role the CSEP played in disseminating research and moving the work forward. Grants awarded to CSEP from the McCormick and Wallace Foundations helped to provide staffing for meeting facilitation, development of research briefs and policy summaries, and funding to bring in national experts to engage in discussions with stakeholders.

One faculty member asserted, CSEP "enabled the work to go beyond that which the state could have provided and was a compelling force that drove the effort forward." Another faculty member stated the external funding was not exclusively focused on policy solutions but also aimed to increase stakeholders' understanding of best practices that could be adapted to fit a program's specific context. She stated, "involvement with the LINC project has taken us to incredible places with our programs. We knew that we needed to cover early childhood, ELL, and special education. . . . Principals need experience in those areas. LINC gave us a systematic approach."

In an effort to ensure transparency among stakeholders involved, and to disseminate information to an even broader group of stakeholders, CSEP developed a website that included meeting announcements, agendas, and minutes; research explored by the group; presentations from subject matter experts; research and policy briefs compiled for the group; legislative progress reports, timelines, and summaries of regulations; other state policy examples; and resources and tools for program improvement. In fact, the website continues to be updated by actors currently implementing the new regulations.

There are at least two reasons why policy-oriented learning occurred between advocacy coalitions involved in the principal preparation program improvement efforts in Illinois. According to Sabatier and Weible (2014), "policy-oriented learning across belief systems is most likely when there exists a forum that is 1) prestigious enough to force professionals from different coalitions to participate, and 2) dominated by professional norms" (200).

In the case of Illinois principal preparation reform, the initial voluntary participation of members involved in IL-SAELP was rooted in the professional practice and norms of both university faculty and district officials. Each group of professionals routinely came together to discuss challenges and opportunities with their work. Many respondents indicated that the reason they remained engaged with this work over such a long period of time was the desire to improve both the profession in general and their institutions in particular.

One department chair asserted,

> We had a strong program, but wanted it to be even better. We don't wait for change to be imposed. We valued the changes that were being made and wanted to be involved with the groundwork. We wanted to be in the forefront, helping to lead the way in the state.

A faculty member from another program expressed a similar reflection: "My first hope was that by collaborating with other universities, we could identify essential understandings and proficiencies that all principals need in order to be effective building leaders."

Stakeholders were clear about the need to create a learning community among the stakeholders involved in this work. As one faculty member reflected, she wanted to tap into the experience and knowledge of others grappling with continuous improvement in substantive ways, "my expectation was, that like all changes in 'the way we do things,' there would be anxiety but also excitement associated with the possibility of growth and improvement."

However, the voluntary nature of the initial improvement efforts changed somewhat once the two state education agencies that had regulatory authority over preparation programs and districts began collaborating in the policy subsystem. Recognizing a shift in power, actors from different coalitions felt compelled to participate to ensure their voices were heard in any policy change discussions. One faculty member stated that she was "afraid not to be at the table."

Similarly, other faculty members and professional association representatives expressed that it was crucial that the state policymakers garnered input from all corners of the state to gain a better understanding of the contextual differences that would impact any implementation of changes. In fact, several key stakeholders interviewed indicated that there was no doubt, after the Illinois School Leader Task Force report came out, that there would be significant policy changes to principal preparation programs. However, no one could be sure exactly what the changes would entail, and for that reason many were compelled to participate.

Absence of Another Forum

According to the ACF, policy change forums are conceptualized as the venues provided by the long-term coalition structures that are likely to influence the short-term constraints and/or resources of the actors. In the case of Illinois, it would be disingenuous to argue that no other forums existed than those provided collaboratively by CSEP, ISBE, and IBHE that provided a platform for actors to participate in improvement efforts involving principal preparation.

Professional organizations such as the Illinois Council of Professors of Educational Administration, Illinois Principals Association, Illinois Association of School Administrators, Illinois Education Research Council, Large Unit District Association and so forth all provided platforms to their members and others to discuss these types of issues. However, most of these efforts were limited to a narrow subset of the overall stakeholder population impacted by principal preparation programs.

Further, the ACF defines a forum as a space where opposing advocacy coalitions interact, debate, and negotiate. "A couple of the most important attributes defining a forum are the degree of openness in participating (open vs. closed forums) and the extent that participating actors share a common analytical training and norms of conduct" (Sabatier and

Weible 2014, 198–199). When applying the ACF's conceptualization of forum, the Illinois case demonstrated that there were at least nine forums that existed over a ten-year period.

Table 2.1 below demonstrates that while there were nine forums, they were formed and disbanded sequentially over the decade with no overlap. For more than a decade, only one forum at a time existed where conflicting coalitions were provided a platform to discuss the state of principal preparation in Illinois. Over eight hundred stakeholders participated in forums in Illinois involving improvements to principal preparation. Many of those individuals were involved in the policy change process for the entire timeline (Baron and Haller 2014).

The forums represented in Table 2.1 provided platforms that allowed actors to come together around a common purpose and acted as a mechanism for opposing advocacy coalitions to debate and negotiate differences. It was the collective efforts of various groups involved in those forums that brought about meaningful change in Illinois. Highlighting the length of time the policy formation phase took, one former superintendent stated, "The process used to get the legislation passed was incremental. We did not move too fast. It was a good process."

According to the ACF, actors involved in a coalition bring their individual belief systems, network contacts, resources, and policy preferences with them. Coalition actors with more moderate beliefs, however, are

Table 2.1 Forums to Discuss Principal Preparation Prior to Passage of Public Act 096-0903

Timeframe	Venue	Number of Participants
2000	State Action for Education Leadership Project (SAELP) Launched	ISU CSEP staff
2001–2004	Illinois Consortium for Education Leadership/IL-SAELP Advisory Body	25 members
2004–2011	IL-SAELP Executive Committee	14 members
2004–2011	IL-SAELP Consortium	120 members
2005	Commission on School Leader Preparation in Illinois Colleges and Universities (Illinois Levine Report)	26 members
2007–2008	Illinois School Leader Task Force	28 members
2008	Leadership to Integrate the Learning Continuum (LINC) Advisory Group	50 members
2008–2010	Illinois School Leader Redesign Teams	50 members
2009–2010	ISBE-IBHE Dissemination Meetings	800+ participants

considered more open to learning from opposing viewpoints than are actors with extreme beliefs. One's belief systems play an important role in filtering and interpreting information, as does the level of diversity within the networks to which one belongs.

Therefore, the statewide forums developed to improve principal preparation in Illinois purposefully included a wide variety of stakeholder roles and perspectives. Interpreting information that is counter to one's belief requires adequate evidence and time to process and incorporate new information into one's existing knowledge framework. The engagement of various actors in the nine iterations of forums over more than a decade provided the time needed for some consensus to emerge that spurred significant policy change.

Levers of Policy Change

The four pathways that promote the development of advocacy coalitions within a policy subsystem do not, in and of themselves, typically result in policy change. ACF scholars hypothesize that the pathways represent conditions that are necessary for change but are insufficient to drive major policy change by themselves. ACF scholars argue that major change involving a government program is unlikely, "except when the change is imposed by a hierarchically superior jurisdiction" (Sabatier and Weible 2014, 204).

Data involving the Illinois policy change process indicated support for that assertion. However, in this case the "hierarchically superior jurisdiction" operated within a robust political environment. Policymakers, including elected officials of the Illinois General Assembly and politically appointed heads of state education agencies, do not operate with unfettered autonomy. They are accountable to the voters and political allies that have provided them, either by election or appointment, with their leadership roles.

Therefore, any major policy change requires a certain level of political will that support the change, particularly from those that would be most directly impacted by the change. To that end, the Illinois policy change process included six identifiable levers of change: (1) funding, (2) policy brokers, (3) research, (4) external pressure, (5) open forums, and (6) involvement by actors with legislative or regulatory authority. These six levers align to the identified pathways that resulted in the formation of advocacy coalitions and influence consensus within and across advocacy coalitions.

Funding

Grants provided by the McCormick and Wallace Foundations were essential to the policy change process. As one IBHE official remarked,

"I believe that we were fortunate to have the right people, in the right place, at the right time to advance the work." Further, the official suggested that to ensure the right people were in fact in the right place, at the right time, and supported with the right information required a certain level of staffing.

Another state agency official claimed, "We simply would never have had the personnel needed to complete the work of IL-SAELP." Funding provided staffing to take on responsibilities such as communicating with stakeholders, securing various data from state agencies, compiling research briefs, identifying and engaging national experts, disseminating information from ongoing meetings, coordinating the logistics of regular statewide meetings, facilitating consensus and drafting reports, and other administrative functions. Without funding, these responsibilities would have fallen to state agency employees who already had overwhelming workloads. That would have caused progress to dramatically slow down and would have diminished the focused efforts of the group.

Funding to staff the improvement efforts and engage external experts provided the state with the capacity needed to bring together a broad representation of stakeholders, with different backgrounds, experiences, and organizational priorities. They came together around a common purpose, which was a true desire to do what they believed was in the best interest of children. Many respondents expressed that the collaborative effort allowed the group to capitalize on specific windows of opportunity over the course of more than a decade.

Policy Brokers

According to ACF scholars, some actors choose to be advocates within the subsystem aligning themselves or their organization with one coalition or another, while others actively take on or emerge in the role of policy brokers who help to mitigate the level of conflict by attempting to negotiate agreements between opposing coalitions. "There are no predefined criteria defining who can or cannot be a broker within a subsystem; indeed, a broker can be affiliated with any organization type, from academia to government to the private or nonprofit sectors" (Sabatier and Weible 2014, 199).

However, actors with centrist views and large, diverse networks are most likely to serve as brokers. Representatives of administrative agencies and researchers were found to be particularly effective brokers in facilitating learning between opponents, as their positions generally required a degree of neutrality (Ingold and Varone 2012). In the case of Illinois, state education agency officials played a vital role as policy brokers, meeting regularly with opposing coalitions, seeking feedback on solutions that met all or most needs and interacting with elected officials to gauge the feasibility of specific policy approaches.

Additionally, policy brokers involved in Illinois also included staff members of CSEP that supported various stakeholder forums by drafting reports, designing conferences and symposia, and organizing meetings where research and data were presented by state and national scholars and practitioners involved in principal preparation. CSEP staff met with actors from all advocacy coalitions, represented their views in reports, and attempted to provide alternative compromises to bridge the groups.

Private foundations that supported these efforts recognized the strong potential for impact based on the ability of stakeholders to work collaboratively with state agencies to bring about meaningful change. National foundations selected CSEP as a grantee because of the qualifications of CSEP staff, the organization's proven ability to facilitate consensus-building among disparate stakeholder groups, and its track record with projects involving collaborative improvement efforts. In fact, CSEP has a long history of informing education policy in Illinois by engaging state-level policymakers and stakeholders in their efforts.

Consistency in engagement with this work by the state education agencies and support by CSEP was essential in moving the work forward over the course of a decade. One department chair stated, "Accolades to the Center [CSEP]. The staff helped steer the boat and deal with the opposition. Without their guidance and support, we wouldn't be where we are now." Another faculty member concurred saying that "the formal workshops, symposia, and conferences offered by the Center [CSEP] and the many resources provided helped keep this effort moving. But the most significant levers were provided by supportive leadership at the state and local/regional levels."

Research

ACF scholars have considered research as a critical lever in changing views. As highlighted previously, quantitative and empirical research was viewed as most effective in changing actors' policy beliefs, particularly when used to dispel a perceived causal relationship. However, "even when the accumulation of technical information does not change the views of the opposing coalition, it can have important impacts on policy—at least in the short run—by altering the views of policy brokers" (Sabatier and Weible 2014, 200). This was certainly the case in Illinois.

After the release of the scathing Levine Report in 2005, local policymakers took notice and began voicing concern about the state of principal preparation in Illinois. However, some stakeholders questioned whether the national sample included in that study was representative of Illinois. IBHE responded to that faction by charging the Commission on School Leader Preparation in Illinois Colleges and Universities with collecting and exploring local data.

Using similar metrics as Levine (2005) and NCATE findings from a similar study, the Commission found Illinois principal preparation program largely mirrored findings from the national sample in the Levine Report (Commission on School Leader Preparation in Illinois Colleges and Universities 2006). The Commission's report, along with the appointment of a new state superintendent, spurred quick action by ISBE and IBHE. The two agencies requested that the Illinois General Assembly establish a task force to explore the problem and make policy recommendations to improve principal preparation programs.

Evidence of the influence of research on policy brokers and policymakers can also be found in the alignment of the state policy requirements with the growing body of literature on effective program elements for principal preparation. The research lever was found to be somewhat interrelated to the funding lever, as faculty and professional association representatives highlighted the importance of financial support for this work to allow them to engage with scholars who provided research-based strategies for principal preparation. Additionally, the ability to engage subject matter experts in early childhood, special education, and English Language Learners resulted in specific course and internship requirements involving knowledge and experience with subgroup populations.

External Pressure

Education policy involving principal preparation is no different than any other public policy arena, in that no reform effort operates in isolation. Rather they tend to interact with many other policies or reform efforts—sometimes complementing, coexisting, or conflicting. Policy researchers have argued, "policies do not land in a vacuum; they land on top of other policies" (Tyack and Cuban 1995, 76), and it is not uncommon for school leaders to encounter situations in which "each time that they attempted to change governance, they confronted layers of institutional experience and vested interests left by previous reforms" (Darling-Hammond 1990, 346).

Similarly, the principal preparation program improvement efforts that took place in Illinois over the course of a decade experienced the influences of policy and reform movements from other policy subsystems. As previously mentioned, the onset of NCLB in 2001 ushered in an unprecedented focus on accountability and for the first time laid bare the dismal state of our nation's high-need schools as well as the widening achievement gap found even in schools that had previously appeared to be meeting expectations.

The accountability movement illustrates how an external policy lever can be interrelated to an internal lever involving research. For example, it was NCLB that required reporting on student achievement. That policy led to an explosion of research that demonstrated through analysis of student achievement and school performance data that improvements were needed.

As such, the accountability movement provided stakeholders in Illinois with a plethora of quantitative data involving school and student performance to explore. New school performance data combined with research on the important role of the principal on student achievement, led stakeholders to a broader understanding of what changes were necessary for preparation programs in order to produce school leaders capable of transforming Illinois schools.

Additionally, national and state policies and programs that were essentially external to the principal preparation policy subsystem, such as Race to the Top and the Illinois Performance Evaluation Reform Act, placed increased pressure on preparation programs to demonstrate their candidates possess the leadership competencies necessary to positively impact school and student outcomes. These external levers alone would not be enough to spur policy change involving principal preparation. However, in combination with other levers, external pressure contributed to a political environment that was open to change.

Open Forum

The initial catalyst for bringing together various stakeholders started with IL-SAELP, which began as a voluntary group of stakeholders who came together with the specific intention of improving principal preparation programs in Illinois. The initial work entailed identifying and disseminating evidence of effective practices and included support for demonstration sites in Chicago and Springfield that had developed strong university/district partnerships. All principal preparation programs in Illinois, as well as district superintendents, principals, regional offices of education, teachers' unions, professional associations, and other civic groups were invited to participate with the IL-SAELP initiative.

Although IL-SAELP was not officially sponsored or endorsed by ISBE or IBHE, both agencies supported the effort by placing leaders from their organization in membership roles. Over time and through interaction with other levers, this unofficial group of stakeholders grew to become a platform for sharing information among members and a source of feedback for ISBE and IBHE on policy constraints and opportunities. One official stated that IL-SAELP "enabled us to bring people together from across the state. Without this support, we could not have developed the opportunities to convene stakeholders to undertake this work."

As outlined in Table 2.1, eight additional forums subsequently grew out of the initial work of IL-SAELP, each building on previous work and including a fairly stable base of stakeholders over time (Baron and Haller 2014). Additionally, other forums, such as the CSEP administered Leadership to Integrate the Learning Continuum (LINC) forum also engaged numerous stakeholders interested in specific topics involving the integration of knowledge and experience with early childhood in principal preparation and development.

Involvement of Actors with Legislative or Regulatory Authority

While the improvement efforts involving principal preparation in Illinois began through the IL-SAELP project, premised upon voluntary participation, over time a power dynamic was inserted into the open forum when ISBE and IBHE stepped in and began to drive discussions toward policy improvements. The forums continued to be voluntary in nature. However, many felt compelled to participate once leaders from ISBE and IBHE began convening the group.

Several actors viewed the shift in leadership as a crucial lever in the policy change process. ISBE and IBHE took a further step forward in the push for policy change when they engaged the Illinois General Assembly in the improvement efforts. Based on recommendations from the state agencies, the General Assembly established the Illinois School Leader Task Force charged with examining the current status of principal preparation and making specific recommendations to the legislature regarding needed policy changes.

When the engagement of stakeholders transferred from CSEP to ISBE, and IBHE and the state agencies began formally convening the group, it signaled a significant shift and indicated the state was prioritizing improvements in school leadership preparation and development. That shift took an additional step forward once the Task Force was convened and it was established that the group had a legislative anchor for its work. This shift was a major turning point in the policy change process.

A later example of this lever was also found through the identification of the chief sponsors of the legislative bills involving improvements in principal preparation that entered in the House and Senate. Both chief sponsors had participated in IL-SAELP meetings and were known supporters of the policy changes to principal preparation. The original bill was introduced by Representative Mike Smith, who had previously served as one of the legislative representatives on the IL-SAELP Executive Committee. The legislation passed the House on May 26, 2010. Then it went to the Senate where Senator Deana Demuzio, another legislative representative who served on the IL-SAELP Executive Committee, sponsored the bill. That bill passed the Senate with a unanimous vote on May 27, 2010. The two legislators' previous involvement with IL-SAELP and their standing in the General Assembly helped them garner substantial support for the bills.

A response by one principal preparation program illustrates the power of this lever. During the lengthy debate over the proposed changes to the statute and rules, one private school dean took the bold step of terminating his institution's old general administrative program a full year prior to the program being ready to apply for approval under the new regulations. Despite the financial hardship, the dean determined that the proposed changes were essential to preparing effective principals and he wanted the faculty focused exclusively on building new systems, structures, and processes that would dramatically improve outcomes.

The dean indicated that without the leadership of ISBE and IBHE and the legislative anchor established by the creation of the Task Force, he would not have had the political leverage to take that bold move. Other actors also highlighted the role of the leadership of the state agencies in moving these efforts forward. A representative from one of the teachers' unions stressed that it was "the commitment of both ISBE and IBHE working together and the broad scope of representatives and organizations that were important to this work."

Not everyone was eager to embrace the proposed changes. But even those who had expressed concern regarding the extent of the changes made identified the consistent involvement and commitment from ISBE and IBHE as an important factor in continuing to make progress. One faculty member commented that after the state agencies began convening the group, she was afraid not to continue participating as it was clear some form of policy change was going to happen. Another faculty member asserted that the "state went too far with some details that made parts of the program counterproductive." However, he added that he had found a willingness on the part of the state agency representatives to meet and address those concerns.

Conclusion

The requirements established for the new Principal Endorsement in Illinois have had a significant impact on the rigor and relevance of the preparation of principals. Since establishing the new regulations, twenty-eight of the thirty-one previously approved general administrative (Type 75) programs have been approved by the State Educator Preparation and Licensure Board (SEPLB). Opinions expressed by a number of individuals during the public comment period indicated some feared the new program requirements would dramatically decrease the number of programs preparing candidates throughout the state.

Those fears have largely been put to rest. However, the new rigor applied to candidate selection requirements has had an impact on the number of accepted applicants to the new programs and some superintendents have express concern over a potential shortage in the field. Exploring the extent of a potential shortage, the Illinois Association of School Boards (IASB) has been surveying principal preparation programs three times per year to monitor enrollment in new principal preparation programs.

Data collected by IASB demonstrated that enrollments, while initially low in the newly redesigned programs, are increasing. Four hundred thirty candidates were cumulatively enrolled across all approved programs in

2013, which was the first year of implementation. That number increased to 1,332 candidates cumulatively enrolled in all programs as of December 2015. Recognizing that supply and demand for school leaders are not only dictated by candidates in the pipeline, the new principal preparation legislation established a clause that grandfathered holders of the old administrative certificate (Type 75 certificate) with all the rights and privileges previously afforded them.

That strategy was essential to ensure an adequate supply of qualified principals during the critical transition period from the old system to the new one. According to data drawn from the Illinois State Board of Education database, there were 43,728 Type 75 certificate holders in Illinois in FY15. Further, the state averages only 400–450 principal vacancies per year, according to ISBE supply/demand data (CSEP, 2016). Therefore, from an aggregate perspective, there appears to be a more than adequate supply of candidates for school leadership positions. Whether or not candidates prepared in Type 75 programs were adequately trained to take on the challenges of a school principal is an area worthy of research.

While stakeholders across Illinois were engaged for over a decade in efforts aimed at improving principal preparation that resulted in dramatic policy change, not all actors are content with the final regulations. The ACF does not suggest that there must be consensus between coalitions in order for policy change to occur. In fact, complete consensus is highly unlikely with any major policy change. "When policy core beliefs are in dispute, the lineup of allies and opponents tends to be rather stable over periods of a decade or so" (Sabatier and Weible 2014). Such was the case in Illinois, and policy change succeeded despite some opposition.

The chair of the Illinois School Leader Task Force acknowledged, "we know from organizational change theory that systems are by their nature resistant to change and will revert to pre-change ways of doing things if the changes are not nurtured, evaluated, and re-shaped to meet conditions on the ground." In the section of this chapter that outlined how policy changes occurred in Illinois, revisions already made to Illinois Public Act 096-0903 were discussed. As the political and economic environment shifts, so too do advocacy coalitions spring back to life in an effort to capitalize on perceived windows of opportunity.

Technically, Illinois has experienced a full policy change cycle involving principal preparation programs: from policy formation to policy implementation to policy improvement. Nevertheless, to suggest the cycle ends there would be premature. Rather than a finite cycle, policy change in Illinois is conceptualized as an ongoing continuous improvement process that continues well beyond the initial implementation phase.

Evidence collected suggests that opposing advocacy coalitions have continued their work to refine the regulations further to better align with their policy beliefs. One actor interviewed expressed disappointment in the new policy, asserting, "I don't agree with this model, and it is bound to fail in the long run because institutions lack the capacity to do everything in the new legislation with an appropriate level of quality over the long-term." Further,

> My expectations about support from the State have not been met . . . the efforts of the Center [CSEP] to try and bridge the lack of support has been crucial. But I feel strongly that the State must increase responsibilities and accountability for these changes for them to be successful.

Even in dissent, the commitment to this work is evident and illustrates the need for continued engagement of ISBE, IBHE, and a broad group of actors involved in the continuous improvement process

---

Policy Concepts in 1000 Words: The Advocacy Coalition Framework

Paul Cairney

Sabatier and Jenkins-Smith [1993] developed the ACF to describe and explain a complicated policymaking environment which:

- contains multiple actors and levels of government;
- produces decisions despite high levels of uncertainty and ambiguity;
- takes years to turn decisions into outcomes; and,
- processes policy in very different ways. Some issues involve intensely politicized disputes containing many actors. Others are treated as technical and processed routinely, largely by policy specialists, out of the public spotlight.

The ACF's key terms are:

Beliefs. People engage in politics to translate their beliefs into action. There are three main types. "Core" are fundamental and unlikely to change (like a "religious conversion") but too broad to guide detailed policy (such as one's views on human nature). "Policy core" are more specific (such as the proper balance between government and market) but still unlikely to change. "Secondary Aspects" relate to the implementation of policy. They are the most likely to change, as people learn about the effects of, say, regulations versus economic incentives.

Advocacy coalition. A coalition contains, "people from a variety of positions (elected and agency officials, interest group leaders, researchers) who share a particular belief system" and "who show a non-trivial degree of coordinated activity over time."

Policy learning. Coalitions learn from policy implementation. Learning takes place through the lens of deeply held beliefs, producing different interpretations of facts and events in different coalitions. Learning is a political process—coalitions selectively interpret information and use it to exercise power. In some cases, there are commonly accepted ways to measure policy performance. In others, it is a battle of ideas where coalitions "exaggerate the influence and maliciousness of opponents." Technical information is often politicized and a dominant coalition can successfully challenge the data supporting policy change for years.

Subsystems. Coalitions compete with each other to dominate policymaking in subsystems. Subsystems are issue-specific networks. They are pervasive in government because elected officials devolve policymaking responsibility to bureaucrats who, in turn, consult routinely with participants such as interest groups. While the literature on "policy communities" and "monopolies" describes the potential for insulated relationships between a small number of actors, the ACF identifies many actors in each coalition.

Policy broker and sovereign. Subsystems contain actors who mediate between coalitions and make authoritative decisions (although policymakers may be members of coalitions).

Policy change over a "decade or more." We are generally talking about relationships, policies, and change over a full "policy cycle."

Enlightenment. Core beliefs are "normative" and "largely beyond direct empirical challenge"; unlikely to change during routine policy learning in one cycle. However, they may change over decades.

The subsystem contains generally routine policymaking, producing relatively minor policy change: coalitions engage in policy learning, adapting the secondary aspects of their beliefs in light of new information. In most cases, learning follows the routine monitoring of implementation, as members consider how policy contributes to positive or unintended outcomes and whether their beliefs are challenged or supported by the evidence (and how it is presented by their competitors).

This process takes place in a wider system that sets the parameters for action, providing each coalition with different constraints and opportunities. It includes:

- factors that are "relatively stable," such as "social values" and the broad "constitutional structure";
- "long term coalition opportunity structures" related to the nature of different political systems (unitary/federal, concentrated/divided powers, single/multi-party, coalition/minority government) and the "degree of consensus needed for major change";
- "external (system) events" such as socio-economic change, a change in government, or important decisions made in other subsystems.

In rare cases, external events prompt subsystem instability and the potential for rapid, major policy change. Events may set in motion "internal" or "external shocks." An internal shock relates to the effect of major external change on a coalition's belief system, akin to a crisis of confidence. The event prompts a coalition to revisit its policy core beliefs, perhaps following a realization by many of its actors that existing policies have failed monumentally, followed by their departure to a different coalition. An external shock has the added element of competition—another coalition uses the experience of a major event to reinforce its position within the subsystem, largely by demonstrating that its belief system is best equipped to interpret new information and solve the policy problem. In other words, the external event is not enough to cause an external shock; it also has to be exploited successfully by a competing coalition which is well led, and equipped to learn and adapt—using resources to frame information, exploit public opinion, rally support (and, in some cases, secure funding).

Externally prompted change may vary, from the election of a new government with beliefs that favor one coalition over another, to a "focusing event" such as an environmental crisis that undermines the ability of a coalition to defend current policy. While many external factors—global recession, environmental crises, demographic changes—appear to solely cause change, coalitions also influence how sovereigns understand, interpret, and respond to them. External events provide new resources to some coalitions—it is up to them to exploit the opportunity.

The ACF developed initially from case studies in the US, with a particular focus on environmental policy. It has changed markedly to reflect its application to cases outside the US and in other policy fields (and by new scholars). For example, the discussion of "long term coalition opportunity structures" resulted from applications to European countries with proportional electoral systems and/or fewer "venues" in which to pursue policy change. The ACF is also revised constantly to reflect the desire of its core team (now driven by Weible and Jenkins-Smith) to clarify/revise earlier arguments in light of experience. It remains one of the most ambitious policy frameworks which tries to provide an overview of the entire policy process.

Source: Reprinted with permission from Paul Cairney, "Policy Concepts in 1000 Words: The Advocacy Coalition Framework." Blog Post, Oct. 30, 2013 retrieved from: https://paulcairney.wordpress.com/2013/10/30/policy-concepts-in-1000-words-the-advocacy-coalition-framework/

Bibliography

Baron, Debra, and Alicia Haller. *Redesigning Principal Preparation and Development for the Next Generation: Lessons from Illinois*. Normal, IL: Center for the Study of Education Policy, Illinois State University, 2014.

Center for the Study of Education Policy (CSEP). *Statewide Data on the Supply and Demand of Principals as a Result of Illinois' New Principal Endorsement*. Normal, IL: Illinois State University, 2016.

Commission on School Leader Preparation in Illinois Colleges and Universities. *School Leader Preparation: A Blueprint for Change*. Springfield, IL: Illinois Board of Higher Education, 2006.

Darling-Hammond, Linda. "Instructional Policy into Practice: The Power of the Bottom Over the Top." *Educational Evaluation and Policy Analysis* 12, no. 3 (1990): 339–347.

Fry, Betty, Gene Bottoms, and Kathy O'Neill. *The Principal Internship: How Can We Get It Right*. Atlanta, GA: Southern Regional Education Board, 2005.

Illinois School Leader Task Force. *Illinois School Leader Task Force Report to the Illinois General Assembly*. Springfield, IL: Illinois State Board of Education and Illinois Board of Higher Education, 2008.

Ingold, Karin, and Frederic Varone. "Treating Policy Brokers Seriously: Evidence from the Climate Policy." *Journal of Public Administration Research and Theory* 22 (2012): 319–346.

Jenkins-Smith, Hank, Daniel Nohrstedt, Christopher Weible, and Paul Sabatier. "The Advocacy Coalition Framework: Foundations, Evolution, and Ongoing

Research." In *Theories of the Policy Process* (3rd ed.), edited by Paul Sabatier and Christopher Weible, 183–223. Boulder, CO: Westview Press, 2014.

Levine, Arthur. *Educating School Leaders*. New York: Teachers College, Education School Project, 2005.

Murphy, Joseph, Stephen Elliott, Ellen Goldring, and Andrew Porter. *Learning-Centered Leadership: A Conceptual Foundation*. New York: The Wallace Foundation, 2006.

Nowlin, Matthew. "Theories of the Policy Process: State of the Research and Emerging Trends." *Policy Studies Journal* 39, no. S1 (2011): 41–60.

Sabatier, Paul. "An Advocacy Coalition Framework of Policy Change and the Role of Policy-Oriented Learning Therein." *Policy Sciences* 21, no. 2–3 (1988): 129–168.

Sabatier, Paul, and Hank Jenkins-Smith. "The Advocacy Coalition Framework: An Assessment." In *Theories of the Policy Process, Theoretical Lenses on Public Policy Series*, edited by Paul Sabatier, 117–166. Boulder, CO: Westview Press, 1999.

Sabatier, Paul, and Hank Jenkins-Smith. *Policy Change and Learning: An Advocacy Coalition Framework*. Boulder, CO: Westview Press, 1993.

Sabatier, Paul, and Christopher Weible. "The Advocacy Coalition Framework: Innovation and Clarifications." In *Theories of the Policy Process* (2nd ed.), edited by Paul Sabatier, 189–222. Boulder, CO: Westview Press, 2007.

Sabatier, Paul A., and Christopher M. Weible (eds.). *Theories of the Policy Process*. Boulder, CO: Westview Press, 2014.

Tyack, David, and Larry Cuban. *Tinkering Toward Utopia*. Cambridge, MA: Harvard University Press, 1995.

Waters, Tim, Robert Marzano, and Brian McNulty. *Balanced Leadership: What 30 Years of Research Tells Us About the Effect of Leadership on Student Achievement*. Aurora, CO: Mid-Continent Research for Education and Learning, 2003.

Weible, Christopher, and Paul Sabatier. "A Guide to the Advocacy Coalition Framework." In *Handbook of Public Policy Analysis*, edited by Frank Fischer and Gerald Miller, 123–136. Boca Raton, FL: CRS Press, 2006.

Weible, Christopher, Paul Sabatier, Hank Jenkins-Smith, Daniel Nohrstedt, Adam Henry, and Peter deLeon. "A Quarter Century of the Advocacy Coalition Framework: An Introduction to the Special Issue." *Policy Studies Journal* 39, no. 3 (2011): 349–360.

Weible, Christopher, Paul Sabatier, and Kelly McQueen. "Themes and Variations: Taking Stock of the Advocacy Coalition Framework." *Policy Studies Journal* 37, no. 1 (2009): 121–140.

Vignettes

New Leaders as a National Advocacy Partner in State Policy Change

Jackie Gran and Alexandra Broin

New Leaders (formerly New Leaders for New Schools) launched in 2000 as a nonprofit organization focused on a two-part mission: (1) preparing the next generation of outstanding school principals, and (2) using its model and lessons to spur changes to the broader field of school leader development and support. In many ways, the impetus behind New Leaders mirrored the origins of the Illinois State Action for Education Leadership Project (IL-SAELP). The founders recognized what emerging research and many practitioners and experts in the field, especially in Illinois, were coming to understand: that the caliber of a school's leader dramatically affected teacher quality and student learning, and that the existing recruitment, selection, training, and support of the nation's principals was insufficient.

In 2004, April Irvin, executive director of New Leaders–Chicago, joined the Illinois IL-SAELP Consortium. New Leaders continued to engage with the IL-SAELP through 2011, during which time Irvin and her successor, Maggie Blinn, represented New Leaders on a working group. In addition to serving as a model-in-action of many of the reforms under consideration (New Leaders' program components are described in greater detail in Chapter 3), New Leaders brought a unique national perspective to the effort that helped coalition members filter and interpret information, opportunities, and challenges in ways that bolstered and advanced the ideas under discussion.

Nationally, the organization expanded from operating in two cities in 2000 to more than ten cities by 2010, bringing data and insights from school systems across the country that could be used to inform and strengthen Illinois-specific strategies. In addition, the organization's focus on addressing the leadership needs of low-performing schools and schools serving large populations of historically underserved youth, especially students of color and children from low-income families, helped put a spotlight on the role of leadership in advancing equity.

Finally, New Leaders was a pioneer in the recruitment of minority leaders, with 64 percent of its program alumni identifying as people of color, compared to just 20 percent of principals nationally (New

Leaders 2018) and other leaders historically underrepresented in the field, including women, who were all too often overlooked for leadership positions by traditional recruitment practices and networks. New Leaders brought to the working group a core belief—backed up by its experience and, over the years, hard data (Grissom, Rodriguez, and Kern 2017)—that strengthening and diversifying the school leader profession were mutually reinforcing.

It is important to recognize that New Leaders was not a neutral participant in the Illinois reform process; the organization had a vested interest in many of the new policies under consideration. For example, under the previous state requirements New Leaders needed to partner with an institution of higher education to sponsor program graduates for a school administrator license. In its founding documents, New Leaders explicitly anticipated that principal licensure requirements would adapt over time to accommodate innovative models to prepare principals capable of attaining measurable improvements in student achievement, and the movement in Illinois was a natural avenue for New Leaders to play a direct role in advancing this policy change.

At the same time, New Leaders' support of the Illinois reforms was also central to its mission: the organization sought to train and support a cadre of highly effective principals *and* to disperse strong leadership practices outside of the New Leaders network to "help all of our young people—not just a few—reach high levels of achievement and knowledge." New Leaders was intentionally structured to support the growth and expansion of its program, yet the organization equally relied on like-minded institutions and strong advocacy partners to achieve its vision for large-scale, national impact.

In fact, New Leaders was organized as an entity outside of the existing traditional principal preparation infrastructure specifically so it could more easily test out new ideas (including those explored and eventually adopted in Illinois), learn and adapt based on what worked (and what didn't), and then bring proven practices back into the larger system. In its early years, this information-sharing often took the form of informal conversations with other preparation programs as well as formal public presentations. Later on, New Leaders began providing more robust technical assistance to federal, state, and local policymakers and publishing open-source materials to help others apply lessons from New Leaders' programs, research, and system-level support to further strengthen leadership policies and practices across the sector.

Ultimately, while New Leaders operated with a sense of urgency to leverage strong leadership to address persistent, inequitable, and unacceptable gaps in educational opportunity and outcomes, the organization was and remains equally committed to investing the time and resources needed to share what it has learned in order to support necessary reforms. Essentially, we've taken that approach so that many more students, teachers, schools, and communities—in Illinois and across the country—can benefit from well-prepared, well-supported, highly effective principals.

Bibliography

"About Us," New Leaders. 2018. Accessed September 24, 2018, https://newleaders.org/about/

Grissom, Jason A., Luis A. Rodriguez, and Emily C. Kern. "Teacher and Principal Diversity and the Representation of Students of Color in Gifted Programs: Evidence from National Data." *The Elementary School Journal* 117, no. 3 (2017): 396–422.

The District as the Consumer: Shared Ownership among Universities and Districts for the Preparation of Principals

Diane Rutledge

It's all about relationships and communication! When I was superintendent of Springfield School District 186, that mantra was often used throughout our system and community, and was essential in developing an effective partnership for leadership development with Illinois State University's Education Administration and Foundation Department.

When our district was awarded a Wallace Foundation grant in 2002, we were offered the opportunity to collaborate in the development of a new principal preparation program. Other grant recipients explored different models, including school districts granting their own teacher's license. However, this author believed creating enhanced school district/university partnerships had the greater potential to be sustained. Our collaboration with Illinois State University and Department Chair Dr. Diane Ashby was forged. The challenge was to fulfill the needs of both institutions, honoring credentialing mandates, while creating a new model that developed a principal that could create the conditions for school success, with emphasis on a data-rich school improvement process.

No longer could the school district simply accept the university program that was offered without a voice at the table. At that time, existing programs that prepared principals were not adequately preparing candidates to meet the needs of new state and federal accountability requirements, children living in increased poverty, use of technology and data, as well as collaborative school improvement efforts.

Leadership at the university and the school district created collaborative teams to develop a new preparation program that was comprehensive, meaningful, and effective. This occurred by:

1. Creating a shared-entrance policy for principal candidates that met the requirements and expectations of both institutions;
2. Developing a meaningful curriculum that included new courses such as the administrative use of technology, a combination course that included both human and financial resources, and a course focused on organizational dynamics, including managing change;
3. Sharing course instruction between university professors and district administrators;
4. Embedding 270 hours of clinical experiences throughout the program and throughout the district at different grade levels in order to provide a broader perspective for candidates;
5. Including a district-centric capstone course that created the opportunity for action research of problem-based situations for the candidate;
6. Providing yearlong internship opportunities to work with an exemplary principal;
7. Mentoring during the preparation program, as well as the first two years of principalship.

The district/university partnership is integral to the preparation of future school leaders. The early adopters of this strategy have served as a model for other preparation programs that reflect the needs of both school districts and universities. This collaborative approach has informed state policy, as well as institutional practice. We are truly better together!

Why Is Principal Preparation So Important for Statewide Teacher Unions?

Audrey Soglin and Dan Montgomery

The Illinois Education Association (IEA) and the Illinois Federation of Teachers (IFT) were instrumental in redesigning principal preparation because we know the success of our teachers depends greatly on the quality of school principals that supervise and support them. In a 2011 national survey of 40,000 teachers, funded by the Gates Foundation, 96 percent of teachers ranked *supportive leadership* as "absolutely essential" or "very important" to retaining good teachers. To recruit and retain the best teachers for Illinois schools, it is imperative that we have good principals.

The goal of changing principal preparation in Illinois was fairly simple—to improve the quality of the instructional leader in our schools—and IEA and IFT shared that goal. As such, we worked collaboratively to help design, pass, and implement the new state changes. We had a very strong presence throughout the legislative process that led to the new principal endorsement policies.

Unlike the previous general administrative endorsement (Type 75), which broadly applied to a variety of school administrative positions, such as deans, department chairs, athletic directors, and others who evaluate staff, the new Principal Endorsement focuses exclusively on preparing high-quality principals and assistant principals. For the first time, Illinois principal preparation programs were required to incorporate new content and field experiences to ensure that principals are capable and effective leaders of school communities, and have the skills they need to address student learning and school improvement for early learners (i.e., students in early childhood programs), English Language Learners (ELLs), and students with disabilities (i.e., have a quality Individualized Education Program [IEP]).

The new PK-12 Principal Endorsement programs were also required to include an intensive internship experience with mentors who have been successful administrators and performance-based assessments that evaluate the candidate on their work. As a result, our members are seeing more candidates coming into the job with some much-valued experience versus learning on the job, which is what so often happened in the past.

The goal of the new Principal Endorsement programs is to ensure candidates develop the critical competencies necessary to improve instruction, establish positive school cultures, and engage families, all of which lead to increased student achievement. These are all skills that matter to us and our members. Wherever they work in Illinois, our members recognize the importance of knowledgeable principals who collaborate with and welcome feedback from teachers, paraprofessionals and school-related personnel as well as the unions who represent them. Thus we continue to engage with state agencies and other education stakeholders to maintain the integrity of new principal preparation programs in our collective effort of serving students.

The Importance of Principals as Leaders in Early Childhood

Joyce Weiner and Elliot Regenstein

Decades of research are clear: high-quality early childhood education helps reduce school readiness gaps among children at kindergarten entry and strong, knowledgeable school leaders directly impact student achievement and teaching excellence. Yet very few colleges and universities have included content related to early childhood education in programs responsible for preparing school leaders. The *Every Student Succeeds Act* provides funds that can be used to support the stronger inclusion of early learning—defined as birth through age eight—within the principal preparation process.

Principals are charged with creating school environments that support children's learning and development as well as teachers' development. However, many principals have not had education or experiences that prepare them for being an instructional leader for teachers working in PreK through early elementary settings.

It is important for principals to appreciate that young children are constantly and rapidly developing and attaining new skills, but that the rate at which children progress varies significantly. Successful cognitive and social development for children in PreK-8 can be supported by teacher-led activities focused on play-based exploration and active engagement with materials. Effective instruction for young children involves a mix of activities in large groups, small groups, or individualized structures.

Success for teachers of young children requires the support of principals who can provide instructional leadership for developmentally appropriate instruction. Moreover, it requires principals who understand the importance of engaging with parents and families as partners in supporting a child's development. According to Connors et al. (2018), school leaders can promote quality learning environments and instructional practices for young children when they:

- Instill expectations that families be engaged and classrooms reflect the races, cultures, and languages of those attending the school;
- Provide teachers with reflective supervision to help them identify opportunities for improving their practice and individualizing instruction;
- Expect staff to design lessons based on student data—including results on the state's Kindergarten Individual Development Survey—to build on children's current knowledge and skills;
- Solicit input from staff on preferred topics for professional learning;
- Schedule consistent blocks of time that allow teachers to participate in job-embedded professional development and collaborative planning activities.

Illinois has been a national leader in preparing principals to provide instructional leadership to early childhood teachers. In the years ahead, the state can continue to strengthen its systems for preparing and supporting principals, so that schools can maximize their positive impact on *children ages birth through eight years*.

Bibliography

Connors, Maja, Angela Farwig, Beth Kenefick, Maureen Wagner, and Debra Pacchiano. "A New Approach to Policy: The Case for Strengthening Organizational Conditions to Improve Early Childhood Care and Education Quality." *The Ounce*, March 2018.

3 Policy Transfer from Local to Statewide

Scaling Evidence-Based Principal Preparation Practices in Illinois

Diane Rutledge and Steve Tozer

More than two decades after the 1983 publication of *A Nation at Risk* (1983) triggered the modern school reform movement, Teachers College Columbia President Arthur Levine released *Educating School Leaders* (2005), a similarly scathing lambasting of school leader preparation in the United States. The first decade of the school reform movement had focused largely on issues of teacher quality, curriculum standards, and state and district reforms in school governance—and very little on school leadership. Yet by the time of Levine's broadside twenty-two years later, significant principal preparation reform was beginning to take shape at national, state, and local levels—and Illinois became a prominent example.

The year 2005 also marked the publication of *Scaling Up Success*, the proceedings of a Harvard Symposium that noted, twenty-two years into the modern school reform movement, how difficult it was to take successful local innovation "to scale" in education. As the authors wrote:

> One of the greatest challenges in education improvement is the immense difficulty of "scaling up": adapting a locally successful innovation to a wide variety of settings while retaining its effectiveness. In contrast to experiences in other sectors of society, scaling up successful programs has proved very difficult in education. Insights from changing operations at one fast-food location may easily transfer to every store in that franchise and perhaps to any comparable type of restaurant. However, a new type of teaching strategy that is successful with one practitioner often is difficult to generalize even to other instructors in the same school, let alone to a broad range of practitioners.
>
> (Dede et al. 2005, xiii)

However, by 2012 Illinois had implemented a statewide policy to scale up from four successful principal preparation programs in two Illinois districts. What lessons can be learned from this effort?

Conditions for Change

Nationally and in Illinois, it was evident that new school leader initiatives were products of the school reform movement that began in 1983 with the publication of *A Nation at Risk*. By 1987, while school reform was still gaining momentum, Secretary of Education William Bennett declared the Chicago Public Schools (CPS) to be the "worst school system in America." Chicago's school reform movement had already begun in earnest through the Chicago School Reform Panel in 1982, state legislation in 1985, and Mayor Harold Washington's education "summit" in 1986, so most observers would say that Bennett's comments fueled an already burning fire.

At the state level in Illinois, the national school reform discourse had begun to push initiatives to establish student learning standards and teacher quality standards. These initiatives would lead to new state legislation by the mid-1990s, including new Illinois learning standards and new teacher licensure standards. It was widely agreed that although the language of *A Nation at Risk* might have been extreme in comparing America's schools to a hostile enemy act, student learning outcomes in Illinois were not something of which the state could be proud. Further, in the early years of school reform, school leadership was at best an afterthought.

As the twenty-first century approached, national shifts in the discourse on school improvement and the role of principals began to inform school leader policy change in Illinois. Leading up to Levine's report in 2005, the second decade of school reform literature was beginning to note that if the quality of classroom instruction matters to student learning, then school leadership must matter too. In the early 1990s, the Danforth Foundation began funding innovative school leader programs at the University of Washington and elsewhere, and researchers such as Ken Leithwood and Richard Elmore were publishing empirical and theoretical work on the impact of school leaders on student learning outcomes. Elmore's 1999–2000 American Federation of Teachers (AFT) article, published largely for a teacher union audience in the *American Educator*, closed the decade by mapping out "a new conception of school leadership" that would more directly affect student learning. In Elmore's ambitious vision, school leaders could influence student learning outcomes by building the organizational capacity of the school to support teacher learning toward better instructional performance.

The five-year period of ferment from 1996 to 2001 illuminates the intersection of national, state, and local initiatives in Illinois. In 1996, the National Commission on Teaching and America's Future published *What Matters Most*, which made a compelling case that the single most important in-school influence on student learning was the quality of classroom instruction. That same year, the Interstate New Teacher Assessment and

Support Consortium (INTASC 2017) published new standards for high-quality instruction for novice teachers. These were adopted in many states, including Illinois, as state standards for teacher performance. Also that year, the Interstate School Leader Licensure Consortium (ISLLC 1996) published the first set of national standards for school leadership performance. Illinois would soon adopt these as state standards for principals. Finally, 1996 was the year that the Illinois State Legislature granted permission to the Chicago Public Schools to impose eligibility standards for school principal candidates above and beyond state licensure requirements.

Five years later, by 2001, emerging school research and policy began to crystallize into new programs and practices in Illinois. One less than promising national development was the reauthorization of the Elementary and Secondary Educational Act, known as No Child Left Behind (NCLB), which focused on teacher quality and new requirements for student performance assessment but gave virtually no mention to school leadership as a lever for improving schools. Nonetheless, work continued on the ground. Despite the NCLB's failure to emphasize school leadership development, a substantial number of states by 2001 had adopted the ISLLC standards for school leader preparation, Illinois included. At the same time, the Wallace Foundation began a national campaign to fund select states that were seeking to improve school leader preparation and development as a matter of state policy and state action; again Illinois was included. The Illinois State University Center for the Study of Education Policy received a Wallace Foundation grant in 2001 and initiated the Illinois State Action for Education Leadership Project (IL-SAELP). The Wallace funding would lead, in the following year, to the launching of a new, next-generation principal preparation partnership between ISU and School District 186 in Springfield, the state capital. Also by 2001, as the state's largest district with over 400,000 students, Chicago had three different school leader development initiatives underway, representing partnerships in three different stages of development: one led by the Chicago Principals and Administrators Association, one by New Leaders for New Schools (later rebranded as New Leaders), and one by the University of Illinois at Chicago.

Turning Point for Illinois: 2005–2006

In 2005, the year that Arthur Levine's report attracted highly publicized national attention, it also attracted resistance from some colleges of education. It is worth quoting Levine at some length to capture the sharpness of his critique:

> This study found the overall quality of educational administration programs in the United States to be poor. The majority of programs range from inadequate to appalling, even at some of the country's

> leading universities. Collectively, school leadership programs are not successful on any of the nine quality criteria presented. . . . Their curricula are disconnected from the needs of leaders and their schools. Their admission standards are among the lowest in American graduate schools. Their professoriate is ill-equipped to educate school leaders. Their programs pay insufficient attention to clinical education and mentorship by successful practitioners. The degrees they award are inappropriate to the needs of today's schools and school leaders. Their research is detached from practice. And their programs receive insufficient resources. . . . This can only be described as "a race to the bottom," a competition among school leadership programs to produce more degrees faster, easier, and more cheaply.
>
> (Levine 2005, 23–24)

However, instead of taking a defensive stance, the Illinois Board of Higher Education that year initiated a thirty-two member PreK-20 Commission on School Leader Preparation in Illinois Colleges and Universities: "The Commission's purpose was to consider and evaluate the findings and recommendations of Educating School Leaders (Levine 2005), examine how principals are prepared in Illinois, and propose goals for improving principal preparation throughout the State of Illinois" (2006, 2).

Before turning to its recommendations for change in Illinois school leader preparation, *A Blueprint for Change* offered a disturbing picture of the lagging elementary and secondary school achievement levels throughout the state of Illinois. The report began:

> Student achievement in Illinois is in crisis. The 2005 National Assessment of Educational Progress (NAEP) results show Illinois with the largest gap between low-income and non-low-income student performance in fourth-grade mathematics, and the largest gap in fourth-grade reading scores between these two groups compared to neighboring Midwest states. Illinois is also among the worst six states in the nation for reading and math gaps between fourth-grade white students and their black and Hispanic peers (Sandel and Batchu 2005). Overall, Illinois students consistently perform poorly on the national measure, with roughly 60 to 65 percent of students unable to score at the "proficient" level or above. On state tests, which may be considered to have lower standards than NAEP, very little improvement has occurred over the past seven years.
>
> (2006, 14)

The Commission went on to document student achievement deficits at length and argued that improving student performance in Illinois schools required a greater commitment to high-quality principal preparation programs in colleges and universities.

By the time that *Blueprint for Change* was released in 2006, four programs in Illinois were demonstrating what the next generation of principal preparation in Illinois might look like, and the report identified three of the four as "model programs" to inform state innovations in policy and practice. In Springfield, the program model implemented a partnership between the district and the program provider—in this case, District 186 and Illinois State University, respectively. Three different partnerships were also demonstrating results in Chicago, and all, like the Springfield/ISU model, emphasized school-based leadership learning and partnerships between the providers in the school district. In addition, all four emphasized careful candidate selection into formal cohorts as a key program component.

Springfield District 186 and Illinois State University Partnership

The Springfield model was developed as one of the twelve LEAD districts funded nationwide by the Wallace Foundation in 2002. It was based on the premise of the school district as the consumer of principal preparation programs; therefore, it was a logical extension that a district/university partnership had the most potential for sustained reform. The initiative provided a means to develop aspiring principals through a collaborative entrance process, relevant curriculum, shared course instruction, embedded clinical experiences, yearlong paid internships, and ongoing mentoring throughout the program and the first two years of novice principalships. The program created a district pipeline for principals and other school leaders while focusing on continuous school improvement. As *Blueprint for Change* (2006) noted in identifying the Springfield/ISU partnership as a model:

> LEAD has numerous components, each critical to improving student achievement in the district. One of the main components is a two-year master's degree cohort program developed and implemented through a partnership with Illinois State University. Each semester one course is taught by an Illinois State faculty member and one is taught by a District #186 administrator. All course materials are tied to the district's needs, and each course contains a one-year internship with a district principal. The program also provides new principal mentoring for first- and second-year principals. Current and retired master principals meet weekly with new principals and also attend monthly professional development sessions with them. As a result of LEAD, the District #186 office notes that school principals have become more committed to spending half their time being instructional leaders.
>
> (2006, 74)

Chicago Public Schools (CPS) and Chicago Principals and Administrators Association (CPAA)

In Chicago, the three models were different in the origins and in partnerships. The first one, LAUNCH, was established in the late 1990s by the Chicago Principal and Administrators Association (CPAA) in partnership with CPS, which provided substantial funding for the initiative. The LAUNCH program selected assistant principals and teacher leaders who applied through a competitive-admissions program. Selected candidates were provided with fully paid, one-semester internships, completed under the supervision of mentor principals who were selected by the LAUNCH program on the basis of their leadership quality. A remarkably high percentage of LAUNCH candidates were hired as CPS principals in a competitive process in which each school's local school council had authority to select the principal. This high hiring rate was a significant departure from standard practice in principal preparation programs in Illinois, where typically a small percentage of graduates achieved principalships reasonably soon after graduation from their certification programs.

Chicago Public Schools and New Leaders Partnership

The second of the Chicago programs, also a partnership with the school district and also highly selective, was identified in the *Blueprint for Change* report as a model national program. New Leaders for New Schools, later abbreviated to New Leaders, began accepting cohorts of approximately twenty-five to thirty candidates in 2001, providing a full-year, fully paid residency with a salary substantially above the average for CPS teachers but below the average for Chicago assistant principals. Like LAUNCH, a high percentage of New Leaders' graduates were hired as principals immediately upon their completion of the certification program residency. Also, like LAUNCH, the New Leaders program was not fundamentally a university-based program, though it was required by the state to have a formal accrediting relationship with a local university. In this case, New Leaders partnered with National Louis University, so that candidates could earn university credit for their New Leaders academic and field experiences. The Commission noted:

> The three-year program is highly selective and rigorous. In the first year, participants attend classes, experience ongoing instructional and leadership skill development, and complete a full-time, one-year residency program in an urban school. During the residency program, participants are assigned a mentor principal, meet regularly with leadership coaches, complete numerous projects based on their needs and the school's needs, and develop a portfolio documenting how they fulfill principal leadership competencies. During the second

and third years, participants receive coaching and mentoring tailored to their individual needs.

(2006, 75)

Chicago Public Schools and the University of Illinois at Chicago (UIC)

The third Chicago-based program, unlike New Leaders or LAUNCH, was similar to the Springfield model in that it was a university-district partnership. The University of Illinois at Chicago began its formal partnership with CPS in 2002 and accepted the first cohort in 2003. Like New Leaders, UIC candidates experienced a full-time, fully paid internship in their first year of the program, while being coached by high-performing former CPS principals. After receiving the state administrative certification, UIC candidates competed for leadership positions in the district and then continued their coaching in the UIC program, taking additional coursework and assessments as they progressed toward an EdD degree. In identifying the program as a model, the Commission wrote:

> The program integrates theory with practice through a three-year clinical curriculum that is designed and taught by UIC faculty in conjunction with principals and system-level instructional officers with experience as successful urban school transformers. . . . The Ed.D program in Urban Education Leadership is highly selective and assessment-driven. Candidates are evaluated frequently on their commitment, knowledge, and performance as change agents in urban settings. Students who satisfactorily meet all assessment criteria may qualify for the Type 75 after one year of full-time, clinical internship and coursework.
>
> (2006, 74)

Despite the evident differences among the four models that were producing principals, they had a number of things in common:

1. All programs represented partnerships between the program providers and the public school system for which principals were being produced, giving voice to the school system in program design, implementation, and assessment of program outcomes.
2. All were designed expressly to produce school leaders who could improve student learning outcomes in schools, which led to relatively small programs designed not to produce maximum numbers of credentialed candidates but to produce results in schools.
3. The programs were selective in their admissions, and all admitted their candidates to cohorts to take advantage of the benefits of a cohort model.

4. All programs emphasized school-based leadership learning through leadership residencies, with mentoring and coaching as essential to the pre-service phase and, for three model programs, continuing into post-certification leadership roles.
5. All programs used the intensive school-based field experiences for more in-depth candidate assessment than would otherwise be possible.
6. All programs expressly based their academic and field-based learning experiences on current standards and research in the field of school leadership, but in addition to these inputs, they kept *output* data on candidate hiring into leadership roles and candidate performance in these roles.

While the Commission lauded these in-state programs, *Blueprint for Change* also reported that the variation in program quality throughout the state was a problem that needed to be addressed if the goal was to improve K-12 learning outcomes in Illinois:

> The considerable variation in quality between school leader preparation programs in Illinois is a significant obstacle. While many programs are high quality and others are in the process of making improvement, there is still wide variability in admissions standards, coursework, clinical experiences, student assessment, and faculty qualifications across the state. This variability poses a problem, as not all aspiring leaders have access to the same high-quality programs that will prepare them to improve the quality of schools and raise student achievement, especially in high-need schools.
>
> (2006, 8)

As a consequence of this variation among the state's "model" programs, and others that the Commission analyzed, *Blueprint for Change* submitted six recommendations for state action. These focused recommendations were a significant turning point for the state because the Commission's thirty-two members (including IBHE staff) were broadly representative of many significant constituencies: large and small districts, public and private colleges and universities, teachers and principals' associations, business and community members. The findings were based on the Commission's shared assessments of the research literature, policy critiques of principal preparation, and in-state as well as out-of-state models of what next-generation programs might become. These were the Commission's recommendations:

1. Restructure admission criteria and recruit high-quality principals;
2. Improve programs using rigorous assessment data;
3. Create meaningful clinical and internship experiences;

4. Establish a rigorous certification exam;
5. Revise the certification and endorsement structure;
6. Coordinate a rigorous program review and approval process.

From Blueprint to Policy Change: 2007–2012

Blueprint for Change represented a turning point for Illinois not just in the content of its recommendations, but in the level of intrastate collaboration to which it led. At this time in Illinois educational history, the "big four" state agencies in Illinois education governance—IBHE, ISBE, Illinois Community College Board (ICCB), and the Governor's Office—were not known for their ability to work productively together across their different jurisdictions. For *Blueprint for Change* recommendations to be implemented, however, collaboration would be needed among at least three of the four—the ICCB did not have a horse in that race.

For some time, a number of related cross-sector collaborations had been initiated in Illinois, and in some cases, they persisted, from a mid-1990s statewide task force that changed state teacher licensure, to the subsequent Illinois Governor's Council on Educator Quality, to IL-SAELP, to the IBHE Commission. These different cross-sector coalitions, engaging PK-12, higher education, foundations, the business community, teachers' unions, and others, sometimes successfully passed legislation to change the Illinois School Code. But *Blueprint for Change* was led and "owned" largely by the IBHE (with IL-SAELP and ISU support), and the Illinois State Board of Education did not embrace it. More than a year after it was released, no action was taken on *Blueprint for Change*.

In 2007, however, this would begin to change. Newly appointed (2006) Illinois State Superintendent of Education Christopher Koch was familiar with the potential power of cross-sector work in Illinois from his experience a decade earlier as an ISBE staff member on a joint ISBE–University of Illinois at Chicago task force on teacher licensure in Illinois that led directly to substantial changes in the Illinois School Code. Instead of remaining distant from the IBHE Commission report, he worked with IBHE, ISU, and UIC to draft a legislative resolution expressly to examine the potential for recommendations from *Blueprint for Change* to be implemented in legislation and practice. The resolution formed a legislative task force charged with the responsibility to

> Prepare a report to the General Assembly, the Office of the Governor, the State Board of Education, and the Board of Higher Education that details an action plan for strategically improving school leadership preparation in Illinois, based on, but not limited to, the measures detailed in the report of the Commission on School Leader Preparation: A Blueprint for Change.

This stage of the process is succinctly captured in Redesigning Principal Preparation and Development for the Next Generation: Lessons from Illinois (Baron and Haller 2014):

> Both IBHE and ISBE leaders were instrumental in moving this work forward. Bringing the combined voice of the two regulatory agencies together to work on this issue made the topic of leadership preparation a real priority in the state. As a result, the *Illinois School Leader Task Force* was convened in 2007, after the Illinois General Assembly passed unanimous resolutions supporting its creation. HJR66 and SJR56 established that ISBE, IBHE, and the Office of the Governor would jointly appoint a task force charged with developing an action plan to improve school leader preparation in the State of Illinois. Chaired by Steve Tozer, a professor at UIC, the Illinois School Leader Task Force was comprised of 28 members, representing public and private universities, public school districts, teachers' unions, professional associations, both chambers of the state legislature, ISBE, and IBHE. . . . Operation of the Task Force (fiscal oversight, administration of meetings, management of workflow, etc.) was supported by staff from CSEP, along with staff from IBHE and ISBE. The design of the task force as a co-commissioned effort by both education agencies set the course for the future success of this work.
> (Baron and Haller 2014, 10)

In fact, this chapter's co-authors took leadership roles in Task Force deliberations, because each had led one of the three IBHE "model programs" that were influential in the Task Force discussions. The resources the Task Force had to draw upon were both internal and external:

1. Membership: key leaders from any sector that had a stake in school leader quality in Illinois;
2. Data on student learning outcomes in Illinois: was there really a problem that needed to be addressed;
3. Research and professional standards: the CSEP staff were instrumental in assembling an ever-growing binder of resources for each Task Force member so that members were informed about developments in the field's research, theory, professional standards, and innovative professional programs in other states. Also, the Illinois Council of Professor of Educational Administration conducted a gap analysis to see where the state's preparation programs might be falling short of the needs of leadership in schools;
4. External expertise: for example, the Southern Regional Education Board conducted a policy inventory on Illinois policies for supporting school leadership preparation and development;

72 *Diane Rutledge and Steve Tozer*

5. Examination of the design and impact of the four Illinois programs that appeared to be leading the state in principal preparation innovation.

The preceding list reveals two significant gaps that the Task Force had to confront. One of these was the gap between (a) student learning outcomes in Illinois and (b) clear evidence that highly competent school leaders are able to improve student learning outcomes significantly. By that measure, it could not be said that leaders in Illinois were, for the most part, highly competent. In fact, similar to *Blueprint for Change*, the Task Force began its *Final Report* with the following achievement update:

> Illinois schools have many things to be proud of, but our students are losing ground against the rest of the nation on key indicators of student achievement. The most recent (2007) results from the National Assessment of Educational Progress show that only 32.2% of Illinois 4th-graders and 29.8% of 8th-graders are proficient in reading. Not only are 26 states above Illinois in each of those categories, but Illinois lost ground against the average gains of the rest of the states over the past four years, 2003–2007. In fact, Illinois lost ground against national averages over the past four years not only in 4th and 8th-grade reading but also in 4th and 8th-grade mathematics—all four of the student achievement measures reported in a current study by Quality Counts (January 2008). It is little wonder that Illinois received a grade of D+ for student achievement in the Quality Counts report.
>
> (2008, 5)

The second gap is a perennial one in educational improvement: the gap between successful models and practice at scale. The Task Force had to decide whether innovative models in principal preparation, from Illinois or elsewhere, were, in fact, successful—and whether they had elements that could be brought to scale in Illinois. As a consequence, in addition to looking at state policies and practices outside Illinois, the Task Force heard presentations on each of the four Illinois programs—the Springfield District 186 partnership and the other three CPS partnerships—to learn about their practices and results.

These two gaps, between research and practice on the one hand, and between exemplar and scale on the other, are to some extent both captured in a concluding remark from Edmonds's influential article in *Education Leadership*:

> We can, whenever and wherever we choose, successfully teach all children whose schooling is of interest to us. We already know more

than we need to do that. Whether or not we do it must finally depend on how we feel about the fact that we haven't so far.

(Edmonds 1979, 23)

In his conclusion to that article, Edmonds reminded us that the first thing we know about schools that produce strong academic outcomes for low-income kids is that they are led by capable principals. One key question for the Task Force was whether the four innovative models in Illinois were teaching us anything valuable about producing such principals. As leaders of each of the four programs presented that model and its data to the Task Force, and as members of the Task Force interrogated each of them, the evidence presented began to support a number of points of consensus:

1. *As expectations for schools have increased, so must expectations for school leaders and their preparation increase.* Model programs presented evidence that expectations for school leadership preparation could be raised by focusing programs on the principal's distinct role in the school, on candidate selectivity, by integrating rigorous academic work with extensive clinical experiences, and by leadership coaching beyond the certificate program. The Task Force further recognized that NCLB had codified what we already knew as a field: that it was no longer acceptable for sizeable portions of our population to fail to learn to read or to drop out of school. The twenty-first century would place a cultural and economic premium on all children learning well in school, and this posed new challenges to school leadership and the preparation of school leaders. Among those challenges are the importance of systematically documenting the outcomes of school leader programs, so the public will know whether increased expectations are being met.
2. *Partnerships improve program quality.* Each program presented evidence that its preparation and development work strengthened through close partnership with the school district. The Task Force came to the view that the work of strong school leader development is so challenging and so important that it should not be left up to higher education or not-for-profit providers (such as New Leaders) alone. In the past, districts had lived with the consequences of principal preparation programs in their schools, but higher education has not. Strong district-provider partnerships in the model programs established reciprocal relationships, enabling districts to have input into the content and quality of preparation programs, including providing and shaping the site-based learning experiences that providers cannot by themselves provide.

3. *School-based learning improves leadership development.* All programs presented evidence that their one-semester to multi-year clinical experiences were strengthening candidate preparation and development. One indicator was the extraordinarily high percentage of candidates, in some programs 95–100 percent, who were taking assistant principal and principal roles immediately after the residency. The Task Force members came to share the view that just as medical preparation had undergone a dramatic transformation almost exactly a century earlier, moving from exclusively classroom-based training to a blend of academic and clinical experiences, so could school leader preparation benefit from a similar increase in school-based leadership learning experiences.
4. *Programs should focus on the specific learning needs of principals.* All programs emphasized the value of focusing limited program resources on preparation for the distinctive, instructional leadership role of principal. The task force shared the view that the Illinois general administrative certificate, intended to prepare candidates for a wide range of school leadership roles including department head, dean, and athletic director, resulted in thousands of candidates receiving leadership credential who never aspired to be principals. Therefore, program resources were being attenuated across thousands of candidates instead of being focused in intense ways on the preparation, development, and assessment of far fewer candidates.
5. *Programs could track evidence of leadership impact on improved student outcomes.* By 2007–2008, the four model programs had been in place long enough that early impact on student outcomes was identifiable—in such leading indicators as measures of school culture and climate as assessed by the Consortium on Chicago School Research and student attendance; freshman-on-track; and lagging indicators, such as annual high school dropout rates and standardized test scores (Chicago was beginning to demonstrate standardized test score increases that at that time were not convincing, but that would later become compelling as Chicago sustained these increases over a fifteen-year period) (Reardon and Hinze-Pifer 2017; Zavitkovsky and Tozer 2017).

Program Diversity and Scalability

In short, the programs offered an "existence proof" to conduct principal preparation programs more effectively in the largest district in the state and in a medium-sized district, and that there was not just one right way to do it. Two of the programs were higher education/district partnerships while the other programs were not. One of the programs embedded its administrative certificate in a doctoral program while one of the programs was not a degree program at all. One program had a one-semester internship while the others had yearlong residencies. Yet together, the programs pointed toward principles of partnership, practice-based learning, and candidate selectivity that the Task Force found were potentially transferable to the state scale.

The final recommendations of the Task Force, therefore, allowed for considerable flexibility and local decision-making in program design. As was recognized explicitly in the Task Force language, it was not only the details of each model that mattered, but that engaging local partners in collaboratively co-designing models that would respond to local conditions was critical. This would replicate what each of the four model partnerships had gone through in co-designing their programs. The Task Force recommendations included specific language indicating that partnerships should be engaged collaboratively in the "design, implementation, and assessment" of their programs, not the replication of some model being put forward. But the recommendations did suggest a set of decision-making rules, or parameters, within which programs should operate, if we were to have a coherent statewide approach to redesign principal preparation and certification in Illinois. For example, while the Task Force was virtually unanimous that practice-based learning was an important lesson learned from the model programs, the nature and duration of the residency should not be overprescribed, but rather that the purpose of preparing leaders to improve student learning should remain central:

> While some Task Force members urged that residencies should be an academic year in length as practiced in some programs in Illinois and elsewhere, others disagreed, arguing that duration of residencies should be left to program providers under state approval guidelines. What was clear from Task Force deliberations was the purpose of the residency: that principal preparation should include a substantial opportunity for hands-on, practical leadership experience in which candidate performance could be meaningfully evaluated.
>
> (2008, 9)

The Task Force addressed the tension between state-level coherence at scale and over-prescription of local practices with three broad design principles that would provide new direction for the state. These design principles were intended to create a systemic approach that would ensure that the state would provide the necessary supports for local partnerships to establish more rigorous next-generation programs in Illinois—and that would tie this systemic approach—explicitly to student learning outcomes. In a section titled simply "System," the Task Force Final Report attempted to capture that systemic approach as follows:

> The members of this Task Force believe that efforts to improve pre-K-12 student learning in Illinois must include focused and strategic

measures to improve the consistency of school leadership quality throughout the state. Further, we believe that three primary instruments for improving leadership quality are most likely to result in real gains in student learning:

(1) State Policies that set high standards for school leadership certification and align principal preparation, early career development, and distinguished principal recognition with those standards;
(2) Formal Partnerships between school districts, institutions of higher education, and other qualified partners to support principal preparation and development; and
(3) Refocused Principal Preparation Programs committed to developing and rigorously assessing in aspiring principals the capacities that are most likely to improve student learning in pre-K-12 schools.

These three instruments must be understood as components in a systemic approach to achieving consistently high-support for the career-long development of Illinois school leaders, from aspiring to novice to master principals.

(2008)

It is not the purview of this chapter to describe in detail the process by which the Task Force recommendations became law, as was elaborated in previous chapters. However, it is worth noting that the collaborative, inclusive processes of the Task Force, together with nearly two years of subsequent work teams and local hearings that engaged higher education and school districts from throughout the state in debating and modifying Task Force recommendations, created advocates for the provisions of the Final Report, modified though they were. Higher education deans and faculty, leadership of such district superintendent organizations as the Large Unit District Association, policy groups such as Advance Illinois, and both ISBE and IBHE leadership all worked with the State Legislature as the Task Force recommendations went through a relatively tedious process of bill-writing and rules-making. By 2010, more than two years after the Task Force completed its work in January 2008, the Illinois Legislature resoundingly passed Illinois Public Act 096-0903.

Policy Change versus "Change at Scale"

To pass a new state law is a significant step in changing institutional practice, but it is not the same as change *at scale*. Certainly, Illinois Public Act 096-0903 was a laudable and hard-won step in the change process. In fact, the new state policy began rather quickly to attract national attention, recognized in 2014 by the Education Commission of the States for the Frank Newman Award in Policy Innovation. In 2015, two national studies—one by Dr. Paul Manna and one by University Council for Educational Administration—each recognized Illinois as one of the two leading states in principal development policy. But that is not the end of the story, as the 2016 ISLAC Final Report stated:

> While Illinois has been recognized as a pioneering state in its focus on school leader preparation, there is still much more work to do. A key message of this report is that policy implementation requires even more attention than policy formation, and that implementation needs to be reworked and refined over time to be successful.
> (ISLAC Final Report, 2016)

There is no doubt that Illinois has been moving forward since the passage of the new state law in 2010—sometimes at state scale and sometimes in enhanced local initiatives. A study conducted collaboratively in 2015 by the Illinois Education Research Council and the Consortium for Chicago School Research showed encouraging implementation progress statewide. At the time of the ISLAC Final Report in 2016, local initiatives included twenty-six partnerships between principal preparation programs (including New Leaders as a non-IHE provider) and school districts winning approval to launch next-generation programs in Illinois. And some of these partnerships, including multiple universities and multiple districts from Quincy to Bloomington to Chicago, have received substantial federal grants to deepen and extend their work. In addition, supplemental legislation was passed to address omissions or oversights in PA 096-0903, such as reciprocity agreements with other states.

While it is not necessary to detail the recommendations of the ISLAC Final Report here, it is worth noting that their focus on committing Illinois to continuous improvement of the state's policies and practices in principal preparation and development is consistent with the set of studies with which we began this chapter, *Scaling Up Success* (Dede, Honan, and Peters 2005). The opening chapter of the book is "Moving from Successful Local Practice to Effective State Policy: Lessons from Union City," in which the authors write:

> Our analysis is grounded in three broad assumptions:
>
> - There is limited understanding of how to take a successful local educational model and convert it into a state-level policy that achieves similar results throughout the state.
> - Coherence and support across state, district, and school levels are essential to the scaling-up process.
> - Ultimate success is anchored in the opportunity schools and districts have to localize practices while maintaining high levels of

coherence and consistency concerning the goals and principals of a given policy.

(Carrigg, Honey, and Thorpe 2005, 1)

To contribute to that literature on scaling up, we would, first, affirm those three broad assumptions, stated more than a decade ago. Second, we would add that the process takes time. The Wallace Foundation began funding Illinois for statewide principal preparation change in 2000, and nearly two decades later we are not yet where we want to be, as the ISLAC report emphasizes. Third, Illinois is demonstrating that scaling up is worth the struggle. Not only are we seeing next-generation programs gaining traction in multiple areas of the state, but also in the state's largest district, the one that has invested by far the most in these programs over time. The results in student achievement gains and high school graduation rates are so significant and so sustained that they have received national attention in the scholarly and mainstream media publications. Finally, we must therefore, remain committed to continuously improving our capacity to increase the quality of principals that our PreK-12 students deserve.

Bibliography

Baron, Debra, and Alicia Haller. *Redesigning Principal Preparation and Development for the Next Generation: Lessons from Illinois*. Normal, IL: Center for the Study of Education Policy, 2014.

Carrigg, Fred, Margaret Honey, and Ron Thorpe. "Moving from Successful Local Practice to Effective State Policy: Lessons from Union City." *Scaling Up Success: Lessons from Technology-based Educational Improvement* (2005): 1–26.

Commission on School Leader Preparation in Illinois Colleges and Universities. *School Leader Preparation: A Blueprint for Change*. Springfield, IL: Illinois Board of Higher Education, 2006.

Dede, Chris, James P. Honan, and Laurence C. Peters. *Scaling Up Success: Lessons Learned from Technology-Based Educational Improvement*. Indianapolis: Jossey-Bass, 2005.

Edmonds, Ronald. "Effective Schools for the Urban Poor." *Educational Leadership* 37, no. 1 (1979): 15–24.

Elmore, Richard F. *Building a New Structure for School Leadership*. Washington, D.C.: Albert Shanker Institute, 2000.

Illinois School Leader Advisory Council. *Final Report*. Springfield, IL: Illinois State Board of Education, Illinois Board of Higher Education, 2016.

Illinois School Leader Task Force. *Illinois School Leader Task Force Report to the Illinois General Assembly*. Springfield, IL: Illinois State Board of Education and Illinois Board of Higher Education, 2008.

Interstate New Teacher Assessment and Support Consortium. *Model Core Standards for Teaching*. Washington, DC: Council of Chief State School Officers, 2017.

Interstate School Leaders Licensure Consortium. *Interstate School Leaders Licensure Consortium: Standards for School Leaders: Adopted by Full Consortium, November 2.* Washington, D.C.: Council of Chief State School Officers, 1996.

Levine, Arthur. *Educating School Leaders.* New York: Teachers College, Education School Project, 2005.

Manna, Paul. *Developing Excellent School Principals to Advance Teaching and Learning: Considerations for State Policy.* New York: The Wallace Foundation, 2015.

National Commission on Teaching & America's Future (US). *What Matters Most: Teaching for America's Future: Report of the National Commission on Teaching & America's Future.* Arlington, VA: NCTAF, 1996.

Reardon, Sean F., and Rebecca Hinze-Pifer. *Test Score Growth Among Public School Students in Chicago, 2009–2014.* Palo Alto: Stanford Center for Education Policy Analysis, 2017.

Sandel, Kathryn, and Bindu Batchu. *The Gap Persists: Closing Illinois' Achievement Divide.* Chicago: A+ Illinois, 2005.

Zavitkovsky, Paul, and Steven Tozer. *Upstate/Downstate.* Chicago: Center for Urban Education Leadership at the University of Illinois, 2017.

Vignettes

Chicago Public Schools Story

Janice Jackson and Zipporah K. Hightower

Great schools cannot exist without great leaders, which is why Chicago Public Schools has made investing in principal preparation a top priority for more than a decade. In 2012, Chicago Mayor Rahm Emanuel bolstered these efforts with the creation of the Chicago Leadership Collaborative (CLC).

The vision behind this initiative was to pool the resources, practices, and expertise of universities and other organizations that prepare principals to serve in CPS schools. Since the creation of the CLC, the district's Department of Principal Quality (DPQ) has met monthly with external partners to review principal competencies and ensure the district's efforts are aligned to expectations from the State of Illinois. Our external partners share best practices that benefit the entire district. Additionally, CPS works collaboratively with our partners to complement the education they provide by offering professional development workshops tailored to meet the needs of new leaders.

The hallmark of the CLC is our Principal Residency Program. The CLC offers aspiring leaders the opportunity to participate in a twelve-month residency within a CPS school, all while continuing to receive instruction and support from their university program. The selection and placement of principal residents is a deliberate process which begins with our university partners identifying potential talent and submitting recommended candidates to the DPQ, which then conducts a careful selection process to determine who will be granted a CPS residency. Matches are made based on what each school can offer our prospective principals as they continue their leadership development.

After residents are placed in CPS schools, the district works closely with these future leaders to help ensure their success. The DPQ works collaboratively with the CLC to evaluate how the combination of classroom instruction and hands-on experience contribute to building a strong pipeline of prospective principals. We also track residents well beyond their first year of school-based service and utilize their feedback to shape and improve our practices.

Throughout their year of residency, the DPQ provides prospective school leaders with the opportunity to work with district leadership. This opportunity, along with feedback from our preparation partners, allows the Office of Network Support to utilize a best-fit approach to match new leaders to schools with principal vacancies.

The most compelling evidence of the CLC's success is recent data released by the Chicago Public Education Fund, which is one of our district's most critical partners for educational leadership research. In September 2017, the Fund reported that CLC alumni are significantly more likely to remain in principal roles than their non-CLC peers. This data reaffirms our continued investment in the Chicago Leadership Collaborative as consistency in leadership critical to the success of our schools.

The UIC Story: Starting with a Question

Steve Tozer

The University of Illinois at Chicago (UIC) EdD Program in Urban Education Leadership is a university-based school leader preparation program conducted in close partnership with Chicago Public Schools (CPS). A number of events between 1996 and 1999 contributed to initiating this lasting partnership. In 1996, the Illinois General Assembly granted CPS the right to impose requirements above and beyond the state's General Administrative Certificate (Type 75) before candidates could be eligible to be hired as principals in Chicago. UIC College of Education Dean Vicki Chou served on the CPS Committee that pushed for this legislation, and UIC then became one of the designers and providers of the additional urban education leadership curriculum that CPS required. In 1999, UIC faculty co-chaired one committee of the CPS "Human Capital Initiative" charged with examining how CPS might develop stronger pipelines of teachers and principals. One conclusion of that initiative was that CPS needed to work more effectively with Institutions of Higher Education (IHEs) to prepare principals who were able to improve student learning outcomes in neighborhood schools.

With UIC's record of strong collaborations with CPS, a significant trust was built between the two organizations. In 2001, Chief Education Officer Barbara Eason-Watkins and CEO Arne Duncan agreed to partner with UIC in rebuilding the principal preparation program from the ground up. The UIC faculty, with CPS input, collaboratively designed an EdD program in 2001–2002 and accepted the first cohort in 2003. From the beginning, the UIC faculty framed the development of the new program as a question to be answered through continuous improvement of our practice: *what would it take for the University to prepare school principals who improve student learning outcomes in schools as a rule, and not as a rare exception to the rule?*

Program Design

The new program explicitly shifted its view of who its main clients would be—not graduate students needing a credential—but P-12 students needing effective principals. In 2003 the UIC College of Education and the UIC Graduate College approved a redesigned program that would grant the state administrative certificate only upon the completion of a full-time, fully paid, intensively coached residency in a CPS school, with the district paying the salary for the year the candidate spent in residency. The new program, a professional doctorate, would be at least three years long with site-based leadership coaching provided throughout the program. Over time, this developed into a 4.5-year doctoral program. The commitment to a doctoral degree was not predicated on the belief that principals need a doctoral degree to be effective. Instead, we believed that learning to be an effective principal would take several years of intensive study, school-based leading, and sustained coaching that would provide expert feedback on leadership practice.

While the program has evolved significantly in the fifteen years since the first cohort of thirteen candidates was admitted (Cosner, Tozer, and Smylie 2012), a number of program design features have defined the program since the beginning. They are:

- *Close collaboration with the district* in program design, implementation, and assessment;
- *Clear outcome-based goals* that integrate all program components;
- *Selective recruitment and admissions into cohorts* of twenty or fewer students, with a demonstrated commitment to counseling students out of the program for underperformance;
- *Full year, full-time, paid leadership residency* leading to state endorsement after eighteen months;
- *Support for competitive placement* in high-need schools;
- *Post-licensure one-on-one leadership coaching* (that grew to a minimum of three years);
- *Sustained, longitudinal data collection* on each UIC-led school's performance, enabling data-based continuous improvement of the program and information to improve the field;
- *Earned EdD degree* on the basis of ability to demonstrate and analyze improved school organizational capacity and performance.

The UIC program could not have been started or sustained without external funding, because IHEs typically do not invest sufficient resources in principal preparation programs. Every IHE with a teacher education program, for example, invests in field supervision of student teaching, if not also in early field experiences prior to student teaching. This has not been so in principal preparation programs (Tozer et al. 2015). The UIC program has been continuously funded by external sources for fifteen years. Because this external funding has helped demonstrate the power of a clinically funded program, UIC has steadily increased its university-funded support of the program, institutionalizing field supervision of aspiring and practicing leaders as well as the labor-intensive work of selective admissions and assessment processes. The university also founded the UIC Center for Urban Education Leadership, which supports and disseminates program practices (www.urbanedleadership.org).

Impact

This continuously improving partnership with CPS has produced significant outcomes for CPS and UIC. In the first fifteen cohorts, 207 students completed their residency and achieved state certification. Of these, 155 became urban school principals, 112 of them in Chicago. The remaining program completers are assistant principals or system-level leaders, including superintendents and associate superintendents of urban districts—most recently the CEO of Chicago Public Schools, Dr. Janice Jackson. UIC has worked closely with CPS, New Leaders, the funding community, and others to improve school principal policy and practice in Chicago, contributing to CPS achieving national recognition for student achievement gains that outstrip all other large school districts in the nation (Reardon and Hinze-Pifer 2017). Evidence of UIC program progress includes:

- *Retention*: over the first decade of principal preparation, 75 percent of UIC principals retained their principalships (or were promoted specifically to principal supervision positions), largely in high-need CPS schools.
- *Overall school improvement metrics*: in 2014–2017, UIC-led schools increased their CPS school quality rankings at all levels more often than comparison CPS schools over that three-year period.
- *National impact:* In 2016 UIC was selected by the Wallace Foundation for multi-year funding to mentor two universities in other states through a new initiative in higher education; and UIC is also featured in a Wallace Foundation video on program processes and impact: www.wallacefoundation.org/knowledge-center/Pages/Series-Shows-How-Illinois-Successfully-Revamped-Requirements-for-Principal-Preparation.aspx.

Beginning with its initial proposal to the Illinois Board of Higher Education in 2003, the UIC program has sought to prepare the principals that students in our public schools deserve, but we have also sought to inform the field about what we are learning. Over the past fifteen years, our published research and evolving practices have led to our working with district and state agencies in twenty states. Our commitment to continuous improvement continues to inform our work in Chicago, in Illinois, and in the field at large.

Bibliography

Cosner, Shelby, Steve Tozer, and Mark Smylie. "The Ed. D. Program at the University of Illinois at Chicago: Using Continuous Improvement to Promote School Leadership Preparation." *Planning and Changing* 43 (2012): 127–148.

Reardon, Sean F., and Rebecca Hinze-Pifer. *Test Score Growth Among Public School Students in Chicago, 2009–2014*. Palo Alto: Stanford Center for Education Policy Analysis, 2017.

Tozer, Steve, Paul Zavitkovsky, Samuel P. Whalen, and Peter Martinez. "Change Agency in Our Own Backyards: Meeting the Challenges of Next Generation Programs in School Leader Preparation." In *Handbook for Urban Educational Leadership*, edited by Grant Khalifa and Arnold Witherspoon Arnold, 480–495. New York: Rowman & Littlefield, 2015.

New Leaders as a Model for Principal Preparation Program Reform in Illinois

Jean Desravines and Alexandra Broin

New Leaders is a national nonprofit dedicated to preparing school leaders capable of delivering breakthrough results for students. It was conceived in response to the school leadership research and student achievement data that helped catalyze the Illinois State Action for Education Leadership Project (IL-SAELP) and related advocacy efforts in 2000. There were several aspects of New Leaders' aspiring principals' program that made it, along with several forward-thinking programs in the state, a model for the policy changes ultimately codified in Illinois state law and subsequent regulations:

First, New Leaders placed a strong emphasis on *rigorous recruitment* of highly effective teachers and employed a *competency-based selection process* to admit candidates with strong potential to lead dramatic student achievement gains as school principals. In an effort to identify the very best talent, New Leaders was open to recruiting former teachers who had previously achieved success in the classroom and were active leaders in other industries. The organization never actively recruited noneducators, and nearly all program participants were accomplished teachers recruited directly from the classroom or other school-based roles. New Leaders' selection process established demanding admissions requirements by focusing on deeply assessing (through performance tasks and data on their effectiveness) prospective leaders' instructional expertise and leadership potential. The Illinois reform package borrowed from this model, raised the bar for entry into principal preparation programs across the state, by requiring in-person interviews of each candidate along with evidence of applicants' track record of improving student achievement over multiple years.

Once admitted, every participant in New Leaders' program engaged in a *full-time, yearlong residency*, learning from an effective principal, shouldering authentic leadership responsibilities within a school, and receiving regular, *ongoing feedback on their performance* from *skilled mentors and program staff*. The residency was among the most important aspects of New Leaders' model and the most difficult, practically speaking, to incorporate into state requirements. This was due to the financial and logistical challenges associated with paying a stipend or salary for an additional school employee. Though the Illinois reforms stopped short of requiring a full-time internship—the 2008 recession and subsequent years of financial strain on state and local budgets all but doomed the prospect of additional public financing to support such a mandate—the state did adopt robust requirements to ensure meaningful newly required school-based learning. This was accomplished by demanding specific experiences (e.g., hiring and evaluating teachers) and ensuring supervisors have the background necessary to support aspiring principals' development (e.g., demonstrated success in improving student achievement over multiple years as a school leader).

The intensive New Leaders internship experience was bolstered by *relevant coursework* aligned to *the most important day-to-day responsibilities of effective principals*: instructional leadership, team management, and other topics critical to cultivating and overseeing a vibrant school community. Of note, while many of New Leaders' program components helped shape the reforms enacted after 2010, state policy developments during this time also influenced the design and delivery of the program. For example, in response to stakeholder feedback, the state expanded the scope of the new principal endorsement to include Pre-kindergarten. As a result, New Leaders built into its curriculum additional content and training specific to early childhood education. Moreover, while the aspiring principals' program had always included discrete sessions on issues salient to particular districts, schools, and student populations, new requirements in Illinois prompted New Leaders to integrate more specific content on English learners, students with disabilities, and other special student populations into its curriculum.

Another aspect of New Leaders' approach that was codified in state law was *school district partnerships*. From the beginning, New Leaders focused on identifying environments in which new principals would be set up for success, for example, by placing a priority on partnering with districts in which school leaders would be granted appropriate autonomy to manage their staff and budgets along with other key conditions (e.g., a sufficient concentration of high-need schools and students, and a strong philanthropic community with a vested interest in the partnership's success, among other factors). The discussions New Leaders had with prospective district partners centered on the idea that school systems, ultimately, would provide feedback on whether program graduates—and the organization itself—were meeting expectations. New Leaders launched in Chicago because many critical conditions were in place, and the local environment became even stronger and more supportive, as the district doubled down on its leadership strategy and investments in the years that followed.

Finally, the learning-and-improvement orientation that characterized the collaboration in Illinois, and that was incorporated into the new principal preparation program regulations, was truly part of New Leaders' DNA. Since its inception, the organization had been tracking and later contracting independent, external evaluators (Gates et al. 2014; Booker and Thomas 2014) to assess graduates' effect on student achievement and other relevant outcomes and *using that data to continuously improve* its program. That Illinois required every program to reapply for approval under the new requirements led to a dramatic shift in the principal preparation landscape across the state. That programs are now required to report on *impact and outcome measures*—and that such data can be used to inform future program renewal decisions—suggests the reforms New Leaders proudly supported will continue to profoundly affect school leader quality in Illinois for many years to come.

Bibliography

Booker, Kevin, and Jaime Thomas. *Impacts of New Leaders on Student Achievement in Oakland*. Washington, D.C.: Mathematica Policy Research, 2014.

Gates, Susan M., Laura S. Hamilton, Paco Martorell, Susan Burkhauser, Paul Heaton, Ashley Pierson, Matthew Baird et al. "Preparing Principals to Raise Student Achievement: Implementation and Effects of the New Leaders Program in Ten Districts." Research Report. RAND Corporation, Santa Monica, CA, 2014.

Districts LEADing Change: The Influence of Springfield District #186 On Illinois' Principal Preparation Changes
Diane Rutledge

Research conducted for more than a decade has confirmed the positive impact that principals can have on student achievement and the importance of keeping the focus of the role of the principal on instructional leadership.

In the late 1990s and early 2000s, the impact of leadership on continuous school improvement was a new concept. The work of the Wallace Foundation and school districts the foundation supported around the country confirmed this impact. The influence of the foundation also encouraged and supported states to re-examine principal preparation program policies to ensure school leaders were prepared to be the creators of conditions to support student achievement and to act as powerful multipliers of effective teaching and leadership practices in schools. Illinois was committed to this work.

The Springfield School District 186 was one of the Wallace Foundation's original ten LEAD districts. As such, we had the unique opportunity to participate in a five-year grant focused on principal preparation. During the grant period, the district implemented strategies to:

- Partner with Illinois State University to provide a principal preparation program in a collaborative model utilizing both university professors and district leaders;
- Collaboratively grant admission to the program based on candidate's proven leadership experiences;
- Redesign preparation program curriculum to reflect school improvement;
- Provide experiential opportunities throughout the program;
- Provide a yearlong internship;
- Require standards-based experiences;
- Create a continuum of leadership development from the classroom to the boardroom.

These strategies resulted in a change of focus to the district as *the consumer and co-provider of the principal preparation program*.

The transition from superintendent of Springfield District 186 to executive director of the Large Unit District Association (LUDA) brought with it an opportunity to inform statewide policy on principal preparation based on Springfield's experiences, as well as efforts in the Chicago Public Schools in partnership with the University of Illinois at Chicago.

The work was complex and developmental. It required the collaboration, experience, and insight of diverse stakeholders with a passion for school leadership. Statewide efforts included both the Illinois State Action for Education Leadership (IL-SAELP) and the Commission on School Leader Preparation (*Blueprint for Change*).

As a result of these statewide collaborations and the work we lead in Springfield, Public Act 096-0903 legislated statewide changes to principal preparation programs that reflected the local changes we sought and enacted in Springfield.

It began with a national foundation asking the question, "Does Leadership Matter?" in the 1990s while investing in school districts and universities in states across the country. This work with supporting research ultimately resulted in a change of policy and practice in Illinois, as well as many other states across the country by the mid-2000s.

Today, preparation programs in Illinois accept only those candidates who are committed to the principalship, providing them with real-world experiences and support from master school leaders throughout the program. The result is a new generation of principals committed to continuous school improvement in support of student achievement and the skills to make it happen. It has been rewarding to observe the work that occurred at the local level impacting state policy and ultimately making a difference for the achievement of students in Illinois.

4 Durable Levers for State Policy Change

Independent Policy Entrepreneurs

Lynne Haeffele and Jim Applegate

Anyone involved in substantive change in state policy knows reform is a long-term endeavor. The change itself can take years. For example, recent successful effort to redesign Illinois' inequitable K-12 funding system was a decade in the making (Lauterbach 2017).

Effecting the change is just the first step. Implementation of the change on the ground requires sustained effort. State policy manuals are replete with significant policy changes gathering dust on the shelf, never having a real impact on the systems they were passed to improve. An example of this can be seen in the significant college transfer legislation that was passed in California in 2010. It aimed at reducing the cost of excess credits by hundreds of millions of dollars and allowing thousands of more students to access college and graduate on time with four-year degrees. Despite aggressive monitoring of the legislation by organizations like the Campaign for College Opportunity, the policy showed uneven implementation across the state resulting in the need for "clean-up" legislation in 2013 to ensure broader and more sustainable implementation consistent with the intent of the 2010 law (Padilla 2010). Those organizations continue to monitor the implementation and outcomes of the transfer initiative.

Even when change is implemented, to sustain the effort advocates must stay in the game to protect reforms in the face of political opposition or changes in the political climate. New Jersey has gone through a thirty-year period in which significant early childhood education programs and funding were implemented and then challenged repeatedly (Education Law Center n.d.). Only through the dogged efforts of advocacy organizations like the Education Law Center, Advocates for Children in New Jersey, and support from philanthropy in the state has the program, recognized as a national model, been expanded and preserved.

Sustained and long-term supports for policy change, implementation, and preservation are unlikely to come from traditional political entities (governors, legislatures, or even the courts in some cases), given the high rates of turnover and the unprecedented degree of partisanship infecting twenty-first-century politics. Though there are always exceptions, like

Tennessee's bipartisan decade-long effort to expand college opportunity to its citizens (Finney et al. 2017), for the most part state capitals are revolving doors with changing agendas. The Education Commission of the States (ECS 2016) regularly documents the staggering levels of turnover in state political and education leadership (ECS 2018). Expecting the sustained, long-term commitments necessary for policy change, implementation, and assessment of impact to come from this sector is unrealistic. Of course, champions are needed from governor's offices, legislatures, and PK-12 and higher education leaders at crucial points in the reform process. Also important is continuing education and re-education of changing leaders and their staffs. The question is, who will provide that education in a credible bipartisan way, and who will bear the torch to light the way to pass, implement, and sustain policy reforms that will produce change at scale?

Enter the Policy Entrepreneur

However inhospitable the political climate is for thoughtful, effective policy reform promoting better lives for the most vulnerable, a livable environment, better civic health, and so forth, the good news is that there are organizations across states and regions that have the expertise, credibility, and even (by far the hardest) the resources to design, advocate for, and successfully oversee implementation and to sustain positive reform over the long term. Though many of these people and organizations may not label themselves as such, they fit the description of "policy entrepreneurs" outlined in the literature on policy change (Kingdon 2003). They come in many shapes and sizes: nonprofits, university centers, foundations, and more. They are defined less by their sector or structure than by what they do. So what do policy entrepreneurs do?

First and foremost, policy entrepreneurs promote policy reforms and innovations that they believe (and ultimately convince others to believe) will produce better outcomes than the status quo. They play a key role in *identifying* policy problems and focusing attention on those problems by important decision makers in that domain. Policy entrepreneurs can operate locally, within a state, and across multiple states. Often, for those operating across states, the focus is on gaining shared agreement on the problem and the need for change (Mintrom and Vergari 1996). Within states and at the local level, entrepreneurs are more likely to engage in deeper change efforts. They present policy solutions and make the case that they are both desirable (better outcomes that matter to decision makers) and practical (providing a path to implementation). In addition, they advocate for the change, mobilize public will, drive policy passage, monitor implementation (e.g., the California example above), and protect the changes made (e.g., the New Jersey example above).

Anyone can identify and argue for policy change. What makes policy entrepreneurship different and effective? What factors contributed to the sustained, successful effort in Illinois to redesign policies and programs preparing education leaders outlined in detail in this volume? First and foremost, effective policy entrepreneurs must establish and continually sustain their *credibility* across sector and party lines. This credibility requires work on several fronts. They must gain stature as experts in their area. Expertise can be validated through a variety of means. It is important to become a reliable and useful "go to" source for decision makers and their support staffs in ways that help them do their jobs more generally and build their own stature. Involvement in national and multi-state networks allows the organization to bring useful exemplars to the table which can be modified and modeled by state leaders. It also helps to gain recognition through grants and awards from generally respected sources (government, philanthropy, publications). Expertise can be validated through the support of influential external groups (e.g., philanthropy, business, and industry).

Credible policy entrepreneurs must not only be experts but also *trusted* experts. Entire books have been written on how to build and sustain trust. Trust can only exist in the context of a relationship. This is why effective policy entrepreneurs are consummate networkers. They are active in multiple policy networks allowing them to understand and adapt to the different perspectives of multiple decision makers (Mintrom 1997). As trusted network members, they avoid surprising colleagues with public positions, commit to transparency, and fight even the perception of a hidden agenda. They consistently demonstrate respect for the various opinions of decision makers, never letting their acknowledged expertise translate into a perception of superiority or bias.

Finally, credibility is built through a dynamic track record of advocacy and effectiveness acknowledged by press coverage and visibility in multiple venues where decision makers live and work. In today's culture, that may involve a strong social media presence and a large set of followers. Sponsorship of meetings and events with strategically targeted audiences that provide useful policy information is another *dynamism* strategy. Decision makers and implementers must encounter the work of policy entrepreneurs regularly and in multiple venues. A few acknowledged policy reform successes along the way are helpful as well.

Using networks and adaptive communication to build trust among decision makers is important. However, effective policy entrepreneurs network up and down the ladder. They know that understanding and support among those who must implement and are most impacted by policy change is crucial to long-term success. Whether it is early childhood educator groups in New Jersey, transfer staff at two- and four-year colleges in California, or superintendent associations and faculty/chairs of education preparation programs in Illinois, the failure to build support among constituent groups involved in implementing policy will almost always lead to powerful opposition and failure, even if the legislature passes a policy. The same principles of credibility, trust, and networking and dynamism apply at every level.

Reforming Principal Preparation in Illinois: Policy Entrepreneurship at Scale

Hopefully, the applicability of these principles of effective policy entrepreneurship to the principal preparation reform effort in Illinois will be relatively obvious to those who read the detailed accounts from the field provided in this volume. Still, it may be useful to draw some direct links here.

Credibility

In order to advocate for needed reforms in the arena of principal preparation, it was imperative to create a cadre of credible experts across both the PK-12 and higher education systems. These included leaders of professional education organizations serving both teachers and administrators, respected faculty of principal preparation programs, education researchers, and high-level staff of the state's education agencies. The staff at the Center for the Study of Education Policy (CSEP) at Illinois State University, with assistance in the form of private foundation grant funds, served as the long-term conveners and facilitators for the work.

Another key strategy to build credibility was to highlight and study the growing body of research on the importance of effective school leaders in improving student outcomes. Rather than focusing on administrative tasks (as the long-standing general administrative certification programs emphasized), these effective leaders took on strong mentoring, coaching, instructional support, and organizational redesign roles (Elmore 2000; Waters, Marzano, and McNulty 2003; Leithwood et al. 2004; Murphy et al. 2006; Marzano, Waters, and Brian 2005), validating a need for concomitant changes in pre-service preparation.

Throughout the process, CSEP and other policy advocates worked to maintain credibility by continuously updating the research base on principal effectiveness and development (Darling-Hammond et al. 2007; Spillane 2009; Bryk et al. 2010). CSEP convened participants for a variety of learning sessions, in which participants shared successful strategies, challenges, and models from other states. When opposing advocacy groups emerged with their own credible arguments, the policy entrepreneurs were able to maintain the focus on research-based improvement and on occasion utilize opposing evidence to improve policy development.

Networking and Advocacy

Networking provides participants with access to relationships and resources, according to social capital theorists (Bourdieu 1986; Rogers

2003; Coleman 1988; Lin 2011). In the case of the Illinois reform effort, a "network of networks" was gradually formed as a variety of education and advocacy organizations worked together on components of the proposed changes. An ongoing and conscious effort was made to continuously identify and recruit key participants into various work groups, committees, and public forums. Some network members had access to financial resources; others had professional relationships with state-level agency staff and legislators. As described in Chapter 2 of this volume, networking policy forums engaged hundreds of stakeholders from 2000 to 2010, engaging in the deliberately incremental process of policy change. Undoubtedly, the collective voices of the network members influenced both political will and the mobilization of resources such as grant funding and were thus more effective in promoting change than any single individual or organization could have been.

Trust

Great care was taken throughout the reform development process to demonstrate integrity in terms of open communication, following through on commitments, and providing a safe atmosphere for debate. Mutual trust developed among participants through processes of research, collaboratively developing and vetting creative proposals, encouraging dissenting opinions, and valuing diverse viewpoints. Proposals were publicly vetted, with a transparent process for stakeholder input, over the course of a decade. In 2009–2010, the Illinois State Board of Education (ISBE) and the Illinois Board of Higher Education (IBHE) held multiple dissemination meetings for public vetting of redesign proposals, attracting over eight hundred participants. The meetings served not only as a platform to explain the redesign proposals but also to allow opposing groups to present their views and engage in constructive debate. Even when disagreements remained, there was general acknowledgment that the process was open and transparent. Specific examples are provided in Chapters 1 and 2 of this volume.

While some points of contention were strongly debated, the process brought about considerable improvements in aspects of the reform proposals. Ultimately, key research-based reforms included:

- A more selective admissions process;
- Preparation for instructional leadership;
- Preparation in supporting student populations with special needs (e.g., early childhood students, English Language Learners, students with disabilities);
- Partnerships between school districts and principal preparation programs for program design and delivery;
- Candidate mentorship and extended internships.

Through the entire process, CSEP as the policy entrepreneur, was able to nurture and maintain the work through continued attention to applying research, securing grant funds to underwrite meetings and other network activities, communicating with stakeholders, and acting as a liaison organization as needed. CSEP maintained close relationships with the key state partners, the Illinois State Board of Education, and the Illinois Board of Higher Education. As a result of their prolonged and successful reform facilitation efforts, in 2014 the partners received the Frank E. Newman Award for State Innovation from ECS. This national recognition added to the credibility of the reform effort (ECS 2018).

A New Wrinkle: Collaboration for Collective Impact

Looking forward, the nature and effectiveness of policy entrepreneurship (especially in education reform efforts) can be enriched by integrating the growing literature on the work done under the rubric of "collaboration for collective impact" (Brady and Juster 2016). The work of policy entrepreneurs to date reflects many of the principles of good collective impact practices. Connecting the two bodies of work will enable a more systemic, explicit framework for implementing policy entrepreneurship and richer strategies for assessing impact in the future (FSG 2012).

The foundation of a successful collective impact effort is the development of a *common agenda* or a shared vision for change among cross-sector participants. For policy change, as the Illinois example demonstrates, participants need to include both policymakers, reform partners in the network, and representation of the community directly impacted by the policy reform and are often responsible for implementation. Not all of these sectors will be equally engaged at all points in the change process but, ultimately, they must be at the table as the process unfolds. Policy entrepreneurs work to identify the problem as a problem, if that is needed, but then build this cross-sector common agenda including the roles and actions for which each partner is responsible. Finally, in seeking collective impact, policy entrepreneurs should make equity a core concern of any common agenda. That was the case in Illinois. Improving the quality of school leaders was directly tied to school performance, especially for underserved student groups.

Policy entrepreneurs should play a role in gaining cross-sector network commitment to *shared measurement*. A limited set of common indicators should be developed to assess progress in the change process as well as, eventually, the impact of the change. Data gathered tied to these indicators can be used to learn continually, adapt, and improve change efforts and, in the long term, make revisions in the policies to improve effectiveness. As noted above, California learned about the need for clean-up legislation through this continued monitoring of implementation. In Illinois, though the school leader preparation reform is relatively recent, strong data on hiring for leaders prepared using the redesigned programs is providing support for changes that have been made. Given the long arc of much policy change, shared assessments of the goals for the change process itself (e.g., when is legislation expected to be introduced?) can inform continuous improvement and redesign of the work when process goals are not met.

Policy entrepreneurs must serve a *coordinating* role throughout the change process. The diverse set of players involved will require continuing efforts to maintain commitments, ensure alignment of activities, and sustain trust and respect among partners. Some have referred to this work as "herding cats." This coordination will be enhanced if policy entrepreneurs can provide or identify and cultivate leaders with strong system leadership skills to support ongoing work across organizations and sectors. These are leaders who can provide safe spaces for difficult conversation, foster compromise and understanding of differences, sustain commitment in the face of setbacks and nonlinear change, and model commitment to the health of whole and the common agenda. The strong facilitation, management, and convening skills help leaders lead at the system level, across sectors.

Policy entrepreneurs must help develop the structures that ensure *continuous and open communication* among members of the network, and with policy leaders responsible for policy change. Collaboration is not a natural human act. It requires structures to ensure adequate engagement of partners. Without continuous communication, coordination of activities and commitment to shared agendas and measurement will be at risk.

Finally, the collective impact literature defines and makes clear the critical importance of what is called "backbone staff," who wake up every morning dedicated to the initiative's common vision, supporting an honest use of measurement and data, keeping the work aligned among partners, building public support and securing funding. The work of the backbone staff is, for the most part, the work of the policy entrepreneurs driving and sustaining change over the long haul. In Illinois, CSEP was the key backbone organization, supporting the "network of networks" and building and maintaining stakeholder support for the dramatic reform in education leader preparation. Collective impact work across the country has made clear success is unlikely without such a commitment. Driving the collective effort cannot be something that is done for an hour late in the day after the "real" work of a particular partner organization is done. Backbone staff and organizations see the change as their real work and help other partners to integrate that vision into their own organization's efforts.

Given the important role that philanthropy plays in supporting collective impact initiatives and policy entrepreneurship, it is important that the funder community understand and target funding for this essential backbone work. Funders lean toward the direct funding of activities tied to initiatives and undervalue the importance of providing capacity-building support to enable policy entrepreneurs and their backbone organizations to carry out the initiative. Often the result is that strategic work is loaded on top of the ongoing demands placed on a typically overburdened agency or nonprofit staff. No wonder many nonprofits and change organizations complain of initiative fatigue. The growing evidence that backbone staff dedicated to improving practice and policy entrepreneurship is crucial to success makes a strong case for more attention to capacity-building support among funders, whether private, corporate, or governmental.

The growing body of exemplars and research in the collective impact space provides useful principles on which to ground policy entrepreneurship. It is the case that much of the actual "collective impact" work is done at the local or regional level: mobilizing stakeholders around change that immediately improves the quality of life in a particular community or region. Policy entrepreneurs more typically focused on change at the system, state, or federal levels as was the case in Illinois. Yet the principles for effective mobilization overlap. Moreover, policy entrepreneurs can gain insight into what broader policies must change by attending to the regional work of many collective impact initiatives. That work provides bottom-up feedback on what state or federal policies make positive change more difficult, as well as what new policies are needed to facilitate change. In short, local and regional collective impact initiatives can help set the policy agenda for policy entrepreneurs operating at a state or federal level.

A Few Final Thoughts

In the United States, at least for the foreseeable future, traditional political avenues for policy change are flooded and largely impassable due to virulent partisanship, rapid turnover in leadership, and short-term reelection motivations. American pragmatism, commitment to fact-based policymaking, and willingness to set long-term goals are hard to find in the current political culture. Yet the problems we face grow larger and the pace of change is accelerating. Climate change, growing income inequality, the accelerating impact of automation and artificial intelligence on the nature of work, the changing role of education in career preparation, and the persistent and growing inequity in the education system itself from preschool to college are all problems that pose real threats to democracy and quality of life. There is no way to put these challenges on hold while our political system comes to its senses. All of this argues for the growing importance of policy entrepreneurs and policy entrepreneurship to develop, advance, and sustain rational policy change that at least mitigates the threats faced by society.

It is hard to imagine, over the last decade, the traditional political establishment in Illinois implementing a dramatic, comprehensive, fact-based reform in education preparation at the scale designed to improve effectiveness and equity in its K-12 education system—a reform that required a significant change in its higher education system. Multiple corruption scandals, leader turnover, massive financial problems, and two years during which partisanship prevented even adopting a basic state budget made survival seem a more realistic goal that productive reform. Yet during that period and in that environment the CSEP and its partners in policy entrepreneurship successfully found funding and mobilized all the right stakeholders in the state to pass legislation and then effectively implement just such a reform, one that has received multiple national recognition for its scale and quality.

The challenge of sustainability remains, as the policy change faces threats aimed to backtrack on depth and quality in the face of educator shortages confronting Illinois, like many other states. Similar to the work on early childhood in New Jersey, improvement and preservation of the reforms will be ongoing. Still, this work should be a source of hope and a model for progress in difficult political times.

One final lesson to be learned from the work Illinois is this: once visions are shared, networks are mobilized, backbone staff and organizations are identified, data and research capacity is engaged, and system leaders are developed—that is, once the infrastructure for policy entrepreneurship in a state or across states is established—the opportunity for ongoing policy improvement is there and is real. Add a success or two, and momentum is added to the mix. Despite all of its challenges, Illinois can find hope in that. Other states have grown similar capacities for policy entrepreneurship. For those that have not, given the current political climate nationally and in many state capitals, it is time do so.

Bibliography

Bourdieu, Pierre. "The Forms of Capital." In *Handbook of Theory and Research for the Sociology of Education*, edited by John G. Richardson, 241–258. New York: Greenwood, 1986.

Brady, Sheri, and Jennifer Splansky Juster. "How Do You Successfully Put Collective Impact into Action?" *FSG*. Accessed April 21, 2016, www.fsg.org/blog/how-do-you-successfully-put-collective-impact-action

Bryk, Anthony S., Penny Bender Sebring, Elaine Allensworth, John Q. Easton, and Stuart Luppescu. *Organizing Schools for Improvement: Lessons from Chicago*. Chicago: University of Chicago Press, 2010.

Coleman, James S. "Social Capital in the Creation of Human Capital." *American Journal of Sociology* 94 (1988): S95–S120.

Darling-Hammond, Linda, Michelle LaPointe, Debra Meyerson, Margaret Terry Orr, and Carol Cohen. *Preparing School Leaders for a Changing World: Lessons from Exemplary Leadership Development Programs*. School Leadership

Study. Final Report. Stanford, CA: Stanford Educational Leadership Institute, 2007.

Education Commission of the States. "School Leadership Matters: Illinois Leading Reforms in Principal Preparation." Accessed October 17, 2016, www.ecs.org/school-leadership-matters-illinois-leading-reforms-in-principal-preparation

Education Commission of the States. "2018 Elections and Changes in State Education Leadership." Updated September 4, 2018, www.ecs.org/2018-elections-and-changes-in-state-education-leadership

Education Law Center. "The History of Abbott v. Burke." n.d., www.edlawcenter.org/litigation/abbott-v-burke/abbott-history.html

Elmore, Richard F. *Building a New Structure for School Leadership.* Washington, D.C.: Albert Shanker Institute, 2000.

Finney, J., E. W. Leigh, R. Ruiz, W. Castillo, E. Smith, and D. C. Kent. *Driven to Perform: Tennessee's Higher Education Policies and Outcomes, A Case Study,* Philadelphia, PA: Institute for Research on Higher Education at University of Pennsylvania, 2017.

FSG. "Collective Impact Forum." http://collectiveimpactforum.org/resources.

Hanleybrown, Fay, John Kania, and Mark Kramer. *Channeling Change: Making Collective Impact Work.* Stanford, CA: Stanford Social Innovation Review, 2012.

Kingdon, John W. *Agendas, Alternatives and Public Policies* (2nd ed.). New York: Pearson, 2003.

Lauterbach, Cole. "Illinois School Funding Reform Signed into Law. *Illinois New Network.* Accessed August 31, 2017, www.ilnews.org/news/schools/illinois-school-funding-reform-signed-into-law/article_bb7ca9de-8e5e-11e7-be5d-ef6185374147.html

Leithwood, Kenneth, Karen Seashore Louis, Stephen Anderson, and Kyla Wahlstrom. *How Leadership Influences Student Learning.* St. Paul: Center for Applied Research and Educational Improvement, 2004.

Lin, Nan. *Social Capital: A Theory of Social Structure and Action.* New York: Cambridge University Press, 2011.

Marzano, Robert J., Timothy Waters, and A. Brian. McNulty. *School Leadership that Works: From Research to Results.* Alexandria: ASCD, 2005.

Mintrom, Michael. "Policy Entrepreneurs and the Diffusion of Innovation." *American Journal of Political Science* 41 (1997): 738–770.

Mintrom, Michael, and Sandra Vergari. "Advocacy Coalitions, Policy Entrepreneurs, and Policy Change." *Policy Studies Journal* 24, no. 3 (1996): 420–434.

Murphy, Joseph, Stephen N. Elliott, Ellen Goldring, and Andrew C. Porter. *Learning-Centered Leadership: A Conceptual Foundation.* New York: Wallace Foundation, 2006.

Padilla, A. *Secretary of State Alex Padilla Reflects on the Importance of Going the Distance on Transfer Reform for California students.* The Campaign for College Opportunity, 2010, http://collegecampaign.org/secretary-state-alex-padilla-transfer-report/

Rogers, Everett M. *Diffusion of Innovations.* New York: Free Press, 2003.

Spillane, James P. "Managing to Lead: Reframing School Leadership and Management." *Phi Delta Kappan* 91, no. 3 (2009): 70–73.

Waters, Tim, Robert J. Marzano, and Brian McNulty. "Balanced Leadership: What 30 Years of Research Tells Us about the Effect of Leadership on Student Achievement." A Working Paper. Aurora: Mid-continent Research for Education and Learning, 2003.

Vignettes

The Influence of Advocacy Organizations: Racing for School Leader Preparation Reform

Ben Boer and Robin Steans

Reforming the way in which Illinois prepares its principals has been an exercise in consensus building and a case study for the value of outside advocacy. The impetus for change came initially from the field itself. The Illinois Task Force for School Leadership—including stakeholders from higher education, school management, foundations, and unions—had met for over a year to discuss how to strengthen school leadership. In 2008, the Task Force recommended that principal preparation needed to be revamped. Despite broad-based input and high-level support for change, concern surrounding a few key provisions coupled with massive financial uncertainty left legislative change far from certain.

Laying the Groundwork

As the School Leadership Task Force considered its options in early 2009, the American Recovery and Reinvestment Act (ARRA), the launch of Advance Illinois, and a PBS documentary changed the dynamic. ARRA included the Race to the Top program, which offered substantial funding for school improvement at the state level, and principal preparation reform promised to make Illinois' Race to the Top application more attractive to federal reviewers. Later that year, PBS released *The Principal Story*, capturing a year in the life of school principals in Chicago and Springfield and driving home both the complexity of the job and the need for capable leadership. As then, US Secretary of Education Arne Duncan aptly stated in the documentary, "*We have no good schools without good principals.*" Finally, in the summer of 2009, Advance Illinois released its founding policy agenda, *We Can Do Better*, which featured a recommendation that Illinois "Invest in Effective Principals and Empower Them to Lead."

Passing Legislation

Going into the 2010 session of the Illinois General Assembly, the goal of all involved was to pass a bill that would create a new PK-12 principal certification to replace the more general Type 75 license that certified a much broader array of school administrators. This change would permit more focus on instructional leadership, raise expectations for prior teaching experience to four years, and require deeper field experience and stronger admission requirements. As important, SB 3610, introduced in early May 2010, would require all universities seeking to offer principal preparation programs to apply for state program approval, and also require existing Type 75 holders in principal positions to get a new endorsement within a set time period.[1]

While many were involved in crafting the substance, few organizations had the ability or inclination to lead advocacy efforts. In addition, some key players expressed concerns over individual provisions: there was worry that field requirements would pull rural candidates away from current positions, disagreement over whether to include nonprofit training programs, and funding concerns, to name a few. While Advance Illinois was still legislatively wet behind the ears, it stepped forward to shepherd the bill. It developed fact sheets to help guide legislative conversations, brought principals and university leaders to meet with key legislators, organized panels of experts and practitioners to testify in Springfield, and organized regular conference calls among proponents to plan and problem solve. When a key legislator quietly moved to pocket the bill, an Advance Illinois-led team of supporters were able to quickly and effectively ensure the bill moved forward.[2] Ultimately, negotiations led to changes (including permitting existing Type 75 certificate holders to be "grandfathered"), and the bill (refiled as SB 226) sailed through both the House and Senate. Governor Quinn signed the bill with a flourish at Bell Elementary School in Chicago.

The Rules Process

While SB 226 was a significant step forward, it did not spell out every element of the reforms at hand but instead provided a framework for principal preparation program redesign. Specifically, it defined key areas for reform: (1) more rigorous selection and assessment of principal candidates; (2) training in teacher evaluation; (3) more intensive field internships; and (4) a requirement for partnership between principal preparation programs and districts. It was ISBE's role to propose the rules, and it was the job of the Joint Committee on Administrative Rules (JCAR) to review and approve the rules. Critically, and with fewer legislators now responsible for the fate and rigor of the new endorsement, the rulemaking process became a second arena for good (or bad) decision-making and action. Knowing that a few key players remained concerned about elements of the bill and knowing that rulemaking could open the door to backtracking, Advance Illinois kept its coalition together—continuing the regular conference calls, talking through proposed rules as they went public, and working with partners to ensure robust public comment.

The coalition proved essential as JCAR rejected ISBE's proposed rules twice. Fortunately, ISBE and others remained engaged, including CSEP, Chicago Principals and Administrators Association, the Illinois Business Roundtable, LUDA, the Ounce of Prevention Fund, University of Illinois at Champaign-Urbana, University of Illinois at Chicago, and Voices for Illinois Children. Similar to its strategy during the legislative phase, Advance Illinois organized supporters to visit JCAR members, prepared fact sheets on areas of controversy, and worked regularly with ISBE and opponents on roadblocks. Ultimately, organization and advocacy paid off, and the rules were complete and approved. The rollout of the legislation commenced, and all principal preparation programs in the state were on notice to be reapproved by July 1, 2014.

Into the Future

Despite the innovative, concentrated, and sustained work on principal preparation reform, support for that piece was not included in the small Race to the Top grant awarded to Illinois in 2011. Nonetheless, reform took hold. Redesigned principal preparation programs were approved, and as expected, fewer programs met the new, more rigorous requirements.

In 2016, key stakeholders and funders again came together to assess the work to date and to plot a path forward, with a focus on ensuring universities and districts had the support they needed to live up to new expectations. The Illinois School Leadership Advisory Council (ISLAC) convened more than fifty stakeholders from school districts, higher education, funders, legislators, professional organizations, and other groups. They reported that many programs were reshaped in accordance with SB 226 and that the first cadres of principal candidates were now graduating and entering the field. As expected, the numbers are more targeted, with roughly two hundred candidates being licensed annually. Recognizing the ongoing challenge of the work, ISLAC also developed a set of recommendations for further supporting and sustaining the pipeline of high-quality principals across the state. Perhaps the most important (and least surprising) conclusion takes the work back to where it started: school leadership is pivotal to student success, and it will take continued coordination among stakeholders to ensure that principals get the rigorous training and support they need to ensure that all schools have high-quality leaders at the helm.

The Use of Data and Messaging to Influence Change

Norman D. Durflinger

Illinois did not have specific licensure rules for principals under the old requirements. Instead, the state had a general administrative credential (Type 75 certificate). This credential was required for anyone who had the authority to evaluate certified school staff, which included department chairs, athletic directors, and deans of students, in addition to principals and assistant principals. Every year, colleges and universities churned out thousands of people with Type 75 certificates; many were teachers with no interest in becoming principals but instead hoped to increase their pay. Others were just looking for administrative jobs, such as department chair, athletic director, or dean of students. In reality, few of the Type 75 certificate holders were explicitly prepared for the role of principal or pursued the principalship upon completion of their certificate program. Today, there are over 43,000 educators in Illinois who hold an active Type 75 certificate.

When it came to hiring principals, there were complaints from superintendents that these programs were too general, they were not preparing principals for the demands of the job, and they did not reflect the research regarding effective programs. Our solution was to design a research-based new Principal Endorsement specifically designed with a focus on the knowledge and skills necessary to be an effective principal or assistant principal. While we worked with a broad range of stakeholders on this effort, the constant challenge facing institutions of higher education was always the fear of lost revenue for universities. In fact, the large revenue that universities brought in through their large Type 75 programs encouraged high enrollments, and it was therefore a big concern to many folks in higher education. However, it was clear the old way was doing little to improve schools or increase student learning. Thus, this mismatch of supply versus demand centered much of our messaging on the need to redesign principal preparation in Illinois to better meet the need of our schools.

The Center for the Study of Education Policy at Illinois State University collected data on the number of candidates enrolled at that time compared to the number of projected vacancies (see Tables 4.1 and 4.2) to make the case that there was an overabundance of educators who were technically qualified to serve as administrators throughout the state. We used the data to counter concerns by the field that an increase in rigor and quality of preparation would affect the quantity of candidates applying to principal preparation programs.

Durable Levers for State Policy Change 103

Table 4.1 Number of Type 75 Certificates Compared with Principal Vacancies

Year	Principal Endorsements Issued	Annual Principal Vacancies
2004–2005	748	437
2005–2006	1,657	581
2006–2007	2,153	614
2007–2008	2,402	522
2008–2009	3,002	342

Table 4.2 Supply and Demand of Administrative Positions in Illinois, 2008 ISBE Supply and Demand Report

Administrator Type	Average New Hires	Needed Through 2012
Elementary Principal/Assistant	272	1,088
Middle Principal/Junior High/Assistant	115	460
High School Principal/Assistant	125	501
Director/Assistant	100	401
Other Administrator	209	836
Total	821	3,286

As the tables indicate, Illinois could well afford to have a decline in program enrollments and still fulfill projected vacancies.

In the end, the new Principal Endorsement in Illinois focuses exclusively on preparing principals and assistant principals. Fewer principals are being licensed, successfully creating a smaller pool of more highly trained principals for schools to select. Before the new principal endorsement, thirty-one approved programs were enrolling approximately 7,610 candidates statewide (using state 2009–2010 enrollment data). Now, there are twenty-six programs with an annual enrollment of approximately seven hundred candidates.

While the number is dramatically less, it is also more predictive of the number of candidates who actually want to be principals or assistant principals and will pursue those positions. Further, in an effort to retain a robust pipeline of principal candidates to prevent a shortage of principals, all Type 75 holders were grandfathered in and remain qualified to serve as a principal or assistant principal, thus maintaining the deep pool of candidates. Both the development of the Principal Endorsement and the termination of the Type 75 helped to address the overproduction of candidates who were narrowly prepared for broad administrative roles.

An additional issue that was addressed by the enactment of the new principal preparation program regulation was a curtailing of mass online programs expanding in Illinois. Prior to the policy change, one of the largest producers of the old Type 75 certificate was an entirely online program that had an enrollment of 1,033 candidates in 2009–2010. That program did not seek approval under the new rigorous preparation requirements to offer the Principal Endorsement. In fact, the program no longer prepares principal candidates in Illinois at all.

To fill the void left behind by the termination of Type 75 programs, a new Teacher Leadership Endorsement was created to prepare teachers who want to serve in leadership roles but not as a principal or assistant principal. Currently eighteen universities have been approved to provide Teacher Leadership Endorsement programs. Regulations also changed that removed the requirement for anyone who evaluated staff (including athletic directors, department chairs, and special education directors) to have a principal license. This change created more autonomy for school districts to hire educators in these roles without the need for the general administrative master's degree credential.

The Shift from Hour-Based Requirement to Evidence-Based Mastery: The Decision Behind Illinois' Competency-Based Internship Requirements

Erika Hunt, Alicia Haller, and Lisa Hood

Prior to Illinois' new P-12 principal endorsement, the number of hours and internship activities a candidate was required to complete varied by institution. While providing autonomy to institutions on how to design their program's internship is not necessarily a bad thing, testimonies were provided by graduates from a wide variety of programs that indicated the types of activities that candidates were completing appeared to be aimed merely at fulfilling the number of hours required, rather than providing authentic on-the-job training that would actually prepare them for a school leader position. Testimony from candidates also indicated that internship sites and experiences were most often self-selected (and almost exclusively based on convenience). Further, the supervision of candidates by principal mentors was minimal, as was any supervision provided by university faculty or staff.

With no consensus, the Illinois School Leader Taskforce and committee members debated ad nauseam the number of hours that should be required by the new regulations. Conversations involving what activities should be required were complicated by estimates of what it would take to complete them. Most agreed the amount of time it would take to complete a given activity would vary based on the experience and background of the individual candidate. Additionally, some members were reluctant to move away from the requirement of a minimum number of hours for the internship. To overcome the stalemate regarding the number of hours that should be required for the internship, the Illinois State Board of Education (ISBE) and Illinois Board of Higher Education (IBHE) brought in Dr. Joe Murphy and Frank W. Mayborn, Chair of Education and Associate Dean at Peabody College of Education of Vanderbilt University, to facilitate a daylong meeting of key stakeholders. Dr. Murphy was regarded as a national expert on leadership and principal preparation and the goal for the meeting was to reach a consensus on the internship requirements so that they could be written into the new state regulations for the P-12 Principal Endorsement.

While a consensus was not reached at this meeting, it appeared from the conversations that the group may not have been approaching the challenge from the right angle. What really mattered was *not* the number of hours one spent in an internship that were important, but rather the kinds of experiences that candidates should have and how they would demonstrate competency with the wide variety of leadership experiences required of a principal. ISBE and IBHE determined that the internship should provide the platform for candidates to gain experience *and* demonstrate they had the knowledge, skills, and abilities necessary to lead schools.

Recognizing this, ISBE and IBHE staff identified competencies developed by the Southern Regional Education Board (SREB). Their *13 Critical Success Factors for Principals* provided a framework of research-based practices of principals who have been successful in raising student achievement. The SREB Critical Success Factors are aligned to thirty-six associated activities that focus on the specific experiences that principal candidates need to be effective as a principal. ISBE and IBHE made the internal decision to integrate the SREB 36 Competencies into the state rules governing principal preparation programs. Illinois' new principal endorsement was structured as a P-12 license, and experiences involving early childhood, ELL, and special education were also added to the requirements.

ISBE and IBHE further determined that the internship experience should be framed in such a way as to require candidates to complete no less than 80 percent of the activities by *doing* the work, not just *observing* the work. This required the candidate to both complete the experience and demonstrate learning with each of the crucial activities. University supervisors, in collaboration with mentor principals, were required to evaluate candidates through competency-based assessments aligned to the internship experiences.

The inclusion of authentic leadership experiences, combined with competency-based assessments, shifted the focus away from an arbitrary number of hours a candidate would need to spend during their internship to the types of activities candidates need to experience to demonstrate their proficiency as a school leader. That approach recognized the varied experience that candidates bring to the internship. Further, in order to provide exposure to the cadence of a full school year, the regulations specified that internships should occur over the course of a year. In order to ensure authenticity and relevance, the yearlong duration was determined to provide candidates with exposure to the principalship in real time throughout the school year. To further support candidates' understanding of the principalship and ensure high-quality supervision of the internship, minimum qualification and training requirements were also included for both the mentor principal and faculty supervisor.

The policy changes made to principal preparation programs in Illinois were a solid first step. But that is not the end of the story. In light of the national adoption of the Professional Standards for Education Leadership (PSEL), Illinois is currently considering how to reshape its internship competencies to align with those new standards. To do this, Center for the Study of Education Policy (CSEP) staff created a crosswalk of the new PSEL standards to the current internship requirements (see Table 4.3).

Table 4.3 Crosswalk of PSEL Standards, ISLLC Standards, and SREB Critical Success Factors

Professional Standards for Education Leaders (PSEL)	Standards for IL Principal Preparation Programs ISLLC Standards 2008 (and Indicators)	13 SREB Critical Success Factors (and 36 Indicators)
PSEL 1. Mission, Vision & Core Values Effective educational leaders develop, advocate, and enact a shared mission, vision, and core values of high-quality education and academic success and well-being of each student. a. Develop an educational mission for the school to promote the academic success and well-being of each student b. In collaboration with members of the school and the community and using relevant data, develop and promote a vision for the school on the successful learning and development of each child and on instructional and organizational practices that promote such success. c. Articulate, advocate, and cultivate core values that define the school's culture and stress the imperative of child-centered education; high expectations and student support; equity, inclusiveness, and social justice; openness, caring, and trust; and continuous improvement d. Strategically develop, implement, and evaluate actions to achieve the vision for the school e. Review the school's mission and vision and adjust them to changing expectations and opportunities for the school, and changing needs and situations of students f. Develop shared understanding of and commitment to mission, vision, and core values within the school and community g. Model and pursue the school's mission, vision, and core values in all aspects of leadership	**ISLLC 1. Develops, articulates, implements, and stewards a vision of learning, shared and supported by all stakeholders** —Collaboratively develop and implement a shared vision —Collect and use data to identify goals, assess organizational effectiveness, and promote organizational learning —Create and implement plans to achieve goals —Promote continuous and sustainable improvement —Monitor and evaluate progress and revise plans	**CSF 1.** Creates a focused mission and vision to improve student achievement 1a. working with teachers to implement curriculum that produces gains in student achievement as defined by the mission of the school. 1b. working with the administration to develop, define and/or adapt best practices based on current research that supports the school's vision. 1c. working with the faculty to develop, define, and/or adapt best practices, based on current research, that support the school's vision. 1d. assisting with transitional activities for students as they progress to higher levels of placement (e.g., elementary to middle, middle to high school, high school to higher education).

(Continued)

Table 4.3 (Continued)

Professional Standards for Education Leaders (PSEL)	Standards for IL Principal Preparation Programs ISLLC Standards 2008 (and Indicators)	13 SREB Critical Success Factors (and 36 Indicators)
PSEL 2. Curriculum, Instruction, and Assessment Effective educational leaders develop and support intellectually rigorous and coherent systems of curriculum, instruction, and assessment to promote each student's academic success and well-being. a. Implement coherent systems of curriculum, instruction, and assessment that promote the mission, vision, and core values of the school, embody high expectations for student learning, align with academic standards, and are culturally responsive b. Align and focus systems of curriculum, instruction, and assessment within and across grade levels to promote student academic success, love of learning, the identities and habits of learners, and healthy sense of self c. Promote instructional practice that is consistent with knowledge of child learning and development, effective pedagogy, and the needs of each student d. Ensure instructional practice that is intellectually challenging, authentic to student experiences, recognizes student strengths, and is differentiated and personalized e. Promote the effective use of technology in the service of teaching and learning f. Employ valid assessments that are consistent with knowledge of child learning and development and technical standards of measurement g. Use assessment data appropriately and within technical limitations to monitor student progress and improve instruction	**ISLLC 2. Advocates, nurtures, and sustains a school culture and instructional program conducive to student learning and staff professional growth** —Nurture and sustain a culture of collaboration, trust, learning, and high expectations —Create a comprehensive, rigorous, and coherent curricular program —Create a personalized and motivating learning environment for students —Supervise instruction —Develop assessment and accountability systems to monitor student progress —Develop the instructional and leadership capacity of staff —Maximize time spent on quality instruction —Promote the use of the most effective and appropriate technologies to support teaching and learning —Monitor and evaluate the impact of the instructional program	**CSF 2.** Sets high expectations for all students to learn higher-level content 2a. developing/overseeing academic recognition programs that acknowledge and celebrate student's success at all levels of ability. 2b. activities resulting in raising standards and academic achievement for all students and teachers. 2c. authentic assessments of student work through the use and/or evaluation of rubrics, end of course tests, projects. **CSF 3.** Recognizes and encourages implementation of good instructional practices that motivate and increase student achievement 3a. using a variety of strategies to analyze and evaluate the quality of instructional practices being implemented in a school. 3b. working with teachers to select and implement appropriate instructional strategies that address identified achievement gaps. 3c. working on a school team to prioritize standards and map curriculum in at least one content area across all grade levels of the school. 3d. working with a group of teachers to unwrap adopted standards and develop assignments and assessments aligned with the standards.

PSEL 5. Community of Care and Support for Students

Effective educational leaders cultivate an inclusive, caring, and supportive school community that promotes the academic success and well-being of each student

a. Build and maintain a safe, caring, and healthy school environment that meets the academic, social, emotional, and physical needs of each student
b. Create and sustain a school environment in which each student is known, accepted and valued, trusted and respected, cared for, and encouraged to be an active and responsible member of the school community
c. Provide coherent systems of academic and social supports, services, extracurricular activities, and accommodations to meet the range of learning needs of each student
d. Promote adult-student, student-peer, and school-community relationships that value and support academic learning and positive social and emotional development
e. Cultivate and reinforce student engagement in school and positive student conduct
f. Infuse the school's learning environment with the cultures and languages of the school's community

3e. working with a school team to monitor implementation of an adopted curriculum.
3f. involvement in the work of literacy and numeracy task forces.
3g. working with curriculum that is interdisciplinary and provides opportunities for students to apply knowledge in various modalities across the curriculum.

CSF 4. Creates a school where faculty and staff understand that every student counts—

4a. working with staff to identify needs of all students.
4b. collaborating with adults from within the school and community to provide mentors for all students.
4c. engaging in activities designed to increase parental involvement.
4d. engaging in parent/student/school collaborations that develop long-term educational plans for students.

CSF 5. Uses data to initiate and continue improvement in school and classroom practices

5a. analyzing data (including standardized test scores, teacher assessments, psychological data, etc.) to develop/refine instructional activities and set instructional goals.
5b. facilitating data disaggregation for use by faculty and other stakeholders.

(Continued)

Table 4.3 (Continued)

Professional Standards for Education Leaders (PSEL)	Standards for IL Principal Preparation Programs	13 SREB Critical Success Factors (and 36 Indicators)
	ISLLC Standards 2008 (and Indicators)	
PSEL 6. Professional Capacity of School Personnel Effective educational leaders develop the professional capacity and practice of school personnel to promote each student's academic success and well-being a. Recruit, hire, support, develop, and retain effective and caring teachers and other professional staff and form them into an educationally effective faculty b. Plan for and manage staff turnover and succession, providing opportunities for effective induction and mentoring of new personnel c. Develop teachers' and staff members' professional knowledge, skills, and practice through differentiated opportunities for learning and growth, guided by understanding of professional and adult learning and development d. Foster continuous improvement of individual and collective instructional capacity to achieve outcomes envisioned for each student e. Deliver actionable feedback about instruction and other professional practice through valid, research-anchored systems of supervision and evaluation to support the development of teachers' and staff members' knowledge, skills, and practice f. Empower and motivate teachers and staff to the highest levels of professional practice and to continuous learning and improvement g. Develop the capacity, opportunities, and support for teacher leadership and leadership from other member of the school community		**CSF 8.** Understands the change process and has the leadership and facilitation skills to manage change effectively 8a. working with faculty and staff in professional development activities. 8b. inducting and/or mentoring new teaching staff. 8c. building a "learning community" that includes all stakeholders. **CSF 9.** Understands concepts of adult learning and provide sustained professional development that benefits students 9a. study groups, problem-solving sessions and/or ongoing meetings to promote student achievement. 9b. scheduling, developing and/or presenting professional development activities to faculty that positively impact student achievement. **CSF 13.** Is a lifelong learner continuously learning and seeking out colleagues to keep abreast of new research and proven practices 13a. working with faculty to implement research-based instructional practices. 13b. working with professional groups and organizations

h. Promote the personal and professional health, well-being, and work–life balance of faculty and staff
i. Tend to their own learning and effectiveness through reflection, study, and improvement, maintaining a healthy work–life balance

PSEL 7. Professional Community for Teachers and Staff
Effective educational leaders foster a professional community of teachers and other professional staff to promote each student's academic success and well-being

a. Develop workplace conditions for teachers and other professional staff that promote effective professional development, practice, and student learning
b. Empower and entrust teachers and staff with collective responsibility for meeting the academic, social, emotional, and physical needs of each student, pursuant to the mission, vision, and core values of the school
c. Establish and sustain a professional culture of engagement and commitment to shared vision, goals, and objectives pertaining to the education of the whole child; high expectations for professional work; ethical and equitable practice; trust and open communication; collaboration, collective efficacy, and continuous individual and organizational learning and improvement
d. Promote the mutual accountability among teachers and other professional staff for each student's success and the effectiveness of the school as a whole
e. Develop and support open, productive, caring, and trusting working relationships among leaders, faculty, and staff to promote professional capacity and the improvement of practice

(Continued)

Table 4.3 (Continued)

Professional Standards for Education Leaders (PSEL)	Standards for IL Principal Preparation Programs ISLLC Standards 2008 (and Indicators)	13 SREB Critical Success Factors (and 36 Indicators)
f. Design and implement job-embedded and other opportunities for professional learning collaboratively with faculty and staff g. Provide opportunities for collaborative examination of practice, collegial feedback, and collective learning h. Encourage faculty-initiated improvement of programs and practices		
PSEL 9. Operations and Management Effective educational leaders manage school operations and resources to promote each student's academic success and well-being a. Institute, manage, and monitor operations and administrative systems that promote the mission and vision of the school b. Strategically manage staff resources, assigning and scheduling teachers and staff to roles and responsibilities that optimize their professional capacity to address each student's learning needs c. Seek, acquire, and manage fiscal, physical, and other resources to support curriculum, instruction, and assessment; student learning community; professional capacity and community; and family and community engagement d. Are responsible, ethical, and accountable stewards of the school's monetary and non-monetary resources, engaging in effective budgeting and accounting practices	**ISLLC 3. Manages the school, its operations and resources for a safe, efficient, and effective learning environment** —Monitor and evaluate the management and operational systems —Obtain, allocate, align, and efficiently utilize human, fiscal, and technological resources —Promote and protect the welfare and safety of students and staff —Develop the capacity for distributed leadership —Ensure teacher and organizational time is focused to support quality instruction and student learning	**CSF 10.** Uses and organizes time in innovative ways to meet the goals of school improvement 10a. scheduling of classroom and/or professional development activities in a way that provides meaningful time for school improvement activities. 10b. scheduling time to provide struggling students with the opportunity for extra support (e.g., individual tutoring, small-group instruction, extended-block time) so that they may have the opportunity to learn to mastery. **CSF 11.** Acquires and use resources wisely 11a. writing grants or developing partnerships that provide needed resources for school improvement. 11b. developing schedules that maximize student learning in meaningful ways with measurable success.

e. Protect teachers' and other staff members' work and learning from disruption
f. Employ technology to improve the quality and efficiency of operations and management
g. Develop and maintain data and communication systems to deliver actionable information for classroom and school improvement
h. Know, comply with, and help the school community understand local, state, and federal laws, rights, policies, and regulations so as to promote student success
i. Develop and manage relationships with feeder and connecting schools for enrollment management and curricular and instructional articulation
j. Develop and manage productive relationships with the central office and school board
k. Develop and administer systems for fair and equitable management of conflict among students, faculty and staff, leaders, families, and community
l. Manage governance processes and internal and external politics toward achieving the school's mission and vision

PSEL 10. School Improvement
Effective educational leaders act as agents of continuous improvement to promote each student's academic success and well-being

a. Seek to make school more effective for each student, teachers and staff, families, and the community
b. Use methods of continuous improvement to achieve the vision, fulfill the mission, and promote the core values of the school

(Continued)

Table 4.3 (Continued)

Professional Standards for Education Leaders (PSEL)	Standards for IL Principal Preparation Programs	
	ISLLC Standards 2008 (and Indicators)	13 SREB Critical Success Factors (and 36 Indicators)

c. Prepare the school and the community for improvement, promoting readiness, and imperative for improvement, instilling mutual commitment, and accountability, and developing the knowledge, skills, and motivation to succeed in improvement

d. Engage others in an ongoing process of evidence-based inquiry, learning, strategic goal setting, planning, implementation, and evaluation for continuous school and classroom improvement

e. Employ situationally appropriate strategies for improvement, including transformational and incremental, adaptive approaches and attention to different phases of implementation

f. Assess and develop the capacity of staff to assess the value and applicability of emerging educational trends and the finds of research for the school and its improvement

g. Develop technically appropriate systems of data collection, management, analysis, and use, connecting as needed to the district office and external partners for support in planning, implementation, monitoring, feedback, and evaluation

h. Adopt systems perspective and promote coherence among improvement efforts and all aspects of school organization, programs, and services

i. Manage uncertainty, risk, competing initiatives, and politics of change with courage and perseverance, providing support and encouragement, and openly communicating the need for, process for, and outcomes of improvement efforts

j. Develop and promote leadership among teachers and staff for inquiry, experimentation and innovation, and initiating and implementing improvement

PSEL 8. Meaningful Engagement of Families and Community

Effective educational leaders engage families and the community in meaningful, reciprocal, and mutually beneficial ways to promote each student's academic success and well-being

a. Are approachable, accessible, and welcoming to families and members of the community
b. Create and sustain positive, collaborative, and productive relationships with families and the community for the benefit of students
c. Engage in regular and open two-way communication with families and the community about the school, students, needs, problems, and accomplishments
d. Maintain a presence in the community to understand its strengths and needs, develop productive relationships, and engage its resources for the school
e. Create means for the school community to partner with families to support student learning in and out of school
f. Understand, value, and employ the community's cultural, social, intellectual, and political resources to promote student learning and school improvement
g. Develop and provide the school as a resource for families and the community
h. Advocate for the school and district, and for the importance of education and student needs and priorities to families and the community
i. Advocate publicly for the needs and priorities of students, families, and the community
j. Build and sustain productive partnerships with public and private sectors to promote school improvement and student learning

ISLLC 4. Collaborates with faculty and community members, responds to diverse community interests and needs, and mobilizes community resources

—Collect and analyze data and information pertinent to the educational environment
—Promote understanding, appreciation, and use of the community's diverse, cultural, social, and intellectual resources
—Build and sustain positive relationships with families and caregivers
—Build and sustain productive relationships with community partners

CSF 6. Effectively communicates to keep everyone informed and focused on student achievement

6a. analyzing and communicating school progress and school achievement to teachers, parents, and staff.
6b. gathering feedback regarding the effectiveness of personal communication skills.

CSF 12. Obtains support from central office, community, and parent leaders to champion the school improvement agenda

12a. working with faculty to communicate with school board and community stakeholders in a way that supports school improvement.
12b. working with faculty, parents, and community to build collaboration and support for the school's agenda.

CSF 7. Partners with parents to create a structure for parent and educator collaborations for increased student achievement

7a. working in meaningful relationships with faculty and parents to develop action plans for student achievement.

(Continued)

Table 4.3 (Continued)

Professional Standards for Education Leaders (PSEL)	Standards for IL Principal Preparation Programs ISLLC Standards 2008 (and Indicators)	13 SREB Critical Success Factors (and 36 Indicators)
PSEL 2. Ethics and Professional Norms Effective educational leaders act ethically and according to professional norms to promote each student's academic success and well-being a. Act ethically and professionally in personal conduct, relationships with others, decision-making, stewardship of the school's resources, and all aspects of school leadership b. Act according to and promote the professional norms of integrity, fairness, transparency, trust, collaboration, perseverance, learning, and continuous improvement c. Place children at the center of education and accept responsibility for each student's academic success and well-being d. Safeguard and promote the values of democracy, individual freedom and responsibility, equity, social justice, community, and diversity e. Lead with interpersonal and communication skill, social-emotional insight, and understanding of all students' and staff members' backgrounds and cultures f. Provide moral direction for the school and promote ethical and professional behavior among faculty and staff. **PSEL 3. Equity and Cultural Responsiveness** Effective educational leaders strive for equity of educational opportunity and culturally responsive practices to promote each student's academic success and well-being a. Ensure that each student is treated fairly, respectfully, and with an understanding of each student's culture and context	**ISLLC 5. Acts with integrity, fairness, and in an ethical manner** —Ensure a system of accountability for every student's academic and social success —Model principles of self-awareness, reflective practice, transparency, and ethical behavior —Safeguard the values of democracy, equity, and diversity —Consider and evaluate the potential moral and legal consequences of decision-making —Promote social justice and ensure that individual student needs inform all aspects of schooling	

b. Recognize, respect, and employ each student's strengths, diversity, and culture as assets for teaching and learning
c. Ensure that each student has equitable access to effective teachers, learning opportunities, academic and social support, and other resources necessary for success
d. Develop student policies and address student misconduct in a positive, fair, and unbiased manner
e. Confront and alter institutional biases of student marginalization, deficit-based schooling, and low expectations associated with race, class, culture and language, gender and sexual orientation, and disability or special status
f. Promote the preparation of students to live productively in and contribute to the diverse cultural contexts of a global society
g. Act with cultural competence and responsiveness in their interactions, decision-making, and practice
h. Address matters of equity and cultural responsiveness in all aspects of leadership

ISLLC 6. Understands, responds to, and influences the larger political, social, economic, legal, and cultural context
—Advocate for children, families, and caregivers
—Act to influence local, district, state, and national decisions affecting student learning
—Assess, analyze, and anticipate emerging trends and initiatives in order to adapt leadership strategies

CSF 13. Is a lifelong learner continuously learning and seeking out colleagues to keep abreast of new research and proven practices
13a. working with faculty to implement research-based instructional practices.
13b. working with professional groups and organizations.

Stakeholders in Illinois realize there is no time to stand on our laurels. Many involved in the efforts to reform the principal preparation program policy recognize that the job does not end with implementation. Just as the job of the principal is ever changing, so too must the training and requirements for preparing principals in rigorous and relevant programs.

Aligning Principal Preparation Redesign to Superintendent Preparation and Teacher Leadership Programs

Dianne Renn and Lisa Hood

Researchers have found that school leaders have a significant influence on student achievement through the instructional leadership they bring to their schools (Leithwood et al. 2004; Waters, Marzano, and McNulty 2003). After legislation was passed in spring 2010 (Public Act 096-0903), standards for principal licensure changed and principal preparation programs in Illinois redesigned their programs to include new content areas in early childhood learning, special education, gifted education, and English Learners.

At the same time, there was an understanding that principals operate within a broader education system and their effectiveness depends on the leadership they receive from their superintendent. Recent research on leadership has extended the effect on student achievement to include the impact of district leadership (Waters and Marzano 2006). With that in mind, the Illinois State Board of Education (ISBE) decided that it was important to align the endorsement and preparation requirements for principals and superintendents so that future school leaders are prepared using standards and learning experiences that are aligned between the two roles. The belief was that with an aligned leadership preparation system, newly licensed superintendents will provide effective support to principals and staff according to a shared vision of effective district and building leadership practices.

In 2012, ISBE convened the Superintendent Advisory Group which used the work of the principal preparation redesign efforts to develop new program standards for superintendent preparation programs. Members of the Superintendent Advisory Group met monthly between July 2012 and May 2013, and the group included representatives from:

- Colleges and four-year universities who prepare superintendents;
- State-level leadership organizations (e.g., Illinois Association of School Administrators, Illinois Association of School Boards, and Illinois Association of School Business Officials);
- Practicing and retired superintendents;
- State education agencies (e.g., ISBE and the Illinois Board of Higher Education);
- Teachers' unions;
- Illinois organizations that study or advocate for education issues and programs (e.g., Large Unit District Association, Parent Teacher Association);
- Representatives who participated in reforming principal licensure and preparation in Illinois (e.g., School Leader Task Force, Principal Preparation Advisory Committee).

As a result, new Superintendent Preparation Program Standards were passed in 2013 and superintendent candidates could only enroll in redesigned programs by September 1, 2016. Similar to the principal preparation program redesign process, superintendent programs were designed by collaborative teams that included university and district partnerships (e.g., Advisory Councils). The requirements for these programs include:

- Submission of a portfolio that provides evidence of the aspiring candidate's achievements and an in-person interview process with faculty members and often, Advisory Council members;
- Competency-based learning experiences and assessments derived from the 2011 District Level Educational Leadership Constituent Council (ELCC) Standards;
- Coursework that focuses on topics such as district-level use of resources (financial, human, technology); rigorous standards for all students, including special education students, gifted students, English Learners; building collaborative relationships within the district and with community members; and content areas such as state and federal laws affecting schools; Multi-Tiered Systems of Support; bullying; and evaluation of certified staff;

- In recognition that superintendent candidates enter these programs with varying building and district-level experiences (e.g., principals, district curriculum coordinators, human resource coordinators), candidates can proficiency out of some coursework requirements if they can provide evidence from their on-the-job experiences that their leadership skills in a specific area meets the criteria of the competencies (cannot be a written exam);
- In alignment with the principal preparation programs, the internship requirements stipulate that working under the mentorship of an exemplary district leader, candidates must have a diverse range of experiences at all grade levels (P-12) focused on the following:
  - Creating, evaluating, supervising, and monitoring high quality and rigorous curricular, instructional, assessment, and financial resources;
  - Hiring, supervising, and evaluating administrators, teachers, and other staff;
  - Managing operational activities that promote the efficiency and safe school environments;
  - Collaborating with administrators, faculty, families, and community members that result in decision-making that are based on legal and ethical principles;
- Superintendent candidates must be actively leading district-level activities and not merely participating. Furthermore, their competency in district-level leadership skills are assessed on competencies using rubrics designed for the superintendent preparation programs.

Like the principal preparation programs, the superintendent programs follow the principle that partnerships will ensure rigorous and relevant learning experiences that will lead to more effective district leaders. The university preparation program administrators were advised to convene their partners regularly not just to design the programs, but also to participate in the program's implementation by recruiting partners to teach courses or serve as internship mentors. Program administrators will also get more bang for their buck if they capitalize on their partners' expertise and regularly convene them (e.g., Advisory Councils) to review program data and monitor program implementation and candidates' progress to make continuous improvements to the program. This will better ensure that Illinois will prepare superintendents with the twenty-first-century leadership skills needed to support our schools' principals, teachers, and staff and meet the needs of our families and students.

Notes

1. Prior to reform, roughly 4,000 individuals a year were receiving the Type 75 license, which required two years of classroom experience and which many acknowledged they were using primarily to "bump up" their salaries.
2. The Center for the Study of Education Policy (CSEP) at Illinois State University, the Large Unit District Association, and the Urban School Leadership Program at the University of Illinois-Chicago were particularly tireless in traveling to Springfield, bringing along key leaders and providing compelling testimony to the need for change and its potential impact.

Bibliography

Leithwood, Kenneth, Karen Seashore Louis, Stephen Anderson, and Kyla Wahlstrom, K. "Review of Research: How Leadership Influences Student Learning." The Wallace Foundation, 2004.

Waters, Timothy J., and Robert J. Marzano. "School District Leadership That Works: The Effect of Superintendent Leadership on Student Achievement. A Working Paper." Aurora, CO: Mid-Continent Research for Education and Learning (McREL), 2006.

Waters, Tim, Robert J. Marzano, and Brian McNulty. "Balanced Leadership: What 30 Years of Research Tells Us about the Effect of Leadership on Student Achievement. A Working Paper." Aurora, CO: Mid-Continent Research for Education and Learning (McREL), 2003.

Section 2
Policy Implementation
From Theory to Practice

5 The Role of Policy Networks to Support Policy Diffusion through Implementation
A Multi-case Study of Four Universities Working Together

Lisa Hood, Erika Hunt, Alicia Haller, and Debra Baron

This chapter will explore the use of a policy network of early adopters to support the diffusion of innovation of Illinois' new principal preparation requirements. Through a grant from the McCormick Foundation, the Center for the Study of Education Policy (CSEP) convened four universities and district partners over a period of two years to work on the integration of early childhood, English Language Learner (ELL), and Special Education content into their principal preparation programs per the requirement of Public Act (PA) 096-0903. Framed by the Diffusion of Innovation theory, this multi-case study examines the results of Illinois policies on the change process that four Illinois institutions experienced in their redesign efforts, as well as the impact the policies and redesign process had on the programs these institutions developed and on those who were involved in implementation.

Background

In recent years, Illinois has been at the forefront of a national movement to improve school leadership. The passage of PA 096-0903 in 2011 that changed principal licensure from a K-12 certificate to a P-12 endorsement made Illinois the first and only state in the nation to license principals across the entire grade span from preschool through Grade 12. By broadening the grade span of the endorsement, the legislation required that all principal preparation programs in Illinois incorporate new content and field experiences so principals are prepared to be capable and effective leaders of P-12 school communities and programs that address school improvement and learning for all students, including young children (i.e., students in early childhood programs), students with disabilities (i.e., with an Individualized Education Program), and English Language Learners. The new law required that by June 2014, all programs in Illinois seeking to prepare school principals must be approved under these revised standards or cease operating. This chapter examines the process undertaken by a policy network facilitated by the CSEP to work collaboratively to adopt Illinois' new requirements.

According to Rogers (2003), "an innovation is an idea, practice, or object that is perceived as new by an individual or other unit of adoption" (12). While universities in Illinois had been offering principal preparation programs for many years, the incorporation of early childhood, ELL, and special education content into the new principal license made Illinois the first state in the nation to require this. Without other state models or examples from which to learn, this made Illinois and its principal preparation program a trailblazer in requiring this content.

The recommendation to integrate early childhood content into Illinois' principal preparation programs came from a 2009 report,[1] which recommended that "the Illinois State Board of Education should broaden its principal endorsement to PreK-12." The report came out of an advisory group of early care and learning practitioners, public school educators, researchers, and policy advocates charged with collecting and studying research about gaps in the pipeline between early childhood and K-12 systems, barriers to collaboration and communication, and effective practices currently in use throughout Illinois. The group was asked to develop and implement policies and practices that address the missing links in creating a learning continuum that supports the whole child, from birth and beyond. An additional charge of the group was to examine the role that early childhood and K-12 school leaders play in their efforts to collaborate with families, support agencies, and community and state stakeholders to provide high-quality learning and developmental opportunities for children.

The advisory committee was facilitated by staff in the CSEP. In addition to convening the advisory committee, CSEP staff surveyed early childhood program directors, elementary school principals, and professional development providers to identify policies and practices that both support and pose barriers to creating a seamless learning continuum from early childhood to K-12 education. One of the key findings of the research was that principals are well-positioned to create the conditions for a smooth learning continuum that fully supports children as they progress from early childhood to K-12 schools; however, they lack awareness and practice in bridging the divide between early childhood and the K-12 system. This finding led to the recommendation by the Advisory Council that Illinois' current principal licensure be broadened to include early learning. The recommendations—made at the same time that Illinois policymakers were working to restructure Illinois' principal licensure—leveraged the Illinois State Board of Education's decision to broaden the content and focus of the principal endorsement to a PreK-12 license.

Yet, to avoid making changes only on paper and not substantively in the course and program requirements themselves, the staff at the CSEP knew that a strategy of collaborative support among early adopters[2] to serve as models for implementation was needed. Rogers (2003) also notes that "an innovation diffuses more rapidly when it can be re-invented (modified in implementation) and that its adoption is more likely to be sustained" (17). By forming what we refer to as a "policy network," the intent was to assist with the diffusion of innovation in Illinois' new state requirements to the fidelity of the new law but also to the adaptability needed for authentic implementation. The intent was also to assist and support universities with making such a substantive change with very few models, research, and resources. The universities involved with the policy network, in turn, served as the innovators who could develop the new content and strategies that could serve as best practices to other universities in the state.

Literature Review

Policy networks are often used as an effective strategy in policymaking. Mintrom and Vergari (1998), who define a policy network as "a group of actors who share in some policy area and are in linked by their direct or indirect contacts with one another" (128), studied the role of policy networks with the way in which policy ideas emerge and gain attention. As described in Chapters 1 and 2, policy networks were successfully used in Illinois to gain policy attention to the need to redesign principal preparation programs. Through a coalition of important actors in the policy process, policymakers in Illinois were able to facilitate the exchange and mobility of actors needed to pass PA 096-0903.

While this was a successful strategy for policy development, it is often not as common to continue to engage policy networks within the process of implementation. One reason is that there are often different actors involved in policy enactment versus policy implementation (Moe 2015). While enactment coalitions are most commonly made up of special interest groups, McDonnell and Weatherford (2016) note that implementation coalitions are more commonly made up more of local grassroots groups and affiliates of these organizations—the practitioners. This membership arrangement often results in a disconnect between policy intentions that are agreed upon by the actors in the policy enactment and the intention that is communicated and followed by those implementing the policy as new actors will emerge that were not part of the policy enactment (McDonnell and Weatherford 2016).

In Illinois, CSEP staff were intentional in engaging the local practitioners—faculty and district administrators in addition to the special interest groups—in the policy enactment process, which aided with the interpretation of the new requirements during implementation. However, recognizing that new players would be involved with the implementation process that were not involved with the development of the new requirements, CSEP staff knew that a coordinated effort for implementation needed to happen. Also, for this reason, CSEP staff (who were instrumental in the policy enactment stage) wanted to continue to play a facilitating role in the policy implementation stage.

Recognizing the complexity of policy implementation, McDonnell and Weatherford (2016) characterize a highly complex process of policy implementation that they define as a "policy feedback process" among bureaucrats, special interest groups and the practitioners that must do the implementation (233). Considering the process that occurs, the communication and support strategies that are put into place to communicate and support the interpretation of the policy intentions are a critical piece to support implementation. Open communication with the policy enactors is also key, as McDonnell and Weatherford (2016) note that the perceptions of the policy design and intent have a great influence on implementation. Simply stated, if there is no trust by practitioners in how the policy was developed, there will not be support with implementation. Additionally, if practitioners support the policy, it is harder for opponents to eliminate it (McDonnell and Weatherford 2016). Recognizing this fact, a key focus of the policy network was to nurture and maintain trust in the process.

Another key factor attributed to successful implementation is time. According to McDonnell and Weatherford (2016), more successful implementation is accomplished when local implementers have more time to build their "local infrastructures" of support (236). Granting enough time also gives local implementers time to make sense of the new directives, referring to what Spillane, Reiser, and Reimer (2002) call the "sense-making process" as local practitioners come to understand a policy's meaning and its implications for their practice.

Implementing a new state policy is complicated and challenging. Implementing an innovative state policy is an even more daunting task. As such, communication regarding a new idea takes a different type of communication and approach than more traditional policy implementation (Rogers 2003). Understanding the complexity that it takes for a new innovation to diffuse, Rogers (2003) characterizes what he calls "diffusion networks" that create a larger group of adopters that serve as opinion leaders with swaying the behavior and opinion of others on the new innovation (300). While we characterize the network of four universities as a policy network due to their intentional tie to Illinois' new principal preparation policy, we also want to note the intentionality that was there with also establishing them as key opinion leaders among universities in the state. Using the concept of policy networks, this chapter aims to answer: how did the use of a policy network assist with the adoption and sustainability of Illinois' new requirements for early childhood, English Language Learners (ELLs), and students with disabilities?

Methods

A cross-case analysis was used to examine similarities and differences across four sites that formed a policy network to collaborate and share best practices and challenges with integrating early learning, ELLs, and special education as they redesigned their principal preparation curriculum to align with the new Illinois P-12 principal endorsement. Following case study methods outlined by Robert Stake (1978, 1995) and Robert Yin (2003), the sites were purposefully selected to serve as early adopters and opinion leaders. Faculty members at the "policy network universities" were involved with the policy enactment of the new principal preparation requirements. The universities in which they are employed are representative of public and private universities (two public and two private) and are located in different geographic regions of the state.

Multiple interpretive methods, including semi-structured interviews, narratives,[3] content analysis, and document review, were used to identify common patterns as well as unique findings at the sites (Denzin and Lincoln 2008). An interview protocol was the primary method used to collect data (Creswell 2003; Miles and Huberman 1994). Interview notes were typed and returned to the site contacts for clarification. Narrative drafts were then developed for each site and again sent back to the site staff. Content and format of the narratives were finalized, and program artifacts were submitted by each program's redesign contact and/or team. The four case studies were made available to other universities in the state to influence the opinion and adoption of the new requirements and to provide assistance. The cross-case analysis findings in this article are drawn from the data contained in those case studies along with other lessons learned through the Leadership to Integrate the Learning Continuum (LINC) project.

Sample Baseline/Case Profiles

While the bulk of the description in this chapter will focus on the synthesized findings related to specific elements of the redesign efforts described in the four case studies, a general overview of each university that participated in the LINC project is provided to situate the context in which the changes took place. While the sites were purposefully selected, each one entered into the redesign process from a different starting point.

Case 1: Illinois State University (ISU) is a large, state-supported university that began as a teacher education institution, with an undergraduate enrollment of approximately 18,000 students and over 2,000 graduate students. It is located near the geographic center of the state, surrounded by two urban areas with a combined population in excess of 130,000 people, along with a number of small rural communities. The twin cities serve as a transportation hub, making it easy for students in the area to access the campus. The Educational Administration and Foundations

(EAF) Department within the College of Education (COE) consists of a total of twenty-two faculty divided among four areas.

The overall focus of the COE centers in its conceptual framework, expressed as "Realizing the Democratic Ideal." This mission grounds the conceptual framework developed by the EAF faculty, "Practical Wisdom for Leaders: Connecting Theory to Practice." This framework

> encompasses the following beliefs about leadership preparation: (a) Leadership preparation features a dynamic relationship between practice and scholarship; (b) Courses blend themes of leadership, learning, and social justice in the context of practical wisdom; (c) Faculty honor diverse voices and multiple perspectives; and (d) Graduates are our partners in the field, building inclusive learner-centered communities.
> (Lyman, Hesbol, and Young 2013, 5)

Case 2: Loyola University Chicago (LUC) is a medium-sized, private, Catholic Jesuit university located in Chicago, with three campuses in the city and surrounding area. It has an undergraduate enrollment of approximately 10,000 and around 6,000 graduate students. Located in a large urban center, there is convenient access to the campuses from the entire metropolitan area; additionally, off-site locations frequently host Education Leadership cohort groups. Full-time faculty in the Administration and Supervision program within the School of Education (SoE) consists of two tenured professors, one full-time clinical assistant professor, and a full-time coordinator of coaches.

The School of Education's vision and mission are guided by the teaching traditions of its Jesuit founders.

> Written in 2009 by integrating current research and best practices about innovative educational leadership preparation, the *Transformative Education in the Jesuit Tradition* statement includes six core components: (a) expand horizons and deepening knowledge; (b) self-appropriation or the self who leads; (c) dialogue; (d) moral responsibility; d) care for planet or leading within various school contexts; and (e) promotion of justice.
> (Israel et al. 2013, 67)

Case 3: North Central College (NCC) is a small, private, liberal arts college located in a western Chicago suburb. It has an enrollment of approximately 2,800 undergraduates and 250 graduate students. Its Principal Preparation and Leadership Program tends to attract teachers from its neighboring school districts—both affluent and Title I districts. There are two full-time faculty members on the Leadership and Administration Master's Program team located within the School of Education and Health Sciences.

The Education Department has developed a shared leadership culture based on the work of Joseph Raelin (2003), author of *Creating Leaderful Organizations: How to Bring Out Leadership in Everyone*. Raelin argues that organizations are more effective when they are collective, collaborative, and concurrent. Additionally, the

> graduate programs embrace foundations in liberal arts and interdisciplinary learning, integrating human, ethical and societal issues into their programs. Moreover, there is a strong emphasis on leadership, ethics, and values in both undergraduate and graduate education, designed to blend intellectual inquiry (theory) with essential professional skills (practice).
> (Servais, Vuksanovich, and Young 2013, 130)

Case 4: Western Illinois University (WIU) is a medium-sized public university founded as a teacher's college. It has an undergraduate enrollment around 9,200 and approximately 1,450 graduate students. Located in the west-central part of the state near the Mississippi River, it comprises two campuses aimed at serving students in a wide, rural geographic area. One of the campuses is located in a four-city urban area that straddles the Illinois-Iowa border with a metropolitan population of 376,000. The two campuses attract candidates from several states in addition to Illinois, including Iowa, Wisconsin, and Missouri. Students are attracted to the university because of the College of Education and Human Services, where the Educational Leadership Department is housed. It is strong in distance learning initiatives and integrating technology into teacher education. There are eight full-time Educational Leadership faculty members.

Prior to the redesign process, the focus of the program was to develop principals who were prepared to manage a building or program. However, during the period of redesign, a total commitment to the development of instructional leaders emerged as an expanded focus for the faculty. Constantly revisiting the Illinois School Code enabled the redesign team to regain focus when challenges arose (Halverson et al. 2013).

Our analysis of the data first focused on the policy adoption using the concepts of policy network and diffusion of innovation, including the implementation process that the universities followed and how the new requirements were adopted and where reinvention occurred. Following this, we looked at how the policy network itself was valued by the network members.

Implementation Process

Redesign Team Composition

There was no single model for the redesign teams. Each institution assembled a group that best maximized the resources available to them. For some, all of the Educational Leadership faculty were members of the team. In other cases, a core group intermittently sought input on their work from their colleagues. Some teams comprised only Educational Leadership faculty, while others included representatives from their partner organizations as well as faculty from other disciplines within their institutions. However, as McDonnell and Weatherford (2016) note, an important step of policy implementation is allowing time and flexibility for organizations to build their "local infrastructures" of support (236).

Our analysis did find one common determinant critical to the success of the teams, and that was the presence of a "redesign leader" who could articulate a clear vision of the skills principals needed to support the education of divergent learners, and who understood the expertise needed to help the team achieve that vision. ISU initially designated the Assistant Chair and member of the P-12 area of the EAF Department to lead this initiative. Midway through the process, that individual retired and was replaced as the Team Leader by the Assistant to the Chair for Program Development. The LUC redesign process was co-directed by the two Principal Preparation Program Chairpersons, with the support of the Dean of the School of Education who had been a member of State of Illinois Advisory Task Force on Principal Preparation and advocated the importance of changing the paradigm. The NCC team was led by a member of the Educational Leadership faculty, who also served as the coordinator of education graduate programs. The WIU process was led by the Educational Leadership Department Chairperson.

Since all of the teams had at least one faculty member involved in the earlier state policy enactment work, those connections also helped to set the stage for their own redesign work. They were able to communicate and interpret the original policy intentions to their colleagues who were not involved with the process, thus avoiding the confusion that it often caused among different actors involved with different stages of the policy process (Moe 2015). These faculty members had been sharing process and product recommendations, committee progress, and discussions from the state committees with their faculty colleagues well before formal design work began, so this also helped with the "sense-making process" (Spillane, Reiser, and Reimer 2002). According to one faculty member who was involved since the beginning of the policy enactment process,

> Sharing these insights gave the faculty members a solid foundation of the issues, the focus, and the intent of the new requirements from the beginning. Having this information available from the outset gave faculty members the opportunity to consider various ideas and begin building background knowledge for the work that was eventually necessary for crafting the proposal as presented for state board approval.
>
> (Halverson et al. 2013, 208)

Even though information was readily available in the literature about the changes that needed to be made in principal preparation programs, it was not uncommon for some faculty members at each of the institutions to enter the process satisfied with their existing programs and resistant to making changes. Not surprisingly, the inclusion of content and experiences for early childhood, ELL, and students with disabilities was not viewed by some faculty as having a relative advantage (the innovation is seen as better than the idea it replaces), one of the characteristics that Rogers (2003) states leads to more diffused adaptation of new innovations. However, WIU found that having input from school district representatives involved in the process made it easier to overcome this challenge, as faculty learned more about the needs of practitioners in the field, thus fulfilling another characteristic defined by Rogers (2003) to ease with diffusion adaptability—that of compatibility found in aligning with values and needs in the field. While other teams found that external input helped them to overcome resistance as well, there were other challenges that arose in bringing together diverse stakeholders.

Early in the process, NCC recognized that there were "organizational cultural differences between higher education and P-12. The common bond quickly became the shared values to improve education for the often-underserved subgroups of ELLs, early childhood learners, and students with disabilities" (Servais, Vuksanovich, and Young 2013, 135). In an effort to allow team members to develop their own norms and working guidelines, meetings were moved from the college campus to a teachers' lounge in one of the partner schools and occasionally to more neutral ground, such as area restaurants. An effort was also made to mark milestones with celebratory events to recognize the team's progress.

Essential Elements of the Change Process

A conclusion drawn by the WIU leadership team aptly reflects what all of the institutions experienced.

> Faculty found this somewhat like a puzzle in which you find pieces that seem to be alike, but in the end do not fit. Courses, objectives, outcomes, and standards had to be examined carefully to identify where they fit together to create WIU's "picture" of principal preparation.
> (Halverson et al. 2013, 214)

In an effort to put the "puzzle" together, all of the redesign teams to some extent used backwards design strategies aimed at preparing candidates to be successful as principals. These strategies helped to characterize the new requirements as less complex (easy to understand and implement) as well as observable (results are easy to see when you picture how a successful principal act), two characteristics identified by Rogers (2003) that better supports adaptation of innovation.

Another commonality was that the words used to describe the redesign process indicate that there was much movement. Terms such as "iterative" (LUC), "back and forth" (WIU), "in and out" (NCC), and "a series of adjustments and rethinking" (ISU) reflect the fluid the process. Additionally, teams had to consider interruptions due to staff changes, co-occurring activities, and evolving state policies. Overall, the interruptions provided space and a time for reflection, allowing ideas to percolate so that when the redesign activity resumed, there was less resistance to the new requirements.

The design teams used various versions of a multifaceted approach, which more or less involved the following nine elements, but not necessarily in the same sequence.

1. A review of the research literature and disseminating information to colleagues who would eventually be impacted by the new policies and practices. Efforts were made to establish or utilize existing learning communities within their program areas to discuss new approaches to principal preparation, frequently well before the actual redesign work began.
2. Several of the teams expressed taking time, either intentionally or because of co-occurring review activities by the Council for the Accreditation of Educator Preparation (CAEP), to review and articulate their core beliefs and values for their new principal preparation program. For LUC, this is an essential component of their Jesuit tradition. ISU found that revisiting their conceptual framework contributed to program coherence. For most of the institutions this was a faculty-focused activity, but WIU also involved current students in this process.
3. Throughout the process, teams paid close attention to the Illinois School Code to stay grounded and ensure that they were keeping on track with the outcomes they would need to produce. They also had to consider the Illinois Professional Teaching Standards (Illinois General Assembly n.d., Section 24.130) as well as other institution-specific guidelines.
4. Each institution also had to grapple with myriad professional standards and guidelines. For example, Illinois also requires preparation programs to meet the Interstate School Leaders Licensure Consortium (ISLLC) educational leadership policy standards (National Policy Board for Educational Administration. ISLLC 2008). NCATE requires compliance with the Educational Leadership Constituent Council (ELCC) Standards (National Policy Board for Educational Administration 2011) for accreditation. Per the rule requirements, the internship experience was also grounded on competencies and assessments that also had to be met.

5. Almost all of the institutions sought feedback from practitioners in the field at one time or another, most often involving program alumni. Early in the process, NCC invited alumni to an event where they were asked to complete a written assessment of their knowledge related to the three new content areas (special education, ELLs, and students with disabilities). Midway through the redesign, WIU asked recent program graduates to identify which experiences had been most helpful to "hit the ground running." When the course syllabi were completed, ISU distributed an online Curriculum Survey to representatives of their partner schools and a select group of current students and alumni. This input was described as essential for gaining validation and determining if additional revisions still needed to be made.
6. In one way or another, redesign teams conducted a gap analysis to determine the missing pieces between what was currently being taught and what would need to be taught to meet the new requirements.
7. All of this information, including the standards to be met, best practices and ideas from practitioners, and program values and beliefs, were assembled in one place. The ISU team participated in brainstorming sessions that resulted in curriculum documents. WIU created a spreadsheet to accomplish this task. LUC fashioned a wall of "big post-its" to match chunked areas of knowledge with desired competencies. NCC created a matrix which allowed team members to strategically integrate new content by moving, revising, or replacing old course content with new knowledge.
8. Only after much of the groundwork described above was completed were course syllabi rewritten. Teams used terms like the "principle of redundancy" (ISU) and "a spiraling of content" (LUC) to describe their efforts to ensure that core content and competencies were addressed and assessed multiple times among many courses. The NCC "team members were relentless and provided insights on ways to embed the new LINC curriculum into almost every course, sometimes as a textbook, an assignment or an assessment" (Servais, Vuksanovich, and Young 2013, 137).
9. It is important to note: this work was taking place while the state was still working out the details for implementing the new policies. Therefore, every redesign team needed to conduct a careful review of what it had produced and to adjust, if necessary, to meet the final state guidelines prior to submitting its application to ISBE for approval.

While frequent meetings were a common occurrence, one aspect of the work that varied quite a bit was the organizational approach of the redesign teams. For example, the LUC Redesign Co-chairs conducted one-hour interviews with each of their colleagues in various disciplines within the School of Education, such as school psychology, special education, and early childhood. They asked them to answer the following three questions:

1. In your area of expertise, what should a P-12 principal know and be able to do?
2. Regarding your area of expertise, what field experiences would you suggest a principal be involved in during his/her training?
3. What specific resources would you consider seminal to a building principal's knowledge of this area?

(Israel et al. 2013, 70)

After completing the fact-finding interviews, the Co-chairs were the primary architects of the redesign plan. NCC, on the other hand, moved between working as a committee of the whole and in three subgroups, each focusing on one of the new content areas (early childhood learners, ELLs, and students with disabilities). The same template was used by each subgroup to address the following "program components: (a) key questions; (b) framework and alignments; (c) resources; and (d) recommended course curriculum" (Servais, Vuksanovich, and Young 2013, 135). The work of the subgroups was then discussed in the large group to gain consensus on the proposed changes or to identify needed revisions.

In spite of the efforts to gain multiple perspectives, learn from best practices, and engage in shared decision-making, the resulting redesigned programs still represented new and somewhat untested ways of doing things. According to one of the ISU Redesign Team members,

> We are walking on the line of teaching things that will need to be internalized on the fly; it will be an interesting experience for everyone. The initiative of the faculty member really will make the difference in how each of the courses works. We have explicitly written that we will learn from the reciprocity with our students and partners.
> (Lyman et al. 2013, 12)

Length of Time to Complete the Process

From the beginning of redesign to the final approval took approximately two to three years to complete at each institution; however, McDonnell and Weatherford (2016) note that time to implement new policies is an important element to its success and sustainability. The pace of reform varied by institution, driven largely by their different organizational environments and structures. The size of the institution and its culture related to change appears to have had the most influence on the approval process for principal preparation curriculum modifications, with NCC being the quickest to adopt the new program changes.

Redesign at NCC took place within a "culture that was comfortable with an on-going change process" (Servais, Vuksanovich, and Young 2013, 136). Being a relatively small institution with few levels of bureaucracy contributed to the ease with which curricular changes were proposed and approved. Additionally, NCC was in the habit of regularly examining best practices and seeking input from the field about potential changes to the curriculum.

> For example, a one-year internship was requested as a program change two years prior to the state-mandated internship change. Therefore, the institutional change process in implementing the new Principal Preparation Program redesign requirements were viewed as another continuous process of leadership reform at NCC.
> (Servais, Vuksanovich, and Young 2013, 136)

Two of the most constant challenges for all of the redesign teams were time constraints and meeting deadlines. The LUC team captured the sentiments expressed by others, noting that

> engaging a large number of institutional faculty members and two partners with different operating structures took a lot of time. There were multiple meetings, and many meetings took four to five hours. A lesson learned is to know that if a program is going to undertake this task, then the time and commitment need to be in place to do it well and to do it right.
> (Israel et al. 2013, 73)

One of the approaches taken by LUC to address time constraints was to voluntarily not admit new candidates for a year. This decision, made by the then Dean of the School of Education (SoE), gave the leadership team the time needed to re-examine "the way in which principals were prepared at Loyola" and to develop "a culture of authentic, collaborative and productive relationships between program faculty members and partners" (Israel et al. 2013, 78).

The efforts of the WIU and ISU redesign teams were slowed by two other factors: turnover in faculty and gaining university approval. However, in both instances, the interruptions caused by staff turnover paid fruitful dividends in the end, which will be described later. The time required to get approval for course and program changes within their university systems was a much lengthier challenge than had been anticipated. Extensive accreditation requirements needed to be met and numerous presentations had to be made to various committees. Recognizing that this was going to be a potentially difficult process, the ISU design team chose to seek state approval first before seeking university levels of approval. This decision led to the need for thoughtful planning and leadership to navigate the university approval process. Both of these examples from LUC and ISU reiterate how important time and flexibility was for universities to each build their "local infrastructures" of support.

(McDonnell and Weatherford 2016, 236)

How New Requirements Were Adopted

Focus on Partnerships

Based on the analysis, we found that one of the most essential elements of the new requirements was the development of formal partnership agreements between higher education institutions and local school districts. This finding represents a major paradigm shift in that programs are to be focused on meeting the needs of their school districts as consumers. The importance of authentic, collaborative, and productive long-term partnerships cannot be overstated, as we identified four essential roles that districts can play in the process to create school leaders under the new state requirements:

1. To assist in the initial steps of the redesign process by helping to clarify roles and expectations, to ensure mutually beneficial interdependence and reciprocity, and to determine if there are other potential partners who needed to be involved with the redesign efforts;
2. To support teachers from their school districts as potential principal candidates, and matching candidates to practicum, clinical, and internship experiences within and across the partnerships that might not be available with teachers' own resources;
3. To create multifaceted internships so the candidates can be truly supported in gaining expertise in leading educational communities through the P-12 continuum, including meeting the needs of young children, English Language Learners, and children and youth with disabilities;
4. To assess and evaluate the candidates' leadership skills and eventually hire many of the newly trained principals.

By districts taking ownership and involvement in these roles, they provided "confirmation" or "reinforcement of the decision" that Rogers (2003) describes as a critical step in the "innovation-decision process" (169).

Other district roles may include shaping course content, identifying potential principal candidates, providing field and internship experiences as well as mentor principals, evaluating the performance of candidates, and assessing the quality and value of the programs offered. Each of the institutions approached these requirements in ways that built on expanding existing relationships and, when necessary, forging new ones. More than the practical roles that districts played was the compatibility found in aligning with values and needs in the field (Rogers 2003), which in turn validated to the universities that the new principal preparation requirements were needed and valued.

While WIU developed formal relationships with only one local school district near each of its two campuses to meet the ISBE criteria for screening and program evaluation, additional input during the redesign phase was obtained through the department's standing Program Advisory Council (PAC). The prior existence of the PAC facilitated acceptance of increased collaboration with professionals "in the field." Early in the process, the PAC was expanded to include greater representation from local districts with varying size enrollments and communities. "The value of active partners cannot be emphasized enough. Their perceptions of what critical content and skills needed mastered enabled the redesign team to move beyond traditional course content to more current problems and issues" (Halverson et al. 2013, 211).

ISU elected to work with four local Regional Offices of Education (ROEs) as partners in the redesign efforts, along with twenty-eight school district partners. The ROEs serve as intermediate-level service providers for ISBE and are in an ideal position to serve in a brokering role with the districts within their regions. Initially, the intent was to form a temporary Advisory Committee comprising one of the ROEs and its superintendents. However, the benefits of establishing formal memorandums of understanding with all of the ROEs and districts that cover the geographical area most frequently served by the institution quickly became apparent, particularly in terms of meeting pre- and post-enrollment needs of the principal candidates. A School Districts' Advisory Committee comprising representatives from the ROEs and ten district superintendents has been established to guide the process going forward. Membership on the Committee will rotate among the partner districts.

Although drawing candidates from a smaller area, NCC chose to go beyond the minimum requirements and develop formal agreements with three school districts where many of their principal candidates work. There is a long history of this institution working collaboratively with its community partners through both formal and informal arrangements. This

> has resulted in mutual goals of developing high-quality educators through pre-service education (e.g., placement of student teachers with district teachers, cohorts developed within districts, courses offered in district buildings, etc.), and in-service education (e.g., presentation of district institute sessions and professional development by faculty).
>
> (Servais, Vuksanovich, and Young 2013, 129)

Careful consideration has been given to developing mutually beneficial partnerships that provide value-added benefits to both the institution and the districts so that all learners can benefit through these shared commitments.

Working in a very different environment than the other institutions, LUC has developed two very distinct partnerships. One involves the Chicago Office of Catholic Schools (OCS), operated through the Roman Catholic Archdiocese of Chicago. The other includes the Chicago Public Schools (CPS) through the Chicago Leadership Collaborative (CLC). The CLC includes LUC, the University of Illinois at Chicago, Teach for America, and New Leaders, who work together to develop a cohesive and consistent model for preparing principals specific to the needs and expectations of CPS.

In addition to the formal agreements that resulted, this opportunity was also used to strengthen informal partnerships with alumni and other relevant parties. NCC drew on its alumni and colleagues in its partnership districts to join its working groups, whereas others drew on their alumni as part of a long-standing Program Advisory Group (WIU), as respondents to a survey to aid in revising the coursework (ISU) and as future internship coaches (LUC). These and other examples will be discussed in more detail below.

Coherence of Resulting Programs

One of the common conclusions of the leadership teams was that the redesigned programs are tighter and more cohesive and will provide for a more carefully constructed training experience for the principal candidates. Care was taken to ensure that the course content flows well from one course to another chronologically as well as at any one point in time (e.g., within any one semester), and that prerequisite attitudes, skills, and knowledge are carefully considered in deciding on a course sequence. Another important "change from the previous required courses was a shift from courses dealing with management issues to courses covering teaching and learning—the focus of the instructional leader" (Halverson et al. 2013, 216). An emphasis on producing leaders with the skills needed to promote and enhance student learning across the P-12 span and for special populations now clearly exists.

In order to accomplish this, each of the institutions adopted new and innovative courses. For example, NCC now offers *Leadership for the Twenty-First Century* as an introductory program to individuals considering either the Principal Preparation Program or a Teacher Leadership Master's Degree as a means for helping them to decide which career path they want to pursue. ISU developed *Leading Learning for Stages of Mind* which features "leadership applications of educational neuroscience to enhance learning capacities from early childhood through adulthood"

(Lyman et al. 2013, 15). Recognizing that almost half of their candidates were not teachers in core subject areas, WIU added *Leading the Core Curriculum* to address the national educational agenda, particularly related to literacy and numeracy. LUC gives their candidates the opportunity to gain a global perspective through an optional two-week summer course at its Rome campus or through an experiential course in the neighborhoods of Chicago.

A few other notable efforts are also worth mentioning. To create greater consistency across instructors, NCC developed a "Master Course Outline" for each course and all faculty, regular and adjunct, will need to adhere to the textbook choices, assessments, and so forth, so that all students who enroll in that course will have highly similar though not identical experiences. Similarly, WIU prepared course specification sheets that include course objectives, desired outcomes, and the Illinois School Code specifications and ISBE requirements for adjunct faculty who teach courses. All of the programs also utilized existing resources that had been developed to support principal pre-service and in-service training on effective programming for young learners, such as the training module developed by staff in the CSEP (see http://leadershiplinc.illinoisstate.edu/LINC-Training/).

Another effort described by WIU to create greater cohesiveness was to cross-train the faculty to teach courses so that the faculty members have a greater awareness of the program content that precedes and/or follows a designated course and results in greater flexibility in assigning faculty to teach courses. At LUC,

> once a separate course, school law concepts were now spiraled within multiple courses such as 1. Multi-Tier Systems of Support, 2. School Supervision, 3. Resource Management and Talent Acquisition, 4. ELL Methods and Assessment, and 5. School Law, Policy Formation and Community Involvement.
>
> (Israel et al. 2013, 71)

Emphasis on Field Experience

Not only have the new policies resulted in significant changes in the course content of the principal preparation programs, but the way they are being taught and assessed has also been altered to provide a much greater emphasis on applied learning through coursework related field experiences and a culminating internship. For example, the ISU program now includes twenty-five field experience assessments in its courses. These "were created to prepare students for the internship experiences and will be scored using the state rubric model for the internship experiences" (Lyman et al. 2013, 10). Additionally, NCC requires field experiences in every course and a two-week, full-time summer residency as a part of its internship. These changes are intended to not only provide candidates with real-world challenges but to also ensure experiences across grade levels and not just at the level of the current position of the candidate.

In order to provide the newly required range of field experiences, the institutions and candidates will have to draw upon the expertise of several mentor principals that meet the state qualification requirements. This practice is quite different than the old practice, where candidates tended to complete all their fieldwork in their home schools under one mentor. For the most part, mentor principals will now be located in school districts that have established formal partnerships with the higher education institutions. In some cases, candidates' home schools and districts may not be able to provide all the field experiences required for the coursework and internships. ISU's partner ROEs will help to broker these experiences. NCC will utilize its three partner districts as well as its alumni network to meet these needs. One of the WIU partner districts has adopted a year-round calendar that can provide "interns an opportunity to gain experiences when their districts are not in school that they wouldn't otherwise have been able to do" (Halverson et al. 2013, 217).

Another change is that assessment of the field-based course assignments and internship will involve greater shared responsibilities between the candidates, mentor principals, and institutional supervisors. For example, ISU will require its candidates to keep journals that will be utilized in conjunction with feedback obtained from mentor principals and university supervisors to assess student progress and program quality. WIU will utilize a series of formative and summative assessments that will be scored by the faculty and program partners and placed in the candidate's ePortfolio.

The LUC assessment activities have been crafted to allow candidates, coaches, and faculty to monitor progress on an ongoing basis, with faculty and coaches meeting every other week. LUC employs coaches, who are retired principals from their partner districts, to work with their candidates during their internships. However, one thing all program leaders recognize is that the true assessment of the field experiences and internships will come in the willingness of the partner school districts to hire program graduates.

Faculty Adjustments

Redesigning their programs required the teams to have open and honest conversations with their colleagues, stressing that there were no "sacred cows."

> Everything and anything that had been a part of the Principal Preparation Program would be under consideration for redesign. The alignment of faculty talents and interests to fulfill specific

responsibilities in the delivery process would be determined only after examining how to create the strongest preparation experience for the candidates.

(Israel et al. 2013, 69)

In order to implement the principle of redundancy, faculty could no longer "own" courses. Notions of " 'academic freedom'—the idea that once I'm in my classroom I teach what I want"—had to be put aside (Halverson et al. 2013, 211). Rogers (2003) talks about how system norms like this affect the diffusion of innovation noting that they can often serve as barriers to change. As indicated earlier, WIU noted that having their partners involved in this process "helped the faculty acknowledge where there was duplication, where there were gaps in curriculum, and where assessments were needed" (Halverson et al. 2013, 211). The collaborative support and the friendly competition that was part of the policy network also helped to push the universities beyond allowing system norms to serve as implementation barriers.

At the same time, it was essential to recognize that faculty needed to feel the same collective moral obligation to prepare every candidate for success that was expected in P-12 education. Although

> one can be highly knowledgeable about the dispositions, skills and knowledge for developing strong principals; however, one person does not have all the answers. Each person in the redesign effort needed to know that they had something valuable to contribute and the final product would be better as the result of many individuals' contributions.
>
> (Israel et al. 2013, 69)

In order to sustain the collaborative culture needed to do this work well, WIU planned to

> cross-train faculty members so that the instructor of a course in a particular area can share his/her strengths with another instructor. This model also maintains the big picture of the program and the components within the various courses, so that course articulation develops naturally.
>
> (Halverson et al. 2013, 215)

Another common theme that emerged was the necessity for the leadership of higher education institutions to consider how participation in the redesign process and ensuing supervision and continuous improvement activities will impact faculty achievement recognition. First, there is the issue of allocating sufficient faculty time to engage in the redesign process. "Engaging in time-consuming redesign activities over the course of several years has to be deemed as worthy as delivering high-quality instruction, supervision and coaching of aspiring leader candidates" (Israel et al. 2013, 74). This again hits upon the notion of "relative advantage" described by Rogers (2003) as the "degree to which the innovation is perceived as better than the idea that it supersedes" (229).

For those institutions that did not begin with a continuous improvement process in place, there was the realization that these activities must be balanced with other ongoing faculty expectations. This can have serious consequences at major research universities such as LUC, where "there is an expectation that faculty will engage in conducting original scholarship approximately 40% of their time" (Israel et al. 2013, 74). Even though the redesign and continuous improvement activities may lead to new research opportunities, the time necessary to collect data and publish is in addition to the time spent facilitating the change process. This tension played into the part of many faculty as to whether or not to actively accept or passively reject the innovative policy changes.

Furthermore, the increased emphasis on field experience is likely to necessitate "a shift in workload to balance internship supervisory needs with teaching workload" (Halverson et al. 2013, 215). All four of the institutions anticipate hiring additional full-time or adjunct faculty who will have the requisite principal background to meet Illinois' new requirements for supervision. This component is reflected in the plans ISU and NCC had for new full-time faculty hires. LUC intends to hire retired principals from their partner schools, utilizing one coach for every four candidates; NCC also plans to make use of its alumni network and partner schools as its source for adjunct faculty to meet these needs. Meeting the supervisory and mentoring needs of the new candidates is likely to be among the biggest challenges ahead.

How the Policy Network Was Valued by Network Members

All of the institutions expressed appreciation for the synergy, relationships, and knowledge gained from their participation in the policy network. The importance of a state-level initiative that provides technical assistance funded by an external foundation brings design teams together and awards a small amount of funding to support the principal preparation curriculum redesign efforts cannot be underestimated. According to WIU team leaders,

> The examples of inter-departmental collaboration shared by the Consortium partners and the gentle, persuasive restatement of the law's focus to prepare principals who could effectively lead learning communities along the P-12 continuum, including children with disabilities, ELLs, and preschool-age children, served to awaken an

interest in looking for resources and additional expertise beyond their department boundaries.

(Halverson et al. 2013, 212)

Inviting CSEP staff to participate in a faculty meeting to restate and clarify the intentions of the redesign efforts coming out of Consortium deliberations led ISU faculty to engage in "a brainstorming process [that] resulted in a new 10-course plus internship program that included five completely new courses" (Lyman et al. 2013, 8). Working with members of the CSEP team on prior collaborative projects, such as the design of the *Internship Assessment* document to be used as part of the credentialing process, provided LUC team leaders with valuable insights for framing and answering guiding questions, such as "How can we embed that experience?" and "How can we contextualize that knowledge or skill for the candidate?" (Israel et al. 2013, 71). LUC also consulted with faculty at the University of Illinois at Chicago who "had already led a process of breaking down pre-existing ideas of principal preparation and helping move faculty members away from their 'sacred cows'" (72). Their expertise and unbiased perspective enabled LUC to examine what they were doing and how it could be made stronger.

Conclusion

At the end of the two-year LINC grant, a one-day symposium was hosted by CSEP and the four university partners to share the lessons learned and resources developed with the other principal preparation programs across the state. Although undocumented, there was a clear range on the level of buy-in and commitment among participants regarding the new principal preparation innovation, with the participants of the policy network representing the spectrum on the highest committed. Follow-up research has not been conducted on how the policy network influenced the diffusion and commitment level of participating universities compared to nonparticipating universities, although it is data worth collecting as it may provide useful data to state agencies for consideration of different approaches to the effective implementation of new policy reforms. Rarely is the opportunity to engage in a deep policy network of support and community provided during the implementation phase of education reforms. This is likely due to a higher cost and a slower rate of implementation, although Rogers's (2003) concepts in his theory of diffusion suggest that this is what might be required for new policy innovations to be effectively implemented and sustained.

Notes

1. The LINC report can be found at: http://education.illinoisstate.edu/downloads/linc/lincp12principleprepsymposium/FINAL_LINC%20report.pdf.

2. Rogers (2003) defines five adopter categories: (1) innovators; (2) early adopters; (3) early majority; (4) late majority; and (5) laggards (pp. 282–284).
3. To meet the grant requirements, a report was compiled that included narratives written by each of the university partners on the process and outcomes of their work.

Bibliography

Creswell, John W. *Research Design: Qualitative, Quantitative, and Mixed Methods Design*. Thousand Oaks, CA: Sage Publications, 2003.

Denzin, Norman K., and Yvonna S. Lincoln. *Strategies of Qualitative Inquiry*. Vol. 2. Washington, D.C.: Sage Publications, 2008.

Halverson, Dean, Rene Noppe, Carol Webb, Stuart Yager, and Robin Miller Young. "The Western Illinois University (WIU) Redesign of the Principal Preparation Program." In *The Leadership to Integrate the Learning Continuum (LINC) Tool Kit: Redesigning Principal Preparation Programs Across Four Illinois Institutions*, 207–221. Normal, IL: Center for the Study of Education Policy, Illinois State University, 2013.

Illinois General Assembly. *Illinois Administrative Code, Title 23: Education and Cultural Resources, Subtitle A: Education, Chapter I: State Board of Education, Subchapter B: Personnel*, n.d. Accessed April 8, 2014, www.ilga.gov/commission/jcar/admincode/023/023parts.html

Israel, Marla, Janis Fine, Susan Sostak, and Robin Miller Young. "The Loyola University (Chicago) Redesign of the Principal Preparation Program." In *The Leadership to Integrate the Learning Continuum (LINC) Tool Kit: Redesigning Principal Preparation Programs Across Four Illinois Institutions*, 67–79. Normal, IL: Center for the Study of Education Policy, Illinois State University, 2013.

Lyman, L. L., K. A. Hesbol, and R. M. Young. "The Illinois State University (ISU) Redesign of the Principal Preparation Program." In *The Leadership to Integrate the Learning Continuum (LINC) Tool Kit: Redesigning Principal Preparation Programs Across Four Illinois Institutions*, 4–15. Normal, IL: Center for the Study of Education Policy, Illinois State University, 2013.

McDonnell, Lorraine M., and M. Stephen Weatherford. "Recognizing the Political in Implementation Research." *Educational Researcher* 45, no. 4 (2016): 233–242.

Miles, Matthew, B., and Michael A. Huberman. *Qualitative Data Analysis: An Expanded Sourcebook*. Thousand Oaks, CA: Sage Publications, 1994.

Mintrom, Michael, and Sandra Vergari. "Policy Networks and Innovation Diffusion: The Case of State Education Reforms." *The Journal of Politics* 60, no. 1 (1998): 126–148.

Moe, Terry M. "Vested Interests and Political Institutions." *Political Science Quarterly* 130, no. 2 (2015): 277–318.

National Policy Board for Educational Administration. Interstate School Leaders Licensure Consortium. *Educational Leadership Policy Standards: ISLLC 2008*. Washington, DC: Council of Chief of State School Officers, 2008.

National Policy Board for Educational Administration. *Educational Leadership Program Recognition Standards: Building Level*. Washington, DC: Council of Chief State School Officers, 2011.

Raelin, Joseph A. *Creating Leaderful Organizations: How to Bring Out Leadership in Everyone*. Oakland, CA: Berrett-Koehler Publishers, 2003.

Rogers, Everett M. *Diffusion of Innovations*. New York: Free Press, 2003.

Servais, Kristine, Monica Vuksanovich, and Robin Miller Young. "The North Central College (NCC) Redesign of the Principal Preparation Program." In *The Leadership to Integrate the Learning Continuum (LINC) Tool Kit: Redesigning Principal Preparation Programs Across Four Illinois Institutions*, 129–143. Normal, IL: Center for the Study of Education Policy, Illinois State University, 2013.

Spillane, James P., Brian J. Reiser, and Todd Reimer. "Policy Implementation and Cognition: Reframing and Refocusing Implementation Research." *Review of Educational Research* 72, no. 3 (2002): 387–431.

Stake, Robert E. "The Case Study Method in Social Inquiry." *Educational Researcher* 7, no. 2 (1978): 5–8.

Stake, Robert E. *The Art of Case Study Research*. Thousand Oaks, CA: Sage Publications, 1995.

Yin, Robert K. *Case Study Research: Design and Methods* (3rd ed.). Thousand Oaks, CA: Sage Publications, 2003.

Vignette

Involving Faculty from Disciplines Outside the Department to Redesign Principal Preparation Courses

Adam Kennedy and Diane Morrison

The principal preparation EdD program at Loyola University Chicago was redesigned in 2013–2014 to reflect a more innovative, field-based coaching model emphasizing the growth of administrators along a developmental continuum toward readiness and effectiveness as administrators and instructional leaders. The program was redesigned by faculty in Administration and Supervision (Ad/Su), but they sought input from and collaborated with a variety of stakeholders and members of school communities. Among those stakeholders were faculty outside of the Ad/Su department who primarily represented the school psychology and early childhood special education programs.

Collaboration With Early Childhood Special Education (ECSE) Faculty

In the two years prior to the principal preparation redesign, the teacher education faculty had embarked upon the total redesign of the undergraduate and graduate programs in order to situate teacher preparation in schools and community agencies, with faculty working alongside practicing educators to prepare candidates through field-based modules in a planned developmental sequence. This process involved building and sustaining partnerships of many types over the years of redesign. As early childhood teacher educators' perspectives are rarely sought in national conversations about higher education quality, structure, and redesign, the fact that Ad/Su faculty approached ECSE faculty for input was tremendous and a welcome surprise.

The collaboration began with a meeting at which Ad/Su faculty asked the question "What do principals need to know about early childhood?" The conversations that followed touched upon assessment, developmentally appropriate teaching, the role of families, and the experiences of early childhood teachers in schools that primarily cater to other grade levels. The following needs were shared and ultimately integrated into the redesigned principal preparation programs identifying that principals need knowledge and skill in (1) early childhood development across diverse populations; (2) the barriers to effective and impactful early childhood education, including the challenges faced by families; (3) the responsibilities of the early childhood educator to families; (4) selecting and supporting developmentally appropriate early childhood curricula that do not emphasize isolated "readiness" skills; (5) developmentally appropriate assessment, as well as how to support teachers in continuing to develop assessment skills that drive instruction and support meaningful goals; and (6) ensuring that early childhood educators are meaningful members of the school community, particularly in cases where they may not have a grade-level team of their own, or when (as is the case in many schools serving young children with special needs) the majority of their students leave after preschool in order to attend schools in their own neighborhoods.

These ideas were integrated into new preparation activities and assignments that require future administrators not only to expand their understanding but also to interact meaningfully in the field to apply that understanding and make an impact.

Collaboration With School Psychology Faculty

Ad/Su faculty also solicited the input of school psychology faculty. The outcomes of subsequent meetings further impacted the redesigned principal preparation program. Specifically, Ad/Su faculty greatly expanded and deepened the preparation of future administrators in prevention and intervention initiatives that serve to (1) align with school curricula; (2) better understand students' instructional and social-emotional needs; (3) identify the need for instructional supports and interventions that emphasize collaborative approaches to improving student performance; (4) build collaboration and assessment systems that support the implementation of Multi-tiered Systems of Support (MTSS) for students' academic and social-emotional development; and (5) prevent inappropriate referrals for special education services and reduce strain on special educators and the districts' specialized services.

As a result of this work, courses were added to the principal preparation program that prepared future administrators to implement and support MTSS in their school districts as well as the leadership and systems issues that impact this work. Furthermore, assignments within the program were revised in order for candidates to demonstrate critical developmental knowledge and an inclusiveness of early childhood education priorities, professionals, and standards.

6 Modeling Innovation into Principal Preparation

The Illinois Partnerships Advancing Rigorous Training (IL-PART) Project

Kathy Black, Maureen Kincaid, Kathleen King, Pamela Bonsu, Melissa Brown-Sims, and Matthew Clifford

This chapter will describe the program components, implementation, outcomes, and lessons learned from the Illinois Partnerships Advancing Rigorous Training (IL-PART) Project, a five-year US Department of Education (ED) School Leadership Program (SLP) grant awarded to the Center for the Study of Education Policy (CSEP) at Illinois State University (ISU) in 2013. The three major goals of the grant were (1) to prepare highly effective school principals for partnering high-need districts; (2) to develop meaningful partnerships between university principal preparation programs and high-need districts with the supports designed to build leadership capacity in an effort to improve student outcomes; and (3) to identify and disseminate best practices and empirical research on effective strategies for preparing and supporting school principals and assistant principals and developing meaningful partnerships between universities and school districts (Illinois Partnerships Advancing Rigorous Training 2013).

The district-university partnerships included in the IL-PART grant were (1) East Aurora School District 131 and North Central College (NCC); (2) Bloomington Public School District 87 and ISU; (3) Quincy Public Schools and Western Illinois University (WIU); and (4) the Dioceses of Rockford, Peoria, and Springfield and the Andrew M. Greeley Center for Catholic Education at Loyola University Chicago. Through these partnerships, the intent of the IL-PART project was to build a strong pipeline of principal candidates for the high-need districts through a rigorous and relevant principal preparation program aimed at improving teaching and learning for pre-kindergarten to Grade 12 students. A major component for each of the principal preparation programs was the implementation of a semester-long, full-time, immersive principal internship taking place within the state-required yearlong internship, which will be described later in this chapter.

District-University Partnerships

Multiple studies of effective principal preparation programs identify the importance of district-university partnerships in the preparation of principals (Davis and Darling-Hammond 2012; Darling-Hammond et al. 2007). The partnerships established through IL-PART resulted in a collaboration of college/university faculty, the DuPage Regional Office of Education (ROE), and district administrators, including the IL-PART coordinator, on candidate recruitment and selection, professional development for principals, and training of principal mentors. District administrators and faculty held informational meetings for prospective candidates. Once candidates enrolled in the program, district administrators and faculty conducted interviews for the full-time immersive internship. Training for principal mentors was provided by the DuPage ROE, district administrators and faculty members, and in one partnership the IL-PART coordinator participated in department of education faculty meetings at the university. In other partnerships, district administrators and university faculty conducted instructional rounds and collaboratively debriefed following rounds, and district administrators taught courses in the principal preparation program. The result of these collaborations was the development of deep, rich partnerships among all IL-PART institutions.

Benefits were seen by both district and university partners because of the strong partnerships developed through IL-PART. In one partnership, the university experienced an increase in principal candidates in its programs, including an increase in diverse candidates. The result for the district was the development of a pipeline of highly qualified principal candidates available to the district for hire as leadership vacancies occurred. "Strengthening the educator recruitment pipeline is an urgent issue nationally and in every community across the country" (Coalition for Teaching Equality 2016). Over the five-year IL-PART grant period, one district and university partnership collaborated on strengthening the pipeline of qualified administrators by working together to prepare twenty of their own principal candidates. Because of the full-time immersive internship, these candidates understood the context of the high-need district and would be ready to step into leadership roles in the district upon completion of the principal preparation program. This is significant given the fact that school districts across the country are facing a principal shortage (NASSP 2017).

Selective Candidate Admissions Criteria

Illinois Public Act 096-0903 required that by July 2014, all principal preparation programs have specific screening and admission requirements. Rigorous and selective candidate recruitment and selection have been identified as one of several key components of effective principal preparation programs (Darling-Hammond et al. 2007; Davis and Darling-Hammond 2012). To assure only high-caliber candidates enrolled in principal programs, applicants had to verify education experience, receive an orientation to program requirements, provide an on-site writing sample, undergo an interview by two full-time faculty members in the program, and share a portfolio demonstrating student growth, previous leadership experiences, and exemplary communication skills, among other factors. The higher education institutions involved in the IL-PART grant went well beyond the state-required admission process through the district partnerships that enhanced the rigor and efficacy of the process.

Specifically, the identification of well-suited principal program candidates became a joint process of district-university partnership. Information sessions were initiated to introduce interested teachers and school employees to the explicit opportunities available through the IL-PART grant. It became clear that the best approach to disseminate information to suitable candidates was to "tap on the shoulder" those school employees who had demonstrated great leadership potential and the dispositions necessary for success in an administrative role. Pounder and Crow (2005) identify this method as more effective and purposeful than mailings, visits, or calls for the recruitment of candidates. Though some successful candidates did self-identify, many more were individuals encouraged to pursue the principal preparation program by an administrator who recognized their potential and offered encouragement. In a study of exemplary leadership development programs, none of the districts

> [was] continuing to rely on self-selected applicants who came to them having completed training in which the district had no role. Instead, the districts had all become more purposeful in recruiting and selecting principal candidates and helping shape their development, in collaboration with partner universities.
>
> (Darling-Hammond et al. 2007, 19)

This important practice is applicable to candidate selection in any school, as administrators recognize the importance of consciously identifying and encouraging leadership development.

All the principal candidates, regardless of their manner of recruitment, needed to navigate a multi-part admissions process successfully. Through the IL-PART grant, district involvement in candidate admission did not end at candidate identification but extended through the process of application and interviewing. Because districts were making a commitment to allow IL-PART candidates to participate in the full-time immersive internship, involving a leave from their district employment responsibilities, the interviewing process included district screening. Through the process, colleges/universities determined if a candidate would be admitted to the principal preparation program and districts determined if a candidate would participate in the IL-PART full-time immersive internship experience. This co-screening of candidates led to unprecedented district-university dialogue about candidate leadership potential.

Candidate portfolios also took on great significance in the screening process as the state redesign required candidates to create a portfolio demonstrating specific evidence of their success as leaders. The development of these portfolios was approached in different ways by different higher education institutions. North Central College embedded the development of the portfolio into an introductory course, requiring candidates to complete the course before being eligible to apply for admission to the program. In the course, candidate assignments included the identification of artifacts to demonstrate admission criteria, enabling candidates to determine their own suitability for leadership roles. Illinois State University provided coaching by the IL-PART coordinator, who stressed that well-explained quality artifacts were more important than a large quantity of less developed examples.

Yearlong Performance-Based Internship

Illinois mandates a yearlong internship with four prescribed projects that candidates traditionally complete during hours outside of their full-time teaching position. The IL-PART grant, on the other hand, allowed principal candidates to authentically experience the role of the principal by funding a semester-long, full-time immersive internship as part of the candidate's state-required yearlong internships. Candidates shadowed the principal and were gradually given leadership responsibilities ranging from analyzing data and leading committees in school improvement efforts to planning and presenting professional development based on evaluation results and school-wide goals. Unlike candidates in the traditional internship, grant candidates were engaged in authentic principal duties collaborating daily with an experienced principal mentor and receiving immediate coaching and feedback.

Significant planning was needed to ensure the success of this full-time immersive experience. Some district and university partners chose dates for the internship that were least disruptive to the educational process, particularly for students in the candidate's classroom. Some candidates began their experience at the beginning of the semester while others bridged both semesters. When scheduling the full-time immersive experience, faculty and administrators took into consideration whether the teacher was in an evaluation year, the amount of transition time needed for substitute teachers, and the number of interns assigned to mentor principals. Many interns were matched with mentors in placements outside the intern's regular school building. Exemplary programs identified by Davis and Darling-Hammond (2012) included this component of placement in an internship site other than the candidate's school of employment. In addition to the primary mentor, "supplemental" mentors were often identified for the intern to give them an opportunity to experience leadership across P-12 levels and including special education and early childhood settings.

At the beginning of the immersive experience, it was critical for the mentor and intern to develop a strong working relationship, moving into a partnership where the mentor gradually released leadership responsibilities. One principal likened it to the process frequently used in student teaching, which requires the mentor to gauge when the intern is ready for different tasks, purposely providing interns with experiences that allow them to use their instincts and knowledge in varying contexts and hone their leadership abilities. As the immersive experience progressed, interns gained confidence and "insider" knowledge about the inner workings of the school. Effective mentors regularly shared their thinking and reflections, which had a powerful effect on the intern's growth. This extended experience provided interns with the opportunity to grapple with the daily issues experienced by the principal while under the watchful eye of an experienced principal mentor (Daresh 2001).

Throughout the full-time immersive internship, state-mandated projects were often at the forefront of interns' minds. It became critical for faculty supervisors to stress the importance of fully experiencing the authentic aspects of each project rather than focusing on fulfilling mandated tasks off a list. Regular meetings between the district administrators and university faculty allowed for discussions regarding how interns could complete state requirements while still immersing themselves in authentic leadership opportunities. Although the full-time immersive internship was yearlong in its tenure, principal candidates' "immersive" experience lasted one semester. The state requirements include a full year for the internship so that the candidate can experience activities that occur at different times throughout the year (hiring certified staff, opening the school, administering the annual student assessment, etc.). As a result, candidates completed many components of the required projects but had other requirements that were completed during the semester before or after their full-time experience so additional opportunities were provided after interns returned to their home school. Further collaboration was also needed to determine how the intern could experience leadership at every grade level (pre-kindergarten through high school) and with diverse learners, including students in special education, gifted programs, and English Language Learners (ELLs). In addition, programs had to determine the best time for the candidates to complete the state-mandated teacher supervision modules and assessments (titled Growth Through Learning) to best support candidate work on teacher evaluation in the internship.

While supporting the growth of the interns, it was also essential for university faculty to collaborate with and provide support to mentor principals. Regular professional development and one-on-one meetings were scheduled to develop the leadership capacity of the mentors and address their concerns regarding the internship experience. This resulted in the development of deeper relationships, advancing the immersive experience for future interns.

The immersive experience greatly benefited interns as well as mentors. When asked for feedback regarding their experience, it was not uncommon for both the mentors and interns to indicate the desire for additional time, indicating "it would be better if it were a year-long immersion." The value of such a rich, collaborative, immersive administrative internship was clearly established, so much so that some districts have committed to offering such an experience without grant funding.

Competency-Based Assessment

The assessment process for the internship unexpectedly emerged as a time-consuming, complicated, arduous task that became the focus of many partnership meetings. Illinois Administrative Code (105 ILCS 5) outlined the areas for assessment by institutions and prescribed three distinct rubrics for three of the four mandated projects. IL-PART participating partner universities developed enhanced project rubrics that mirrored the state's version but included an additional column beyond the state-provided "Meets" or "Does not Meet" rating to include an "Exceeds" column to promote further development of skills and abilities beyond minimum requirements.

These rubrics involved the assessment of three of the four mandated projects from the state involving very specific leadership experiences and artifacts, addressing content, process, outcomes, products, and quality for each project. The first project assessment involved evidence of data analysis and school improvement processes. The second assessment focused on teacher hiring, faculty evaluation, and professional development, including alignment to the Learning Forward standards for professional development. The third assessment required evidence of school-wide systems and management of resources. The final assessment, which did not have a state-prescribed rubric, required evidence of individualized education programs, ELL programs, bilingual programs, and the needs of "struggling and advanced readers" (Illinois State Board of Education). In addition, candidates were also required to provide evidence of having met the thirteen critical success factors and thirty-six indicators of the Southern Regional Board of Education—another state requirement. Navigating this myriad of specific criteria became a burdensome aspect of the internship experience, as interns with rich leadership experiences sought ways to translate these experiences to meet the specifics of the state rubric language.

Looking beyond the state rubric requirements, university supervisors involved in IL-PART also sought to assess leadership dispositions and mind frames. Though development of professional dispositions was a major focus of internship work, there was no assessment rubric required by the state that directly captured the presence or absence of critical attributes, such as viewing diversity as an asset, collaborating with all stakeholders, and having a commitment to student learning as a fundamental purpose of school. Various programs integrated the assessment of dispositions in different ways, whether formally or informally, as the development of these attributes was deemed essential.

Collaborative Supervision and Support

Illinois Public Act 096-0903 also included very specific requirements pertaining to the supervision of candidates in the internship. Each intern had to be assigned a principal mentor with two years of success in a school principalship as demonstrated by evidence of positive student growth. These principals were required to undergo an orientation to the mentorship prior to supervising the intern, and the intern supervisor from the college/university needed to have at least two meetings with the principal mentor. The intern supervisor from the college or university needed to meet specific criteria including proof of a valid administrative endorsement and experience as a principal. The supervisor was required to conduct four on-site observations of the intern and four conferences with the intern over the yearlong experience.

IL-PART principal mentors and supervisors far exceeded this state-required criterion. Initially, all potential principal mentors involved in IL-PART were invited to a one-day mentor training conducted by experienced education administrators. Eventually, it proved beneficial to conduct one-on-one training for many principal mentors since the orientation could be adapted to meet mentor concerns and their environments (see "Changing Mindscapes" vignette).

As interns sought to gain experiences across the PreK to Grade 12 spectrum, other school placements became necessary, and some district partners chose to designate specific supplemental administrative mentors to guide interns through experiences in these other school settings. The required experiences with students with gifted, special education, or ELL characteristics also led to assignments with supplemental mentors who could share insights and offer experiences in these areas. In effect, a concerted effort was made to create a team to support candidate development of leadership experiences of both breadth and depth that was unprecedented in previous principal preparatory programming.

Program Outcomes

As the recipient of an ED-sponsored SLP grant, IL-PART was required to have a rigorous program evaluation to answer questions pertinent to its success. The American Institutes for Research (AIR) was engaged to conduct an external evaluation during the five-year (2013–2018) grant. The evaluation was organized around five research questions. AIR and CSEP developed evaluation questions that would supply IL-PART partners with findings regarding the implementation and impact of the program. These research questions follow:

1. To what degree has IL-PART been implemented as planned across participating university and college partners, and why have changes to the implementation plan been introduced?
2. How does principal satisfaction with participation in the intensive pre-service internships compare with traditional internships?
3. To what degree do candidates who completed the intensive pre-service internships seek and obtain positions as principals in high-need or low-performing schools compared to candidates who completed traditional internships?
4. How does pre-service principal skill development (e.g., instructional leadership skills measured by the certification examination) compare between participants in the two internship models?
5. How has student learning changed, if at all, in schools led by candidates who completed the intensive internships compared to student learning in similar schools led by candidates who completed traditional internships?

AIR used qualitative and quantitative evaluative approaches to address the research questions. Data collection activities included the following:

- *Document reviews*. Program records (e.g., recruitment, selection, and enrollment data) from the institutions of higher education (IHEs) were collected to better understand the features of the redesigned principal preparation programs. Licensure and certification data were collected to monitor the rate of success for graduates who received the Illinois Professional Educator License Administrative Endorsement.
- *Interviews*. In the first year of program implementation, AIR captured the progress of district-university partnerships through interviews with school districts, IL-PART coordinators, and university faculty. In later years, graduates who became assistant principals were interviewed and asked to reflect on their careers.
- *Surveys*. Principal candidates (or interns), their principal mentors, and faculty supervisors were surveyed to assess their satisfaction with the internship experience. In addition, AIR gathered surveys on school culture to assess the newly hired principals' impact on the schools.
- *Student achievement data*. AIR requested student achievement data to conduct an impact analysis of newly hired school principals in public schools. Preliminary findings will be included in the final summative report, which is being drafted as this book is being published.

The Value of District-University Partnerships for Program Implementation

An integral component of the program is to develop meaningful partnerships between institutions of higher education and high-need school districts. To gain a better understanding of this collaboration and the implementation of the principal preparation program, AIR gathered program documents, conducted interviews, attended partner meetings, and collected candidate recruitment, selection, and enrollment data. The information obtained led to the development of case studies on each partnership, capturing the way in which partners collaboratively developed and implemented their preparation programs. These case studies revealed that both district and university partners were responsible for the following:

- Selecting and assessing potential principal candidates;
- Establishing internships and field experiences;
- Developing and implementing training programs for mentors and university supervisors;
- Identifying the locations where internships and field experiences would take place;
- Monitoring and evaluating the principal preparation program.

Throughout the course of the program, interviews with IL-PART coordinators and surveys of principal candidates, mentor principals, and faculty supervisors revealed an ongoing commitment to the shared responsibilities outlined. Programs consistently recruited and enrolled qualified candidates, who were then immersed in a program that melded the theory and practice of instructional leadership.

IL-PART anticipated that it would enroll and graduate at least eighty principal candidates from one of the three participating IHEs by 2018. In the first year (2013), with forty-five principal candidates, IL-PART was more than halfway through its enrollment goal. By the end of 2017, candidates totaled 228—nearly three times more than the proposed goal. This higher than expected enrollment was partly the result of the strong relationship between district and university partners and their intentional approach to recruiting candidates for the program. These increased enrollment numbers assuaged the concerns that partners had expressed about enrollment in 2013. At the beginning of IL-PART implementation, partners worried about the challenges of identifying interested or qualified principal candidates because of then recent legislative mandates that strengthened principal preparation program requirements and the distance between their schools and IHEs, which might deter some candidates from applying.

Perceptions of the Internship Experience

The capstone of the principal preparation program is the internship component. Principal candidates selected one of two options: the full-time model, or *intensive* internship; or the part-time model, or *traditional* internship. By a three-to-one margin, principal candidates overwhelmingly selected the traditional internship (159 principal candidates) compared to the intensive internship (48 principal candidates). Early in the project, financial and political constraints were recognized as obstacles to the intensive internship model. The original project proposal did not include the costs of covering both salary and health insurance of temporary substitute teachers for a full year. The funding was structured to pay just the salary of a substitute teacher for one semester, which would not include the added cost of health benefits. That was intentional, as the cost of a full-year substitute teacher would make the model cost-prohibitive beyond the life of the grant. But cost was not the only consideration, as smaller school districts expressed concern over releasing highly effective teachers from their classroom responsibilities to complete the principal internship, particularly those who served in specialized content areas in higher grades (physics, foreign language, etc.). There was also concern about how the intensive internship could affect annual teacher evaluations because teachers would be away from the classroom.

Surveys were administered annually to assess the internship experience from the perspectives of principal candidates, mentor principals, and their faculty supervisors. Survey results consistently revealed that both internship models were an immersive experience. More specifically, survey results revealed that although more than three times of principal candidates completed the traditional internship model (compared to the intensive internship), all stakeholders (i.e., principal candidates, mentor principals, and faculty supervisors) reported that candidates were prepared for the job of the principalship regardless of the internship model selected. For example, mentor principals and faculty supervisors described the traditional and intensive internship models as "immersive," "hands-on," "realistic," "authentic," "real-life," and based on "true experiences" as an outcome of IHEs revamping their principal preparation programs to meet the 2010 Illinois legislative mandate.

Principal candidates were assigned to a mentor principal based on a number of matching factors. Nearly all principal candidates, regardless of their internship option, were assigned to a mentor principal and received close supervision and support. When principal candidates identified the factors on which their pairing was based, differences between internship types were observed. The majority of principal candidates who completed the intensive internship reported each year that they were matched based on a number of factors. These included mentor principal preference, the candidates' expressed preference for working with a particular mentor principal, university input, district input, the availability of qualified mentor principals, the location of the school, areas for growth and development, the candidates' background or content area of expertise, the candidates' interests, and current type of school. Through the internship experience, principal candidates were more than likely to

160 *Kathy Black et al.*

work alongside a mentor principal who, in more ways than one, modeled their near future.

The internship and field experiences that all candidates received also emphasized instructional leadership at all grade levels and with various subgroups (e.g., students with disabilities, English Language Learners, and gifted and talented students). The survey consistently reported principal candidates' participation in most of the internship activities, which included serving students of these various backgrounds, developing and implementing a school improvement plan, observing instructional staff, and participating in the hiring of teachers and staff. Regardless of the internship model, principal candidates were given learning opportunities that were reportedly "immersive," "hands-on," and "authentic."

Postgraduate Pursuits

Since its inception in 2013, the redesigned principal preparation programs at ISU, NCC, and WIU graduated a combined total of 161 principal candidates. Postgraduation, IL-PART coordinators and university faculty tracked the hiring of its graduates across the state of Illinois. Thirty-nine percent of all graduates ($n = 63$) accepted positions as school administrators (e.g., principals or assistant principals). Of this number, approximately 15 percent ($n = 24$) were hired as school principals in either public school districts or parochial schools in the state (Figure 6.1). The difference between internship models is due in part to the difference between the total number of candidates that completed each internship type (i.e., there were far fewer candidates that completed the intensive, full-time internships).

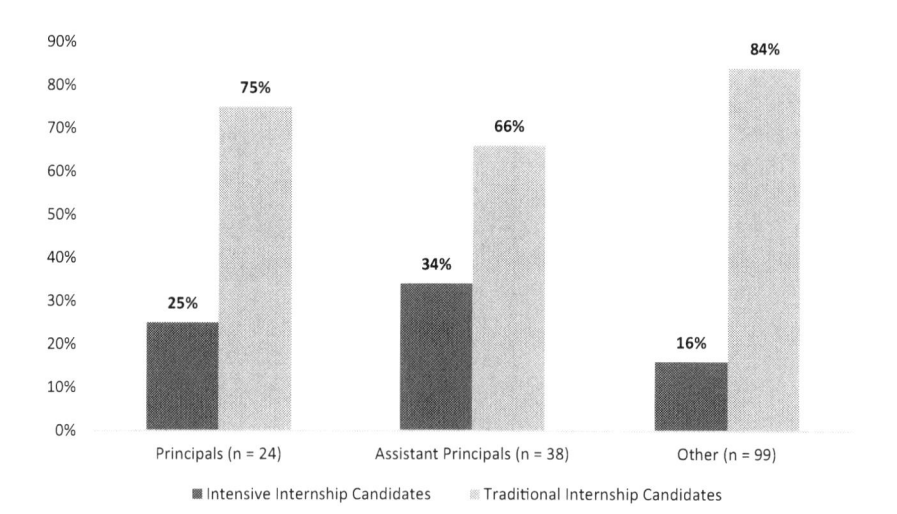

Figure 6.1 IL-PART Graduate Hires: By Position

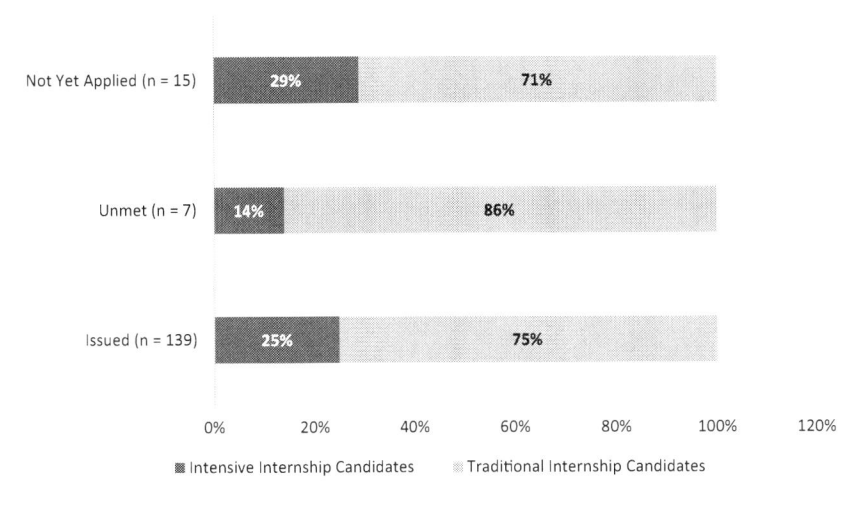

Figure 6.2 Status of Certification Attainment by Internship Type

- Not Yet Applied (n = 15): Intensive 29%, Traditional 71%
- Unmet (n = 7): Intensive 14%, Traditional 86%
- Issued (n = 139): Intensive 25%, Traditional 75%

PEL Administrative Endorsement Achievement

To assess principal candidates' skill development, AIR used publicly available data obtained through the Illinois State Board of Education Educator Licensure Information System to report on certification attainment. As of the 2017–2018 academic year, more than 86 percent of all graduates had satisfied the requirements (i.e., graduation, completion of the Illinois Licensure Testing System Principal as Instructional Leader [195 and 196] exam and training modules) for the administrative endorsement. Figure 6.2 provides a breakdown by internship model of the percentages of graduates who attained certification. The difference in percentages between internship types is due largely to the fact that there are more traditional candidates than intensive candidates overall.

Overarching Lessons Learned

Insights from the principal preparation program emerged over the course of the IL-PART grant. Lessons learned reflect the experience and insight of district-university and evaluation partners. The four lessons learned are highlighted briefly below:

- *Developing a strong district-university partnership is crucial to the success of the district-to-university principal preparation pipeline.* Many of the district and university partners noted that their own existing one-on-one partnerships were already strong because of mutual trust, understanding, and common mission. However, others noted that the grant would afford them the opportunity to strengthen their partner relationships further and to seek information from, collaborate with, and learn from other districts and institutions.

- *Although the intensive internship model was a key component of the redesigned principal preparation program, in practice this option was selected by less than a quarter of principal candidates.* Preference for the traditional internship option may have been influenced by an SLP grant requirement: with a focus on high-need districts, the intensive internship could only be completed at one of the three participating IL-PART districts. Given that a number of principal candidates were from outside the district, and in some cases outside the geographic regions of the district-university partnership, principal candidates were more likely to opt for the traditional internship model, which could be completed in their home district. Moreover, the selection of an internship model was not made solely by the candidate but in consultation with their district's central office.
- *Although the majority of graduates obtained principal licensure, fewer went on to become principals.* Even though more than a third of graduates were hired as school administrators, roughly two-thirds returned to the classroom or assumed other leadership positions in their schools (or districts). Interviews with graduates revealed concerns about the availability of principal positions in rural regions of the state. District and university partners may want to consider enhancing their resources and support for graduates on the pathway to the principalship. Graduates may need exposure to leadership opportunities, as well as sustained training and professional development while in the principal pipeline.
- *Principal identification of prospective leaders is a valuable part of successful succession planning to sustain the principal pipeline.* During the IL-PART grant, it became evident that principal encouragement of strong leaders within their schools played an integral part in candidates pursuing the principal endorsement. Principal mentoring of candidates, combined with the authentic intensive experiences of the internship, led to a well-qualified pool of administrative candidates.

Bibliography

Coalition for Teaching Equality. "Building a Strong and Diverse Teacher and Principal Recruitment Pipeline." 2016, http://coalitionforteachingquality.org/images/upload/201606Recruitment.pdf

Daresh, John C. *Leaders Helping Leaders: A Practical Guide to Administrative Mentoring.* Thousand Oaks, CA: Corwin Press, 2001.

Darling-Hammond, Linda, Michelle LaPointe, Debra Meyerson, Margaret Terry Orr, and Carol Cohen. *Preparing School Leaders for a Changing World: Lessons from Exemplary Leadership Development Programs.* School Leadership

Study. Final Report. Stanford, CA: Stanford Educational Leadership Institute, 2007.

Davis, Stephen H., and Linda Darling-Hammond. "Innovative Principal Preparation Programs: What Works and How We Know." *Planning and Changing* 43 (2012): 25–45.

Illinois Administrative Code 105 ILCS 5.

Illinois Partnerships Advancing Rigorous Training (IL-PART) submission to School Leadership Program for USDE. July 2013.

Illinois Public Act 096-0903.

Illinois State Board of Education, State of Illinois, 23 Ill. Admin. Code 30.45.

National Association of Secondary School Principals. "Position Statement: Principal Shortage." 2017, www.nassp.org/policy-advocacy-center/nassp-position-statements/principal-shortage

Pounder, Diana, and Gary Crow. "Sustaining the Pipeline of School Administrators." *Educational Leadership* 62, no. 8 (2005): 56–60.

Vignettes

Engagement of District Leaders in the Candidate Selection and Placement Process

Brad K. Hutchison

Leadership is about relationships. Armed with this core belief, the design team for our newly revised principal preparation program at Illinois State University (ISU) knew that engaging professional partners would be a key component to the success of the program. Professionals from the P-12 field were called upon to participate in the candidate selection process for the newly designed principal preparation program and to serve on an advisory committee, whose function was to provide meaningful feedback on all the P-12 administrative programs, taught by the Education, Administrative, and Foundations Department (EAF Department).

The EAF Department at ISU has a long history of successfully interacting with educational leaders on research and policy questions, but utilizing these P-12 partners in the application process of the principal preparation program was a new concept. It was our belief that current P-12 educational leaders were the best people to help identify principal preparation candidates with high potential and capacity to lead by engaging others. Subsequently, information regarding the EAF Department's desire to create a formal partnership was shared with area leaders through meetings at the Regional Office of Education, and other professional meetings, in hopes of attracting P-12 educational leaders who would like to be considered for the advisory/interview committee as part of the formal partnership with the Department. The positive response from the P-12 partner committee resulted in area Superintendents, Assistant Superintendents, and two Regional Office of Education Superintendents who were willing to serve on the committee voluntarily.

Members of the EAF Department quickly realized that the selection of principal candidates with input from the P-12 partners was a great decision. The P-12 partners supported the rigorous redesigned interview process with their keen awareness of what today's school leaders need to be able to do to be successful. These P-12 partners brought a wide array of professional experiences, which helped to create a more authentic interview process, as they drew upon their firsthand knowledge of school culture, best instructional practices, budget, and school law. It also provided the principal preparation candidates with the benefit of having an authentic interview process with current P-12 leaders.

Although the main purpose of the partnership with the school district leaders was to help interview and place principal candidates, an unforeseen benefit emerged as the P-12 leaders showed a willingness to serve as an advisory committee to the EAF Department for all of its P-12 programs. The P-12 partners brought a deep understanding of practical experience to meetings and provided faculty with a keen awareness of what leadership skills were needed in the P-12 community. The core value that leadership is about relationships was validated by the P-12 partners, and helped to shape the conversation around the instructional decisions made by the Department regarding its P-12 programs. Additionally, some of these same partners eagerly accepted principal preparation students as interns in their schools, which greatly enhanced the internship experience for our students.

In conclusion, the decision by the EAF Department to engage P-12 partners was primarily initiated for the principal preparation application process. But the P-12 partnerships quickly expanded to have an impact on all of the university's P-12 programs. When asked about engaging P-12 partners in the interview process, a recent graduate of the program, who is serving as a principal, replied, "Yes, the applicant interview process was an authentic passage into the P-12 educational administration program at ISU. It provided me with a glimpse into how the program works and helped prepare me for the interview process at the end of our training." Not only did the principal preparation students benefit from the involvement of the P-12 partners, but the EAF Department found all of their P-12 programs enriched by forming those partnerships.

District Leaders Engaged in Program Coursework and the Value of the District Voice at University Department Meetings

Herschel Hannah, Cindy Helmers, and Mary Kay Scharf

The Bloomington Public Schools and Illinois State University can track their partnership in education for over 150 years. While the concept of partnership is not new, the depth of the partnership between the Department of Education, Administration, and Foundations and the school district has flourished during the last five years. A US Department of Education School Leadership Program grant supporting principal preparation awarded to the Center for the Study of Education Policy at Illinois State University was the catalyst for the deepening relationship between the university and the high-need district. The project, Illinois Partnerships Advancing Rigorous Training (IL-PART), required extensive collaboration between the two entities.

What started out as an agreement to serve as placement sites for principal internships, grew to include significant participation of school district personnel in the university preparation program. Members of the school district administrative team now attend monthly PK-12 program meetings at the university, providing university partners the opportunity to listen to voices from the field. District representatives and program graduates have opportunities to share their insights, perspectives, and experiences in programmatic planning during these meetings. These interactions provide mutual benefits for the partners working together to provide learning experiences for university students and interns that are relevant and robust. Key examples of the expanded role the district plays in partnership with the university include collaboration on the redesign of the superintendent's preparation program, adjustments to the principal preparation program, participation in various routine operations (such as candidate selection), and broadened recruitment for the various programs offered at the university.

It bears mentioning that the initial functions of the partnership described above have grown into a richer contribution connecting theoretical learning to real-world applications. District administrators joined the nontenured faculty ranks, teaching such courses as Current Issues in Education, Issues in Site-Level Leadership, Human Resources Administration, and Supervision of Professional Practice. Additionally, other district administrators in the region have served as guest speakers for many courses to enhance the instructional experience.

Both partners benefit from the internship experiences required by the state and university which are realized in the public school setting. The university is able to place interns in a high-need district, providing a diverse and challenging experience. Interns are required to provide evidence of leadership on thirty-five complex professional competencies such as school improvement, cultural competency, hiring, program evaluation, working with special populations, and many more. The intern and mentor principal work together to facilitate the intern's leadership activities, resulting in real contributions to school improvement.

The authentic experiences designed to prepare the principal interns have consistently benefited the internship sites. For example, an intern's audit of the transition of students between grades five and six resulted in a district-wide improvement effort and expansion of existing programs and strategies. Improved quality in the school improvement process was found to be beneficial in each setting. Principal mentor Jeff Geringer stated, "The increased structure in the school improvement process allowed us to move forward at an accelerated pace." Another principal mentor, Jeff Lockenvitz, mentioned this highly specific benefit: "among other significant contributions, the intern's expertise in special education helped our staff write better goals for students, determine appropriate levels of service, and develop effective supports to promote the success of all students in the general education setting." These are just a few examples of the positive outcomes resulting from the placement of university interns in our schools.

In the school district, an unanticipated benefit was the development of the leadership capacity of existing principals as they were prepared for the role of mentor. Over the life of the grant, a district grant coordinator provided ongoing professional development for principals as well as supported the individual growth and development of these individuals through coaching and mentoring. Each principal engaged in specific mentor training as it related to the internship. All district principals and assistant principals also participated in Blended Coaching training which benefited the supervision of interns and also the supervision and development of teachers. A handful of these administrators went through an even more intensified training in coaching conversations. As mentor principals engaged in the internship process, the expectations of the required competencies often promoted the skills and knowledge of the mentor as well.

The partnership between the university and school district may have been over a century in the making, but the depth of the partnership as it has grown in the past five years has provided rich, meaningful contributions in both settings. The end results include better prepared principals and ultimately higher achieving students.

Changing Mindscapes: How the New Internship Requirements Changed Current Principals' Thinking and Practices

Kathy Black

Throughout the journey of implementing our newly designed principal preparation program at North Central College, we discovered some changes in school leaders' thoughts about the new program requirements, the "immersion" internship experience, and recognition of how the full-time internship actually changed practices.

Planning for mentor in-service training on program requirements and dispositions didn't accomplish what we had originally thought it would. First, since all mentor principals had gotten their administrator licenses via the state's old Type 75 certification system, they thought this would be a similar program and had a difficult time shifting paradigms. Although we reiterated many times that the new program was nothing like their preparation programs, the principal mentors didn't truly understand the extent to which the program requirements had changed until they hosted their first intern. Providing mentors with a copy of the internship handbook (80+ pages) afforded another opportunity to discuss the fieldwork projects, and there were numerous sighs of relief when faculty members told principal mentors that the interns were responsible for documenting the details, not them. The project was daunting at first glance, with four field projects broken down into seventeen focus areas and thirty-six activities, including many other detailed requirements within each component.

The second aspect of the mentor training that did not go as planned related to the format used for training. We efficiently provided the in-service to all principals and assistant principals in the district in a large group setting. Congratulating ourselves on our game plan initially, we realized that our timing was off as faculty began to supervise the internship. Providing the in-service too early resulted in faculty having to repeat much of the information and individual meetings with principal mentors were often needed to review the requirements. Although it was time-intensive, it was well worth the investment, as we began to see how the mentor principals embraced the need to allow the interns space to experience leadership. As one principal mentor stated, "As an administrator, I can jump in and support her, but then I think no—She's got to figure this out on her own. It's a gradual release of responsibility."

Recognition and full understanding of the new program requirements came slowly but were eventually highly respected by the principal mentors. Faculty supervision of interns was paired with gentle support for mentor principals to ensure the interns completed tasks in areas that the mentor principals might not be as informed in themselves. This aspect was evident in feedback from another principal: "Liz brings the latest and greatest ideas, and we want to incorporate all of what she's learned" to improve student learning.

While the main focus of our efforts at North Central College was primarily on the principal candidate's growth through the intensive internship requirements, we also learned of the indirect impact on principal mentors. When asked if the immersion internship affected his practice and leadership, one principal replied, "Why yes, it made me a better principal! I've become more reflective as I know I'm serving as a model for the intern." Another stated, "As the principal of three interns, it has truly helped me grow into a better leader as I reflect upon my practices. The intern has a front row seat for all aspects of being a principal, including what happens behind the scenes, and the opportunity to reflect and dialogue has helped me to synthesize how I handled something and why I handled it that way." And finally, another principal stated, "Having interns has made me a more reflective practitioner. Seeing our systems through the eyes of an individual new to administration has helped to illuminate both our strengths and weaknesses as an organization." The benefits to this internship went beyond the interns themselves and beyond our expectations!

Partnership between University Faculty and District Administrators in Supporting In-District Professional Development Designed to Build the Leadership and Mentoring Capacity of School Principals

Lora Wolff, Dean Halverson, and Carol Webb

Two words really sum up the IL-PART work between Western Illinois University (WIU) and Quincy Public Schools (QPS): collaborative partnership. Throughout the project, the collaborative nature of the work was evident from the beginning, including planning professional development, arranging the internships, implementing instructional rounds, and evaluating the work.

The collaboration began with partners representing the educational leadership faculty at WIU and the QPS administrative team planning the professional development and training component. The first task was to determine how best to prepare the current Quincy principals to mentor the principal interns. Planning continued throughout the grant as we moved to different phases, prepared presentations for conferences, and supported interns and principal mentors.

One of the strongest components of the work was in the professional development. The university partners participated in all training, sometimes as presenters and other times as participants. Regardless of the role, it was evident that the university partners were focused on learning and developing alongside the QPS administrators. The professional development included learning about the internship requirements and how a full-time internship could best be implemented within the QPS context. We learned together about instructional rounds and how we would implement rounds in all the schools in Quincy. Then we learned about the SAMs (School Administration Managers) process. Our focus was on professional growth regardless of individuals' roles in each institution.

Throughout the grant partnership, collaboration, communication, and connection were the three critical elements ensuring the WIU principal interns had the most realistic and comprehensive internship experience possible. QPS and WIU partners reviewed principal applications, conducted interviews jointly, and worked as a team to select outstanding mentors for each intern in buildings where the intern would experience the most growth. In some cases, this meant matching an intern from one grade level with a principal mentor at another level. For example, an elementary teacher was paired with the high school principal. This stretched both the intern and the mentor as they worked together on the multiple tasks required in the internship. We also collaborated in our work with the interns, ensuring they had completed activities and tasks required by the state standards and posted artifacts representing each. The interns met as a group on a regular basis led by the IL-PART coordinator and the WIU faculty supervisor. Through these meetings, we were able to answer questions and guide the interns' understanding and skill development.

Instructional rounds completed the collaborative cycle, bringing the partnership to its deepest level. To strengthen the process, additional partners enriched and enhanced the instructional rounds' process through in-depth training and team visits to all buildings in the district. We took notes, worked in teams to discuss what we saw, and then made recommendations for the building leadership teams. They in turn responded to the recommendations, made changes, and reported progress. The partnership and collaboration around instructional rounds continued for over two years. Instructional Rounds by building teams continue in Quincy as a direct result of this partnership.

Collaboration and partnership are words that slip off peoples' tongues easily. In the case of the IL-PART grant, the collaboration was deep and ongoing, which made for a partnership that was authentic and mutually beneficial. This rich collaboration continues even though the grant has reached its end.

Thinking Creatively about the Internship

Carol Frericks and Michaela Fray

During participation in the Illinois Partnerships Advancing Rigorous Training (IL-PART), Quincy Public Schools District 172 (QPS) engaged in an innovative design process to provide high quality, full-time principal internship experiences. The shift from a traditional, part-time principal internship to an intensive full-time internship required a purposeful partnership with Western Illinois University (WIU), and intentional planning by QPS administrators and the IL-PART coordinator. Thinking creatively was vital to the success of implementation of the full-time, semester-long internship.

QPS and WIU had a mutual understanding that the internship experience had to be a win-win-win for all stakeholders: a win for the aspiring principal engaged in the internship as preparation for a future school leadership position; a win for the practicing principal serving as the principal mentor that receives assistance from a capable aspiring school leader; and a win for the vacancy that was to be filled by a substitute teacher for one semester while the principal intern was actively participating in the full-time portion of the internship. This mindset was the primary driver to thinking outside the box when selecting principal mentors, matching interns to mentors, and securing substitute teachers for the principal intern.

Previously, QPS provided traditional internship experiences where the principal intern completed their internship with their building principal, while teaching during the day and engaging in internship experiences outside of the school day. The intern was required to log a designated number of hours, regardless of learning or mastery of necessary competencies. While commonly practiced, this was not necessarily beneficial for authentically preparing educators for the principalship, nor did it provide in-depth opportunities to complete the leadership competencies of the new principal preparation requirements. Occasionally, QPS principal interns were given the opportunity to serve as the Summer School Teacher Leader, which provided a four-week experience in a small-scale school leadership role. QPS leaders recognized the need for more opportunities like that for principal interns to serve in a full-time leadership role. Transitioning from a traditional internship to the new full-time internship meant revisiting how principal mentors were selected and assigned. That sparked conversation about the possibilities of completing the principal internship outside of the principal interns' current building. In partnership with WIU, it was determined to invite practicing principals who met the state requirements to apply to serve as a principal mentor. QPS administrators and WIU faculty together interviewed the candidates and selected principal mentors.

After the selection of principal mentors, the team worked strategically to determine the assignment of each intern with a principal mentor. This process entailed critical conversations and multiple perspectives on rationales for potential assignments. The assignment decisions aligned with the win-win-win understanding for all stakeholders. The matches were not what the interns and mentors anticipated, but through the internship the intentional matching proved to be a very positive component of the internship.

During implementation of IL-PART, there were principal interns who had specialized teaching positions, which made it difficult to find long-term substitutes. These principal interns were eager to serve as a full-time principal intern but were adamant that their positions be filled by quality, trained individuals. Building principals were equally concerned about the quality of substitutes who would fulfill these specialized roles during the full-time internship. It became abundantly clear that finding and securing high-quality substitute teachers would take very creative thinking. Examples of those hard-to-staff specialized teaching roles included a Reading Recovery teacher and interventionist, a Career and Technical Education (CTE) teacher who taught multiple engineering courses, a transportation discipline officer, a quasi-dean of students, and the high school marching band and music director.

QPS embraced the challenge to find quality substitutes as an opportunity to provide experiences for other educators to engage in development of his/her professional interests. QPS utilized a recently retired Reading Recovery teacher who was still qualified to provide those services and multiple small group interventions. When searching for a substitute for the transportation discipline officer and quasi-dean of students, QPS administration invited and encouraged future leaders to serve in this role. It was a game of chess, and moving one educator to another required the filling of additional positions. A para-educator served as the quasi-dean of students and the following year transitioned to a similar leadership role. An elementary P.E. teacher and head basketball coach served as the transportation discipline officer. It provided the teacher an opportunity to see potential leadership roles in their future. His strong relationship with the community enhanced his ability to step in and immediately make a positive difference. The P.E. schedule in his building was modified and his role was filled with a retired teacher who came in and taught part-time. Through schedule modifications and enlisting retired educators, the principal interns were able to step away from their role and feel confident in the services their students would receive in their absence.

Securing substitutes for the band director and CTE teacher were more complex. Due to limited qualified candidates and specialized need, these two interns' full-time internships were modified to span an entire school year. The interns taught a portion of their day and then traveled to their internship site for the remainder of the day. It was equivalent to a full-time, semester-long internship, just modified to meet the needs of the students.

Through a variety of creative approaches, principal interns experienced a meaningful, authentic full-time internship. The approach created a win for the interns, a win for the principal mentor, and a win for the students, who continued to receive high-quality instruction.

Competency-Based Assessments: Using Standardized Rubrics Driving a Shared Understanding between Districts and Universities (and Interns) Regarding What Constitutes Effective Leadership Practices aka Looking for a Little R&R?

Kathy Black

Looking for a little traditional R&R? Well you're not going to find it in the newly redesigned principal preparation programs in Illinois. Instead, you'll find a different sort of R&R—rigor and relevance. Starting with the required rubrics outlined by the state of Illinois to evaluate the components of the principal internship, college professors and districts began to deconstruct the focus areas. There was much discussion on how various assignments and experiences matched the state's requirements. Slowly we all came to a consensus on what was an effective leadership experience. The rubrics used at our college came out of work begun with Illinois Partnerships Advancing Rigorous Training (IL-PART)[1] partners, and then the district administrators and principal mentors weighed in on them. Meetings occurred on a regular basis as we reviewed assignments and projects for accuracy (meeting the state's requirements) and mastery.

What we didn't expect was how the candidates internalized the "rigor" mentality and began to lead us in developing high-level experiences and artifacts of their work. For example, three interns worked on evaluating a budget and presented their findings to their principal. He was so impressed with their analysis that he tasked them to overhaul the process in which requests would be approved and monitored within the building. Another intern revamped how disciplinary infractions were codified and managed in the school. Yet another worked with her principal on the importance of linking the school's mission to the school improvement plan. Her principal responded by changing his practices to regularly remind faculty and staff of the school's mission and its connection to all their efforts with school improvement. Interns pushed themselves and often raised the bar on their own, and they also left a legacy.

Faculty were struggling with the challenge of supporting interns with incorporating, documenting, and tracking the thirty-six critical success factors of the Southern Regional Education Board and corresponding activities in the internship experience, only to find a candidate had created a color-coded rubric/template and shared it with other interns to assist them in completing this requirement. Faculty and administrative staff from other IL-PART partnerships then shared examples of what they and their candidates had developed. The end result was the development of expanded tools and resources that represented the high level of work being done in the field. The collaboration allowed us to take the state's two-column rubric (with two ratings: "completed" or "did not complete") and expand it to three columns with more descriptors, thus providing a more nuanced understanding of a candidate's performance.

When completing the internship requirements, professors and mentor principals collaboratively challenged the candidates through authentic leadership experiences, ensuring rigor and relevance were embedded in their practice. What began as a program partnership between universities and districts evolved into our most effective strategy—the work being done within the triad of the principal intern, the principal mentor, and the university supervisor. The reciprocal transformation of the three representatives involved in the triad ultimately results in the greatest impact as it influences the understanding of this work by the university, the school, and the student.

The Role of the Regional Office of Education as a First Team Player in Illinois School Leadership Reform: One Example (of Many)

Gail Fahey

The DuPage Regional Office of Education (DuPage ROE), specifically its regional superintendent, Dr. Darlene Ruscitti, was invited to serve on the statewide Illinois School Leadership Advisory Committee (ISLAC) because it was one of the four entities named to develop the statewide Illinois New Principal Mentoring Program (INPMP) authorized by the General Assembly in 2006. ISLAC was successful in recommending deep changes in Illinois' outdated principal preparation program requirements to the General Assembly. One of its recommendations was to require principal preparation programs to provide mentoring and development of pre-service principal interns by qualified, practicing principals who are familiar with the new law, are skilled in conducting professional conversations, and have a proven record of student growth in their schools.

In Illinois, ROEs are led by an elected regional superintendent and assist the Illinois State Board of Education and the Board of Higher Education in implementing legislation passed by the General Assembly and signed into law by the governor. From the beginning of ISLAC's deliberations, it was clear the DuPage ROE had an important role to play in the rollout of the new, game-changing principal preparation rules. Historically, the DuPage ROE had exhibited a keen passion and expertise for professional development of school leaders. Its partnership with the Center for the Study of Educational Policy (CSEP) at Illinois State University provided the DuPage ROE with the opportunity to focus on statewide delivery of school leadership professional development rather than being localized to DuPage County, which had been the customary practice.

The DuPage ROE professional development role with the CSEP was to support the IL-PART grant through the development of an administrator academy for principal mentors (IAA1093, The Supervision of Principal Interns) and launch its delivery statewide to all grant identified universities and school district partners. The academy, designed as a daylong course, covered the specifics of the new law and its impact on practicing principals who elected to serve as mentors. An emphasis was placed on the real-time, real-life instructionally related experiences the intern was to engage in while working alongside their principal mentor. A focus on conducting professional conversations, which encouraged the intern to reflect on their day-to-day progress, was a major part of the mentor training.

Another component of this academy, and perhaps its most important element, was the requirement that the principal mentors work together with the district to develop a PK-12 plan to assure that the thirty-six required Southern Regional Education Board (SREB) activities, which Illinois adopted as part of the new law, were experienced by the principal intern. Prospective mentors were encouraged not just to think district-wide but also regionally due to the number of dual district arrangements in Illinois. Most mentors discovered that no one building could deliver all the required PK-12 experiences. Thus, collaboration among colleagues was paramount.

The lesson here is that some ROEs in a large state such as Illinois must be relied upon to assist other ROEs, ISBE, and IBHE when any of these or other entities lack the capacity to support equity and excellence in education. For example, organized structures such as "leadership hubs" could provide the vehicle for collaborative work across ROEs and other entities. Another lesson learned was that a one-day academy was perhaps necessary, but certainly not sufficient, to launch this project and fully prepare the principal mentors. For example, additional training on coaching strategies was provided to all participating principals. Further, follow-up professional development on deconstructing the requirements and processes discussed in the academy could have been offered to ease the transition expected of the principal candidate and principal mentor.

District and University Partnerships to Provide Comprehensive Principal Preparation

Mark Daniel

Being a school leader is a large-scale responsibility to students, families, staff, and the community. Given the magnitude of responsibility, a candidate for school leadership should have the very best training possible. The Illinois State University (ISU) Principal Preparation

Program (PPP) is the gold standard for principal candidates. The ISU PPP includes a robust curriculum covering relevant topics coupled with problem-solving strategies focused on real-world scenarios that build the skills necessary to navigate what are often emotionally charged situations. In the two and a half years of coursework prior to the internship, professors masterfully generated opportunities for thinking about necessary paradigm shifts and approaches to school-based issues. Areas that each PPP candidate is required to master include the use of data to assess and communicate school improvement initiatives, the implications of cutting-edge neuroscience, facilitating cultural competency, helping teachers grow through evaluation, and applications of legal findings.

Would any school district consider hiring a new teacher who had not completed on-site student teaching? Of course not! Why would a district want less for the building leader? The full-time internship is an invaluable experience. During the internship, each candidate is supported based on their unique needs in the internship setting by the school principal and an ISU supervisor. Not only do candidates get a behind-the-scenes view of the principalship, but they also get to participate actively and engage with staff, parents, students, and other stakeholders in the learning community.

Experience in any profession allows an individual the opportunity to not only gain knowledge but to also live out real-life situations and circumstances. Without this experience, one is limited to what he or she has read in a book or heard from others. Experience allows an individual to see, hear, and feel in authentic situations, and it provides moments when an individual must gather information, make decisions, and respond in a manner that is best for all those involved. In education, many of these moments collide rapidly, requiring school leaders to multi-task and prioritize. The only way to truly develop the skills to handle these complex situations is through experience.

The role of a school leader comes with much responsibility as one takes on day-to-day tasks and yearlong goals. A principal preparation program that provides experience for a candidate transitioning out of the classroom and into an administrative role is not only beneficial but it is imperative to the growth and development of the candidate as a leader. Likewise, a program that allows candidates to practice real-world scenarios alongside a mentor principal provides a support system for a new leader having to make both broad and detailed decisions that affect the learning community.

In order to maximize the growth and development of a leader, yearlong administrative internships provide both an appropriate duration of time and a variety of problem-solving opportunities from start to finish. The beginning of the year tasks lay the foundation for staff and student goals and expectations and the end of the year tasks circle back to explore those prior goals and success along the way. All parts of the school year share equal importance and require unique tasks, responsibilities, and priorities. Additionally, the need to use problem-solving skills occurs many times throughout a given school day, as building leaders face numerous and various issues that arise unexpectedly. New leaders must learn how to prioritize issues as they also learn how to professionally support all invested stakeholders while working to do what is best for students. These types of skills require practice, and many times they affect other decisions made throughout the year. For these reasons, it is important for an individual to experience all parts of a school year from an administrative perspective.

In addition to a yearlong principal internship, the relationship with the assigned principal mentor is crucial to the development of principal candidates. Yearlong internships allow for these two individuals to build a strong relationship while working side by side, which is critical to the principal candidate's growth. When problem-solving, principal candidates who have strong relationships with mentor principals also develop trust, which allows for individuals to speak and listen openly with a confidence that ideas will be heard and suggested changes can be made. It is critical and takes time for the principal candidate to reflect on feedback and make adjustments to further develop skills that are best facilitated through a strong relationship between the mentor principal and the principal candidate.

Providing funding for a full-time internship for principal candidates is a cost to the district, but the value in the quality of the administrator we receive is immeasurable. Staff members who have graduated from the PPP indicated that they gained exposure and expertise in topics vital to the principalship while being taught by faculty members who had previous experience as principals, superintendents, school board members, and directors of education. Learning from experienced faculty members, along with the opportunity to work closely with a mentor principal and experience all elements of what it is like to be a building principal, provides candidates with the knowledge and skills they need to be successful school leaders.

Preparing Leaders of Faith-Based Schools:
The Case for Both/And

Michael Boyle and Patricia Huizar

It is no secret that there is a leadership challenge at all levels in Catholic schools. In the public school arena, Doyle and Locke note that "Ever-rising accountability standards, limited authority over key decisions, and mediocre pay make the job more and more demanding and less and less attractive to talented leaders" (2014, 2). The issue is even more critical in Catholic schools. In Catholic and other faith-based schools, the challenge of finding qualified principals is compounded by the simultaneous responsibility of the principal as a spiritual leader as well as an instructional and managerial leader (Ciriello 1996). As lay leaders replace religious women and men in Catholic schools and dioceses, congregational sponsors can no longer assume that principal candidates will possess a working knowledge of the Catholic faith and Catholic school governance structures or the skills needed to build a faith community within the educational community (Boyle, Haller, and Hunt 2016).

In order to address this concern, Catholic school systems must systematically work to create leaders for all levels. Standard 6 of the National Standards and Benchmarks for Effective Catholic Elementary and Secondary Schools (NSBECS) (Ozar and Weitzel-O'Neill 2012) states: "An excellent Catholic school has a qualified leader/leadership team empowered by the governing body to realize and implement the school's mission and vision" (19). Further, Benchmark 6.1 states: "The leader/leadership team meets national, state and/or (arch)diocesan requirements for school leadership preparation and licensing to serve as the faith and instructional leader(s) of the school." The significant phrase in Benchmark 6.1 is "faith and instructional leader," and the effective Catholic school principal is charged with being both.

With the rise of leadership standards like those of the Interstate School Leaders Licensure Consortium (ISLLC) (2008), university principal preparation programs must understandably focus on program alignment with such standards in order to meet licensure requirements. The issue then becomes, how do university programs also prepare candidates in the necessary faith leadership components that are so critical to leading effective Catholic schools? With the ever-increasing focus on the enrollment of students in graduate schools, there is an inherent tension between new approaches to principal preparation for public school principals and balancing the unique needs of preparing effective Catholic school principals. Often, aspiring Catholic school principals can feel that their professional preparation needs are not addressed. As Cook (2008) described one aspiring principal's observation: "My peers in public schools need only concern themselves with students, discipline, and parents. Everything else is done for them at the district level. I, on the other hand, take care of budgeting, personnel, curriculum, grant writing, school calendar, school maintenance, student recruitment, and the list goes on" (3).

Rooting the Program in Standards

Standards are effective at providing a clear description of the role of the principal, an organizational frame for the program, and a means for assessment. Yet the ISLLC standards (2008) and Southern Regional Education Board (SREB) critical success factors to anchor programs do not fully address the preparation needs for leaders of faith-based schools. Although not specifically a set of leadership standards, the NSBECS can offer guidance for the development of necessary skills and competencies relevant to the development of the Catholic school administrator.

NSBECS was designed through a two-year collaboration among stakeholders from PK-12 Catholic schools, the Church, diocesan offices, universities, educational networks and partnerships, and funders (Ozar and Weitzel-O'Neill 2013). The purpose was to develop a universal set of characteristics and criteria to define how "mission-driven, program effective, well-managed, and responsibly governed Catholic schools operate" (Ozar and Weitzel-O'Neill 2012, vi). Of all four domains, governance and leadership are central and determine the level of success in all other areas (Ozar and Weitzel-O'Neill 2013). Therefore, a strong principal must possess an understanding of all of the standards of excellence as well as the skills to lead school improvement across all four domains.

The NSBECS describe effective school functioning and are not specific to the skills and responsibilities of the principal. The faculty of the Greeley Center for Catholic Education (GCCE) at Loyola University Chicago developed a process to use the NSBECS as a blueprint to guide the development of leaders for faith-based schools. In collaboration with a veteran Catholic school principal, the staff at GCCE examined each standard and benchmark and determined the requisite skills and experiences the candidates would need to gain in order to meet the standard of excellence (Morten and Lawler 2016). The result of this process yielded the Catholic School Principal Competencies, a list of skills and competencies of a Catholic school principal that are linked directly to the NSBECS. These competencies articulate the unique responsibilities of the Catholic school principal associated with the faith-based mission and the differences in governance, staffing, and funding structures (Boyle, Morten, and Guerin 2013).

Morten and Lawler (2016) provide a detailed account of how the Catholic Principal Preparation Program at Loyola University Chicago used the state leadership standards, the NSBECS, and the Catholic School Principal Competencies as a framework for the university to better prepare principal candidates for the new state changes and to address the needs of leading faith-based schools. Following is an overview of the process used to develop a program that addresses both aspects:

Program standards. In order to comply with state regulations, the ISLLC standards and SREB critical success factors must direct the curriculum and program. It was equally important that the program be based on the Catholic School Principal Competencies to prepare candidates for the reality of leading Catholic schools. The team created a crosswalk between the two sets of standards and recognized the congruence.

Course Alignment. The Catholic School Principal Competencies were aligned with all courses within the Catholic Principal Preparation Program (CPPP). Utilizing the *Understanding by Design* (Wiggins and McTighe 2005) curriculum framework, course instructors created discussion prompts, activities, assignments, field experiences, and assessments to develop the specific skills outlined in the competencies. The alignment ensured that the courses were meaningful and practical, considering the candidates' commitment to serving within the Catholic school system. Furthermore, based on the NSBECS, the focus is not on developing Catholic school leaders but on preparing *highly effective* Catholic school leaders.

Explicit selection process. The NSBECS was also used as a foundation for developing the interview guide and writing prompt for candidates for the CPPP. During the interview, prospective candidates are asked to articulate the role of the Catholic school leader in maintaining both academic excellence and faith formation.

Clinically rich internship. The NSBECS-aligned Catholic Principal Competencies also play an important role in the candidate's internship, tracking candidates' activities using an onboarding plan that was aligned to the SREB critical success factors, ISLLC Standards and Functions, and the NSBECS-aligned Catholic Principal Competencies. Candidates must provide evidence of activities they have observed, participated in, or led that align with each SREB Critical Success Factor and ISLLC Standard, as well as all Catholic Principal Competencies.

Coaching and reflection. The coaching component of the Catholic Principal Preparation Program brings meaning to the standards-aligned activities and facilitates the transformation of the candidates to Catholic school leaders. Ignatian pedagogy inspires the approach to reflection within the CPPP. Through intentional questioning, candidates become more aware of the internal operations that direct their decisions (Hartnett 2009). This framework also encourages the candidate's exploration of the spiritual aspect of leadership.

University-district partnership. Illinois state law requires that principal preparation programs formally create partnerships with districts to ensure that the programs are meeting the leadership needs of the district. To fulfill Loyola University Chicago's mission of serving the inner city and the Church, the CPPP partnered with the Office of Catholic Schools within the Archdiocese of Chicago. Diocesan officials have assisted in recruiting and selecting candidates, as well as mentor coaches for the candidates.

Program oversight. The CPPP utilizes an ePortfolio (electronic portfolio) as a system to capture the growth of the candidate and to showcase the candidate's skills, abilities, values, experiences, and competencies across all the standards of the program. The ePortfolio is organized to mirror the onboarding plan, listing activities aligned with all ISLLC Standards, SREB critical success factors, and Catholic School Principal Competencies.

The use of the NSBECS, alongside ISLLC, helps to unify the vocabulary of principal preparation among both dioceses and Catholic institutions of higher education. Creating a consensus by using a combined structure that incorporates both NSBECS and ISLLC standards assists members of the collaboration by creating common nomenclature and shared understanding of the preparation program outcomes. This has the potential for increasing the quality of communication between Catholic institutions of higher education and diocesan offices of Catholic education (Boyle, Haller, and Hunt 2016) which ultimately will assist in creating highly effective principals who are *both* instructional *and* faith-based leaders.

Note

1. IL-PART was project housed at the Center for the Study of Education Policy at Illinois State University, in which North Central College and the East Aurora School District participated. Funded by a $4.6 million grant from the US Department of Education, it sought to increase principal effectiveness by improving principal preparation and development.

Bibliography

Boyle, Michael J., Alicia Haller, and Erika Hunt. "The Leadership Challenge: Preparing and Developing Catholic School Principals." *Journal of Catholic Education* 19, no. 3 (2016): 293–316.

Boyle, Michael J., Sandria Morten, and Richard Guerin. *The Catholic Principal Preparation Program Participant Handbook*. Loyola University Chicago, 2013, http://luc.edu/media/ lucedu/ccse/pdfs/Catholic%20Principal%20Preparation%20Program%20Handbook.pdf

Ciriello, Maria J., ed. *Formation and Development for Catholic School Leaders: The Principal as Educational Leader*. Vol. 1. Washington, DC: USCCB Publishing, 1996.

Cook, Timothy J. *Responding to Leadership Challenges in US Catholic Schools: The Lived Reality*. Online Submission of Annual International Conference on Catholic Leadership, 2008.

Doyle, Daniela, and Gillian Locke. *Lacking Leaders: The Challenges of Principal Recruitment, Selection, and Placement*. Washington, DC: Thomas B. Fordham Institute, 2014.

Hartnett, Daniel F. *Transformative Education in the Jesuit Tradition*. Chicago: Loyola University-Chicago, 2009, 4–16.

Interstate School Leaders Licensure Consortium. *Interstate School Leaders Consortium: Standards for School Leaders*. Washington, D.C.: Council of Chief State School Officers, 2008.

Morten, Sandria, and Geralyn Lawler. "A Standards-based Approach to Catholic Principal Preparation: A Case Study." *Journal of Catholic Education* 19, no. 3 (2016): 332–349.

Ozar, Lorraine, and Patricia Weitzel-O'Neill. "National Catholic School Standards: Focus on Governance and Leadership." *Journal of Catholic Education* 17, no. 1 (2013).

Ozar, Lorraine, and P. Weitzel-O'Neill. "National Standards and Benchmarks for Effective Catholic Elementary and Secondary Schools." *Momentum* 43, no. 1 (2012): 14–23.

Wiggins, Grant P., and Jay McTighe. *Understanding by Design*. Alexandria, VA: ASCD, 2005.

Section 3
Policy Improvement and Sustainment

7 Monitoring Implementation

Findings and Implications from a Statewide Study

Bradford R. White, Amber Stitziel Pareja, Holly Hart, Michelle Hanh Huynh, Brenda K. Klostermann, and Janet K. Holt

For many decades prior to Illinois' principal preparation redesign efforts, training had typically consisted of administrative courses such as school law, finance, and educational theory, followed by an internship consisting of a set number of hours primarily spent shadowing a principal. Programs varied greatly in the quality of both course content and mentoring, and many had few, if any, candidate selection criteria beyond what was required by the college or university.

Meanwhile, a growing body of research evidence indicated that principals play a critical role in improving student performance and leading effective schools (Hallinger et al. 1983). This research identified the importance of principals as successful instructional leaders rather than simply efficient building managers, and it identified key components of effective principal preparation programs including targeted recruitment and selection; a rigorous curriculum focused on instruction and school improvement; integration of coursework and fieldwork; and robust, sustained internships that allow candidates to gain leadership experience working with an expert mentor (Darling-Hammond et al. 2007).

As a result, many began to perceive traditional principal preparation as providing inadequate training, and as such, principal preparation programs have become the target of intense scrutiny (Levine 2005). In 2010, Illinois required a complete redesign of all its principal preparation programs with the goal of advancing statewide school improvement through strengthening school leadership. The new requirements, which went into effect in 2014, called for the reauthorization of all programs and several radical shifts from the status quo, including:

- A targeted principal endorsement, instead of a general administrative certificate;
- Formal partnerships with school districts in preparation program design and delivery;
- More selective admissions criteria and processes;
- A focus on leading all students, including students with disabilities, English Language Learners, and early childhood education;

- Collaborative support for candidates from highly qualified faculty supervisors and mentor principals;
- A competency-based internship, with an emphasis on demonstrated leadership skills.

Data and Methods

The implementation of Illinois' new principal preparation program was studied for two years to track the changes that occurred because of this new policy. With funding from the Robert R. McCormick Foundation and It is The Wallace Foundation, our mixed-methods study set out to describe stakeholders' perspectives on the policy goals, how programs and their district partners navigated the new state requirements, and the early impact of the state's new principal preparation strategy.

The study consisted of four components, beginning with a policy scan completed during the fall of 2014 and early winter of 2015, which involved a broad sample of stakeholders. To delve more deeply into the themes discovered in the statewide scan, we conducted site visits to twelve of the approved programs.

During these site visits, which occurred between March 2015 and March 2016, program faculty and district partners were interviewed and focus groups were conducted with each program's principal candidates. To include evidence about the implementation of key policy components in coursework, syllabi were analyzed from fourteen programs that volunteered to participate. Finally, an online survey was conducted of all program coordinators (response rate = 75 percent) in fall 2015 to explore themes across the whole population.

Findings

The analysis of the data describes how programs have negotiated the increased demands and complex requirements of Illinois' new principal preparation policy. It was discovered that although the policy brought about real change in these programs, the way that programs implemented the central tenets of the legislation ranged in both depth and breadth.

The remainder of this chapter describes this variation and highlights key implications from the study. We organize the findings across six major functions: partnerships, recruitment and enrollment, curriculum, special student populations, mentoring and internships, and continuous improvement. Within each section, findings are woven from each of the study's components, and additional details are presented in a final report (White et al. 2016).

Partnerships

Prior to the new policy, formal partnerships between principal preparation programs and school districts were quite limited. The redesign strengthened existing partnerships and helped create new ones. These partnerships took many different forms: some were between a program and a single district or Regional Office of Education (ROE), others between a program and several districts, and one was between a program and a partnership board.

Most programs developed formal partnerships with multiple districts while maintaining informal partners for internship experiences. In general, district representatives reported that they communicated with programs more frequently and that programs were more responsive to their needs. Program staff members believed districts provided key input into the redesign and important feedback on program and candidate performance, and principal candidates valued having access to the experience and knowledge of district superintendents and principals. Ongoing communications also helped keep districts and programs up to date.

A few partnerships were able to reach and sustain a deep level of ongoing collaboration. In these highly engaged partnerships, districts shared responsibility for curriculum design, candidate selection and evaluation, internships, and mentoring and felt they had a stronger voice into the preparation of their future principals. Higher levels of engagement produced greater impacts on both programs and districts, but resource limitations undermined the development of deeper partnerships (Figure 7.1).

To what extent is your district partner responsible for the following in your principal endorsement program? (Note: "Not at all responsible" and "Less responsible than program" response categories are not shown.)

Recruitment and Enrollment

Almost all programs experienced a dramatic drop in enrollment, as anticipated by moving from general administrative training to a principal-specific endorsement. In many instances, these decreases were substantial, with several programs citing tenfold declines from the enrollment levels of their prior (Type 75) programs. However, stakeholders generally viewed this as a shift from quantity to quality that benefited principal preparation, specifically by providing more targeted and practical training squarely focused on creating the state's next generation of school leaders.

Program staff viewed current principal preparation candidates as being stronger overall, more committed to careers in the principalship, and no less diverse than those prior to the redesign (although most programs acknowledged they still needed to improve in the area of diversity). One challenge to implementation was that this more intensive approach to preparation strained program resources and stressed relationships with the broader university. In response, programs were forced to rethink and more than double their recruitment efforts (White et al. 2016). Although most program coordinators who responded to the survey reported that their current enrollments were sufficient to sustain their programs (Figure 7.2), concerns about the system's ability to meet the demand for principals *statewide* over the next five years were more widespread.

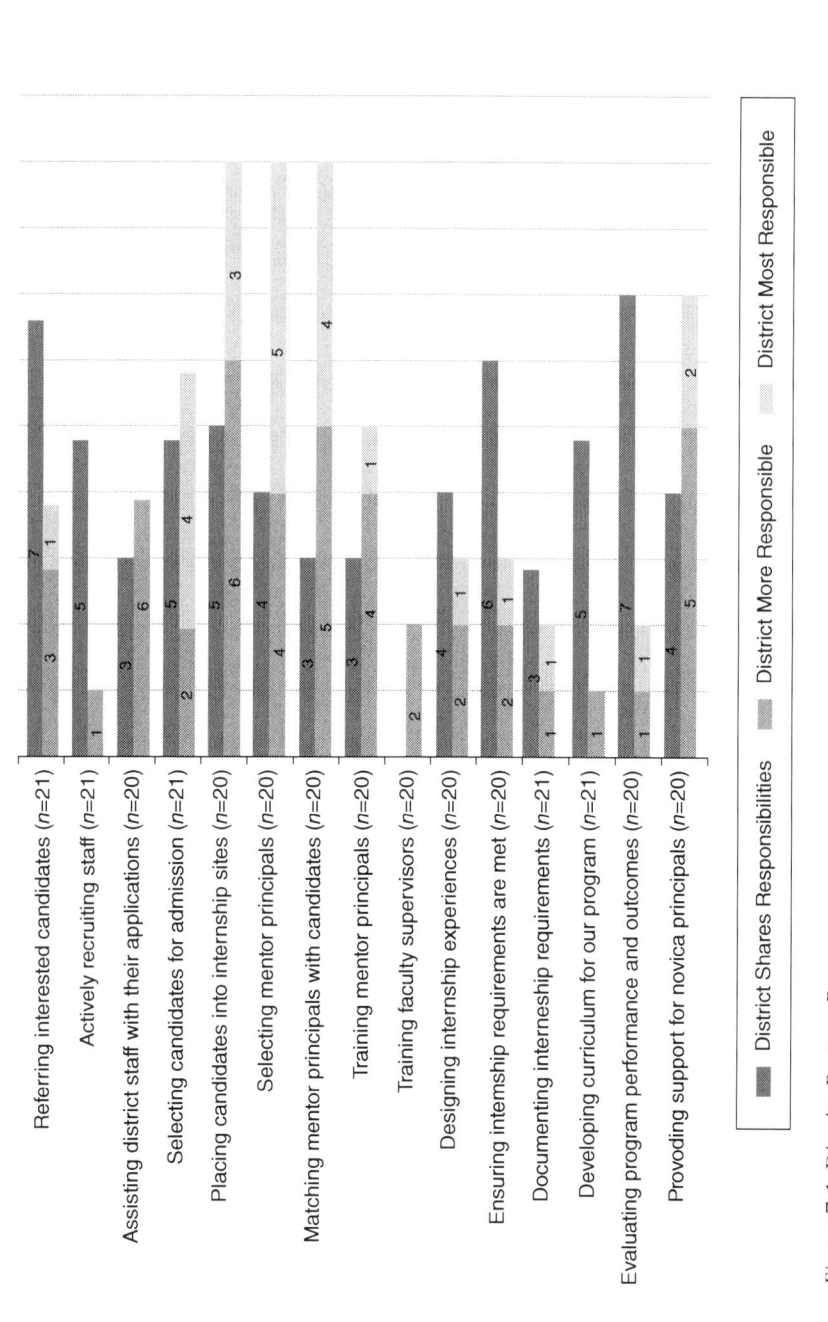

Figure 7.1 District Partner Responses

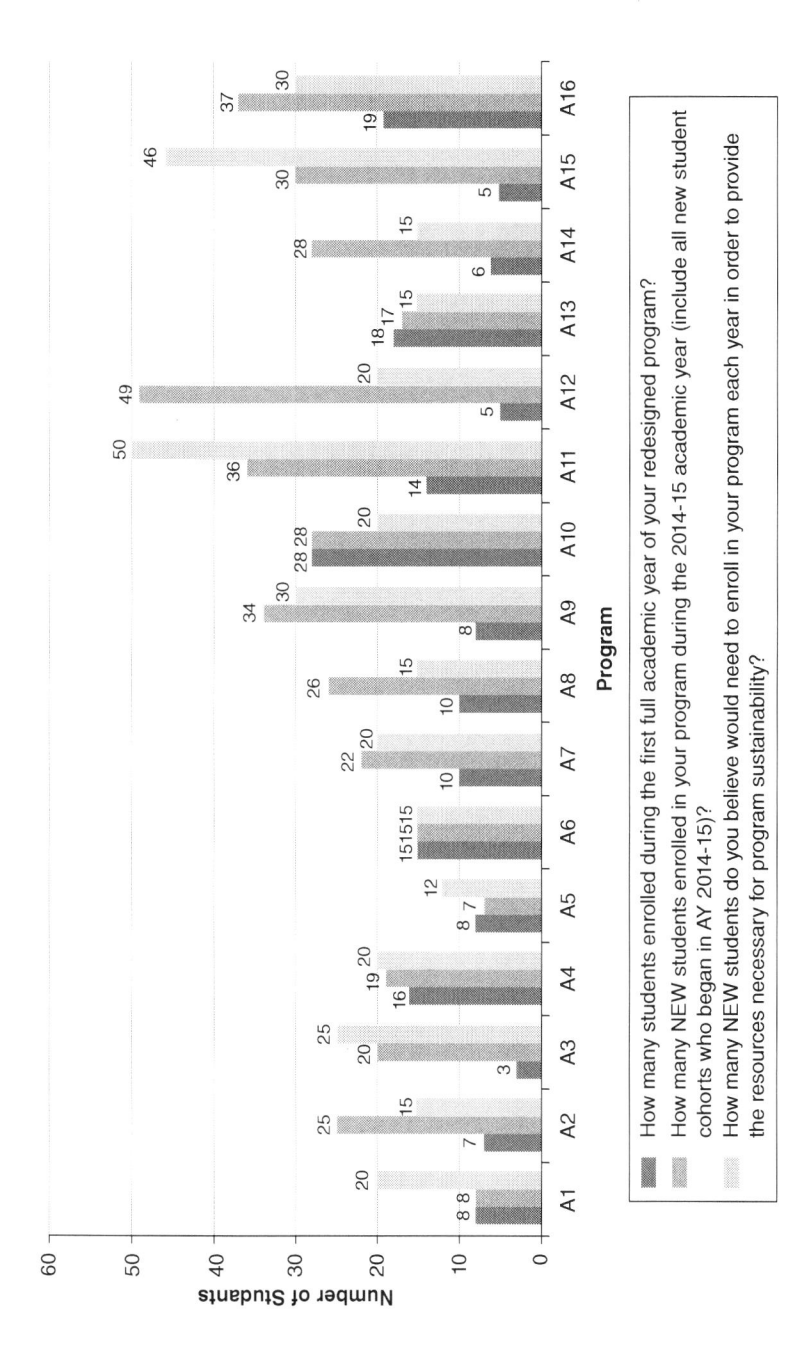

Figure 7.2 Enrollments in Initial Year of Implementation, in 2014–2015, and Needed for Sustainability ($n = 16$)

Curriculum

The principal preparation redesign process provided programs a welcome opportunity to revamp their curricula. Instructional leadership was a clear focus of coursework and the internship in the new programs. However, respondents generally viewed this as part of an ongoing movement in the field and did not necessarily attribute it to the redesign. Participants also noted that school improvement and data analysis became more established parts of the curriculum and that coursework and fieldwork were better integrated into the new programs.

Many candidates and faculty representatives felt that organizational management was overly de-emphasized in the new programs, and some programs were in the process of bringing back key management and finance courses. Our syllabi analysis, however, indicated that organizational management remained a major area of instruction, addressed to a similar degree as instructional leadership in most programs (Figure 7.3).

Special Student Populations

Special education, early childhood, and English Language Learner student populations received increased coverage in both coursework and internships in the new programs. Preparation program representatives generally felt that candidates would be better positioned to work with all students. Whether this preparation would be sufficient to prepare principals to lead in all contexts remained a matter of debate among both policymakers and practitioners.

Further, there were wide variations in curricular coverage between programs as well as among the different special student populations (Figure 7.4). Special education coursework was the most universal because students with disabilities are more widespread throughout the state and this content was traditionally included in school law and other education administration courses. Early childhood education (ECE) and ELL content, on the other hand, proved more challenging to integrate into new coursework and internship placements. Candidates often learned about working with special student populations from their peers, but there was limited collaboration with other departments that could boost knowledge of special populations at most programs.

Mentoring and Internships

Stakeholders believed the competency-based internship better prepared candidates for the principalship. The new internship requirements—including instructional leadership opportunities, more direct leadership, and experiences working with many types of students—were generally viewed as deeper, clearer, and more authentic. Many also believed that mentoring from faculty supervisors and principal mentors improved and further enhanced the internship experience.

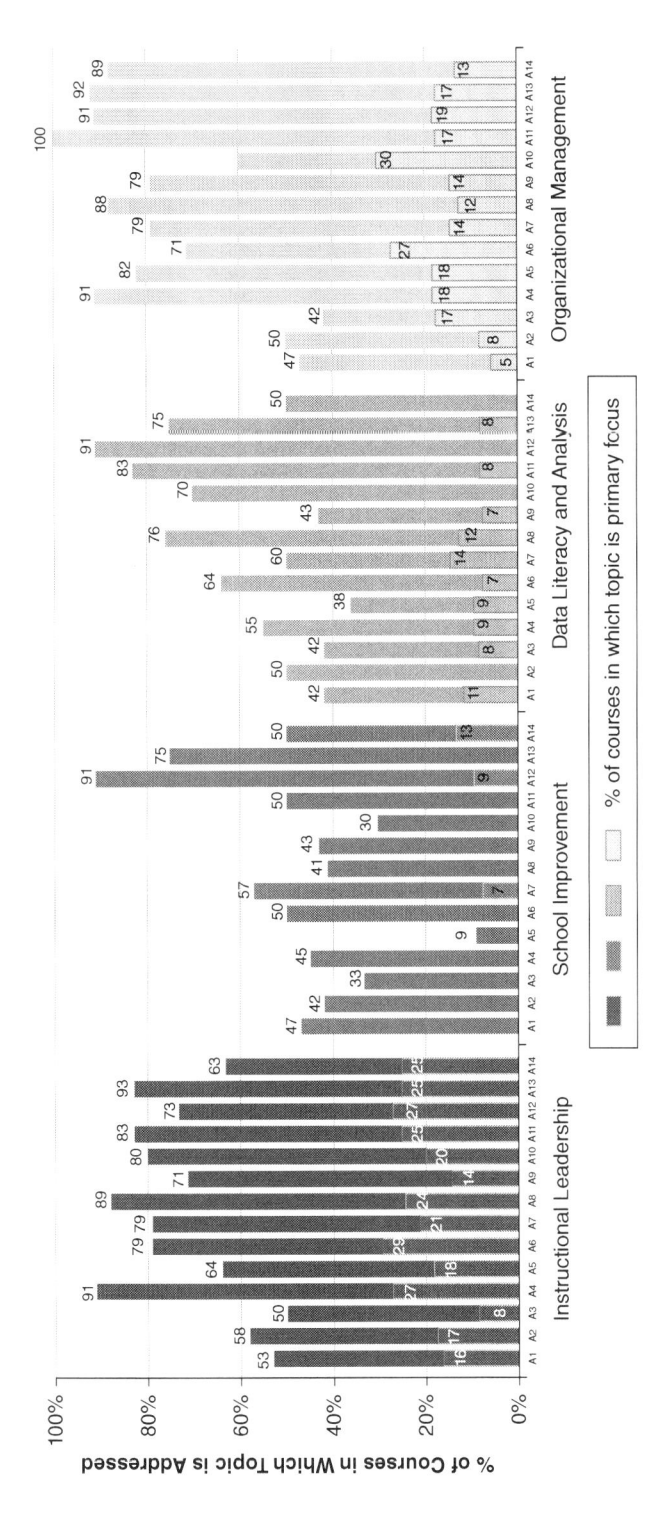

Figure 7.3 Course Coverage of Instructional Leadership, School Improvement, Data Literacy and Analysis, and Organizational Management, by Institution

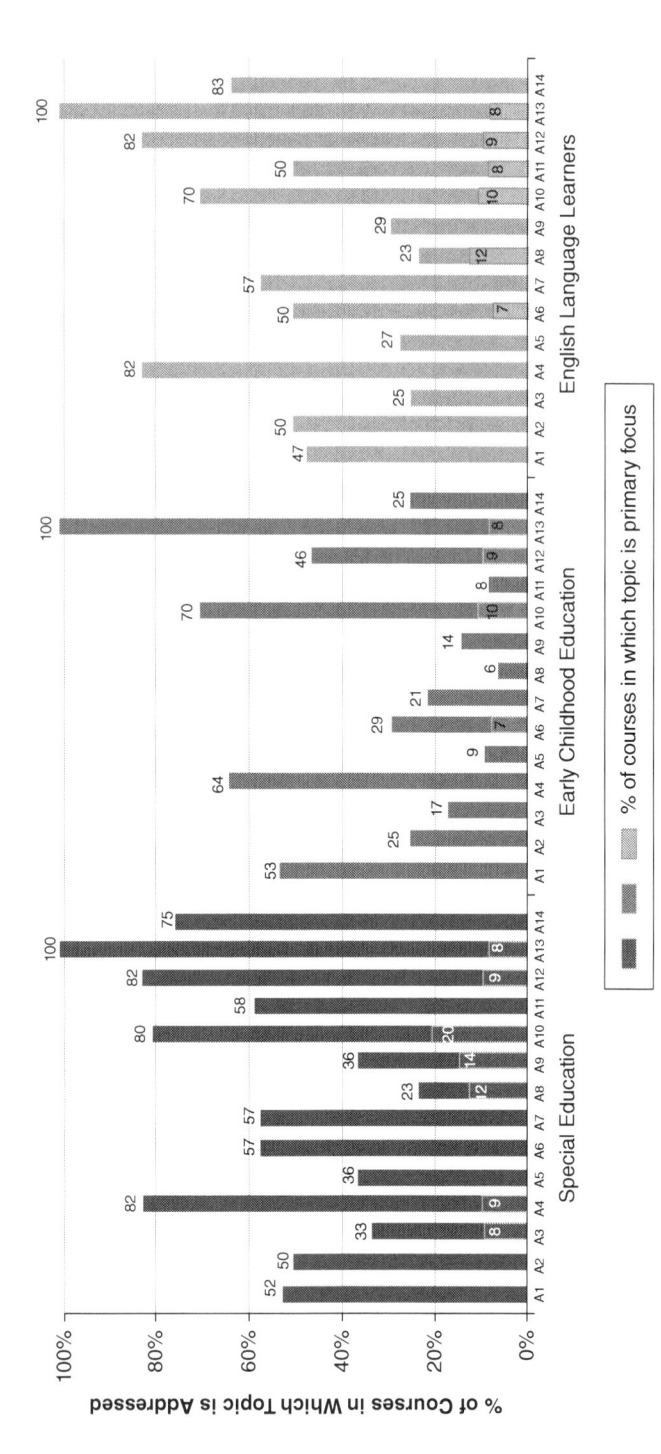

Figure 7.4 Course Coverage of Special Education, Early Childhood Education, and English Language Learners, by Institution

Although the format of the internship typically remained unchanged, many candidates believed a paid, full-time, yearlong internship would provide better opportunities to prepare them for the principalship in a more holistic, meaningful way. Challenges to successful internships included finding a sufficient supply of qualified principal mentors and faculty supervisors, and the intense time commitment required to implement the internship. As one program coordinator noted:

> Four times a year, [the faculty supervisors] go and observe [candidates] . . . participating [in] their leadership role. We observe them and give them written feedback as a part of the evaluation process. That never happened under the old internship. I mean you would go out and meet with them, but you didn't actually observe them in leadership activities.

In addition, some stakeholders felt that the internship activities outlined in the policy were too prescriptive to allow programs and candidates to tailor the internship experiences to meet the needs of candidates.

Continuous Improvement

Most programs collected data on current candidates, but outcome data on former graduates was lacking. The majority of programs collected candidate data such as internship performance data and application, acceptance, enrollment, persistence, and completion rates (Figure 7.5). Programs

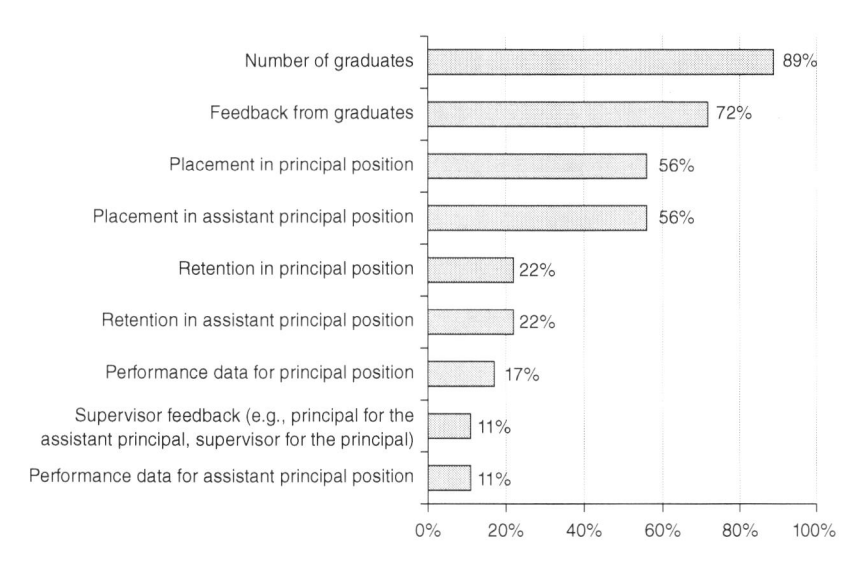

Data Collected	Percentage
Number of graduates	89%
Feedback from graduates	72%
Placement in principal position	56%
Placement in assistant principal position	56%
Retention in principal position	22%
Retention in assistant principal position	22%
Performance data for principal position	17%
Supervisor feedback (e.g., principal for the assistant principal, supervisor for the principal)	11%
Performance data for assistant principal position	11%

Figure 7.5 Graduate Data Collected by Principal Preparation Programs
What data about graduates from your program do you currently collect for program evaluation or program improvement?[1] (N = 21)

utilized these data to modify and improve their programs, although many noted the need to gather these data more systematically and to collect and analyze data on program graduates' outcomes in the future.

Implications

Finally, several key issues were explored that policymakers, principal preparation programs, and other stakeholders need to address to determine the ultimate fate of Illinois' principal preparation redesign efforts. By addressing the following areas, principal preparation in Illinois has a promising future.

High-Engagement Partnerships Can Be Beneficial to Both Programs and Districts, but They Require High Levels of Resources and Supports

Stakeholders believed that more intense partnerships could benefit both programs and districts. However, these high-engagement partnerships required substantial investments of funds, time, and personnel, which made them difficult to engage in and sustain over time. This study revealed that some programs and districts were more poised for high-engagement partnerships than others for various reasons, including capacity and resources, pre-existing relationships, and geographic location. These findings suggest that there could be a role for regional hubs (as suggested by the Illinois School Leadership Advisory Council—ISLAC 2016) to help equalize and optimize resources so that all districts and programs are able to take advantage of the benefits offered by high-engagement partnerships.

Steps Need to Be Taken to Ensure That There Are Enough High-Quality Candidates to Fill Principal Vacancies in Both the Short and Long Term

By design, the new policy required more intensive and focused training for a smaller, more targeted population of candidates, specifically those who aspired to be school leaders. Although most of the program coordinators responding to our survey indicated their enrollments were already at or above the levels needed for sustainability, it is important to ascertain the health and viability of all programs to be able to reliably predict future supply.

Further, there were lingering concerns that too few candidates would be prepared under the new system, and stakeholders worried that this could eventually lead to a shortage in the principal pipeline. It is crucial for the state to understand and continuously monitor the supply of and demand for both the new principal endorsement *and* the reserve pool of Type 75 certificate holders to assess whether Illinois will have enough high-quality principals to staff schools in the short term and long term.

There Is a Need for Both Instructional Leadership and Organizational Management

Numerous individuals interviewed for this study—both faculty and students—spoke of the shift in focus that had occurred between "management" on the one side and "instruction" on the other, with some suggesting the new reforms had caused the pendulum to swing too far in the direction of the latter. There is no doubt that instructional leadership has risen to the forefront over the past decade, and is clearly a focus of educator preparation, not just in Illinois, but nationally.

Recent research on principal effectiveness, however, argues for an *expanded* definition of instructional leadership that goes beyond the principal's involvement with day-to-day instruction and includes elements of organizational management as they relate to improving instruction (Louis et al. 2010). In fact, several of these studies suggest that a principal's time spent in day-to-day instructional activities may be detrimental to important school outcomes (Sebastian and Allensworth 2012). Instead, this line of research suggests the placement of more emphasis on making sure principals have the skills to organize their schools to support teachers and set the stage for good instruction by, for example, promoting positive learning conditions, creating a workplace that supports instructional practices known to be effective, and attracting, hiring, developing, motivating, and retaining better teachers (Bryk et al. 2010).

The extent to which Illinois' new principal preparation policy incorporates this broader definition of instructional leadership—or, perhaps more importantly, the extent to which each program can embrace it—could go a long way toward determining the ultimate effects of Illinois' redesign efforts.

A Focus on Competency and Continuous Development Can Help Resolve Tensions between Comprehensiveness and Specialization

One goal of the new policy was to ensure all principals are prepared to lead all students, from PreK through high school, including students with special learning needs such as students with disabilities and English Language Learners. In concept, the new programs were intended to be competency-based, whereby candidates must demonstrate mastery across a comprehensive array of skills to earn endorsement. In practice, however, candidates were rarely able to test out of an area where they had already demonstrated expertise or receive credit for professional experience. That is, even if the policy was flexible about how candidates demonstrate competency, program administrators interpreted the requirements as quite rigid and were not exercising flexibility.

This confusion points to a broader tension between comprehensiveness and specialization. One strategy for striking this balance could involve increased attention to the full continuum of principal preparation, acknowledging that professional development does not end when candidates enter the workforce. Requiring continual professional development throughout principals' careers— "from aspiring to retiring"—would provide additional opportunities to acquire specialized knowledge and skills that fit changing needs as principals grow.

Further, similar steps could be taken with the pool of Type 75 certificate holders to help identify and fill gaps in their preparation and experience, and thus, ensure that all new Illinois principals possess the competencies needed for success in today's schools.

Many Argue for Transitioning from a Compliance Mindset toward a Focus on Performance

Many of the biggest challenges programs had with the redesign revolved around the volume and specificity of the policy's requirements. Numerous program representatives voiced recommendations for reduced paperwork and increased autonomy in implementation. Some advocated for a move away from concerns of "micro-managing" inputs and toward a focus on holding programs accountable for outcomes.

ISLAC and others advocated for the creation of a state-level office of school leadership charged with formally gathering feedback from the field and evaluating the state's performance and policy around principal preparation on a regular basis. One potential role for this office could be to assist programs with tracking candidates into the field and taking the lead in collecting a range of quality indicators to assist programs' continuous improvement efforts and the state's accountability system.

Conclusion

Illinois has been, and continues to be, a leader in the nationwide effort to improve principal preparation. Although there have been several challenges along the way, and some aspects continue to need improvement, most stakeholders expect this training will produce future school leaders capable of improving schools and student achievement. There are lingering concerns, however, that the supply of principals prepared in the new programs will not be sufficient to meet statewide demand.

In addition, this more intensive way of preparing principals has required programs to invest more resources into each candidate, which was particularly problematic given the state budget impasse that was occurring at the time. What ultimately matters is having sufficient quantity *and* quality of principals to staff all schools successfully. Continued efforts and attention from policymakers, funders, practitioners, and researchers are needed to assess the extent to which the redesigned programs and partner organizations have the supports and resources necessary to engage in intensive principal preparation, and the degree to which these programs are fulfilling the promise of preparing more effective school leaders.

Note

1. Approximately 17% of respondents did not have any program graduates at the time of the survey and were excluded from these calculations.

Bibliography

Bryk, Anthony S., Penny Bender Sebring, Elaine Allensworth, John Q. Easton, and Stuart Luppescu. *Organizing Schools for Improvement: Lessons from Chicago*. Chicago: University of Chicago Press, 2010.

Darling-Hammond, Linda, Michelle LaPointe, Debra Meyerson, and Margaret Terry Orr. *Preparing School Leaders for a Changing World: Lessons from Exemplary Leadership Development Programs*. Stanford: Stanford University, Stanford Educational Leadership Institute, 2007.

Hallinger, Phillip, Joseph Murphy, Marsha Weil, Richard Mesa, and Alexis Mitman. "Effective Schools: The Specific Policies and Practices of the Principal." *National Association of Secondary School Principals Bulletin* 67 (1983): 83–91.

Illinois School Leadership Advisory Council. *Illinois School Leadership Advisory Council Final Report*, 2016, http://education.illinoisstate.edu/downloads/csep/ISLAC-Final-Report.pdf

Levine, Arthur. *Educating School Leaders*. New York, NY: Teachers College, The Education Schools Project, 2005.

Louis, Karen Seashore, Kenneth Leithwood, Kyla L. Wahlstrom, Stephen E. Anderson, Michael Michlin, Blair Mascall, and Shawn Moore. *Learning from Leadership: Investigating the Links to Improved Student Learning*. Minneapolis, MN: University of Minnesota, 2010.

Sebastian, James, and Elaine Allensworth. *The Influence of Principal Leadership on Classroom Instruction and Student Learning: A Study of Mediated Pathways to Learning*, 2012, http://eaq.sagepub.com/content/48/4/626

White, Bradford R., Amber Stitziel Pareja, Holly Hart, Brenda K. Klostermann, Michelle Hanh Huynh, Mary Frazier-Meyers, and Janet Holt. *Navigating the Shift to Intensive Principal Preparation in Illinois: An In-depth Look at Stakeholder Perspectives (IERC 2016–2)*. Edwardsville, IL: Illinois Education Research Council at Southern Illinois University, 2016.

Vignettes

Applying Continuous Improvement Processes to Policy: The Mission and Focus of the Illinois School Leader Advisory Council (ISLAC)

Diane Rutledge and Steve Tozer

Background: Illinois Policy Formation Over Time

Illinois has received considerable recognition in the past five years for policies that support school principal preparation and development.

This recognition has come in the form of top rankings for Illinois principal policy in studies conducted by The Wallace Foundation (Manna 2015) and the University Council for Educational Administration (Anderson and Reynolds 2015). The state's policies also received the 2014 Education Commission of the States' Frank Newman Award for State Innovation.

But it wasn't always so. As documented elsewhere in this volume, in 2006 an Illinois Board of Higher Education Commission sharply criticized the state's school leader policies in *School Leader Preparation: A Blueprint for Change*. And in 2007, a state policy inventory conducted by the Southern Regional Education Board showed that Illinois policy was, like nearly all other states, in need of significant revision. These findings were presented in the legislative recommendations of the Illinois School Leader Task Force in 2008, which by 2010 were codified in Public Act 096-0903. These new requirements were consistent with the recommendations of the 2006 *Blueprint for Change* report. By 2012, no program was allowed to continue operations without receiving state approval under the new law, which required new program components:

1. A professional P-12 endorsement targeted explicitly to principal preparation;
2. Selective admission of candidates;
3. Formal roles for school district partners in program design, delivery, and assessment;
4. Intensive field experiences with mandated assessments of school-based performance;
5. More rigorous requirements for the qualifications of faculty and field supervisors;
6. More rigorous state assessment of candidate qualifications;
7. Data-based demonstration of program impact on schools through program graduates' performance in leadership positions.

Two Post-Legislation Implementation Supports

During the Task Force deliberations, and in two years of statewide study groups that shaped the final legislation that passed in 2010, it was clear that this legislation was contentious. Online university programs recognized that approval of their programs would be difficult, if not impossible, under the new guidelines, and the largest brick-and-mortar programs in Illinois, including one with 1,700 students enrolled, could lose tuition if they had to demonstrate selectivity of candidates. Those who opposed the legislative changes also feared a serious reduction of candidates for the principalship, despite Illinois State Board of Education figures showing that there were, after the legislation took effect, some forty-three thousand administrative certificate holders in a state in which there are approximately four to five hundred vacancies annually.

By 2014, after some twenty-five revised programs were approved under PA 096-0903, reducing the number of programs and sharply reducing the number of candidates enrolled, two additional steps were initiated to support the continuous improvement of principal quality in Illinois. One of these was a study jointly conducted by the Consortium for Chicago School Research and the Illinois Education Research Council, which sought to document implementation perspectives and progress on the new state law. The study acknowledged concerns about unintended consequences of the new policy but concluded that "the majority of program representatives and statewide stakeholders indicated that they support the goals of the new policy and have a positive outlook on its impact in the future of principal preparation in Illinois. Most believe that the redesigned principal preparation programs will ultimately create better-prepared school principals, as well as improved student achievement and more successful schools" (IERC 2015, 10).

The Illinois School Leader Advisory Council

The second implementation-support measure undertaken was the formation of the Illinois School Leader Advisory Council (ISLAC), a joint undertaking of the Illinois State Board of Education (IBHE) and the Illinois Board of Higher Education (ISBE). The Council was co-chaired by representatives from the University of Illinois at Chicago and Springfield School District 186, who had done considerable work developing preparation and support models for principals, thus championing the scaling of these efforts. The Council was founded on the premise that it is easier to pass legislation than it is to change organizational culture, and that it would be important to provide statewide supports for implementation of Public Act 096-0903 if principal preparation in the state were truly to realize the law's potential. As the ISLAC Final Report put it: "One of the key messages of this report is that policy implementation requires even more attention than policy formation, and that implementation needs to be reworked and refined over time to be successful" (25).

The initial ISLAC charge was clear: to develop a *five-year strategic plan* detailing how Illinois would systemically achieve a statewide vision for preparing and supporting school leaders through effective programs to provide high-quality school leadership in every school in the state, regardless of location. Through the collective input of the Council, the charge was further developed to include strategies for program cohesion and continuous improvement, quality assurance, effective partnerships and training, and networked support for the sustainability of high-quality school leadership in every school in the state, regardless of location. (ISLAC Final Report, 26).

The Council included some fifty representatives from virtually all key constituencies in the state that had a stake in principal preparation and development, such as the Illinois Principals' Association, the state's two largest teachers' unions, private and public universities, and representatives from early childhood education, special education, the Illinois State Board of Education, the Board of Higher Education, the education policy group Advance Illinois, and others (full membership list included in the ISLAC Final Report). The work was funded by The Wallace Foundation and McCormick Foundation through the Center for the Study of Educational Policy at Illinois State University.

To achieve its charge, ISLAC met six times between September 2014 and June 2015, often hosting guest presenters from Illinois and elsewhere who were invited in support of a vision statement for the work of the Council, as presented at the initial Council meeting in September 2014.

"Illinois will prepare and support school leaders through effective principal preparation programs . . . and coherent, high-quality professional development" (ISLAC, 26). It was clear from the inception of the Council that this vision would not be achieved quickly, but that we could take important steps toward continuous improvement over time. As the Final Report stated it: "It is *not* the intention of this report to recommend immediate solutions to all problems faced by the complex and ambitious state effort to improve school leader preparation and development. This report recommends permanent mechanisms for supporting, monitoring, and continuously improving school leadership in the state. Our goal is to ensure a statewide commitment to the continuous improvement of school leader preparation and development that respects the voices from school districts, institutions of higher education, professional organizations, state agencies, non-profits, and others who have a clear stake in the quality of teaching and learning in Illinois schools" (ISLAC, 20).

To establish the mechanisms for continuous improvement of school leadership in Illinois, the Council formed four study teams, each charged with collecting data and recommending improvement mechanisms to the larger Council. These study teams addressed (1) program cohesion and continuous improvement; (2) quality assurance; (3) partnerships and training; and (4) network supports. Put differently, each of these study teams was assigned to contribute its best thinking to questions of how Illinois could build capacity to support continuous improvements in programs, in personnel, in partnerships, and in intrastate networks.

The ISLAC Final Report, revised and ratified by the membership, was delivered to the state in early 2016. It provides a five-year plan that addresses the focus of each of the study groups, as well as a proposal for funding the plan. These recommendations are extensive and detailed, providing a "Blueprint for Change," to borrow the title of the 2006 IBHE report on the future of school leadership policy in Illinois. The Final Report summarizes these detailed recommendations in general terms (2016, 3–4):

1. *Program Cohesion and Continuous Improvement*: To ensure the preparation of highly effective leaders, principal preparation and ongoing support will include well- designed, tightly integrated courses, fieldwork, and internships that provide authentic leadership experiences supported by highly qualified mentors. Two important steps will be (a) increasing the diversity of the leadership talent pipeline and improving leaders' cultural competencies; and (b) designing, implementing, and reporting out a continuous improvement process that ensures program cohesion and effectiveness.
2. *Quality Assurance*: Illinois must support data analysis at the program level for purposes of continuous improvement while improving and coordinating data analysis for reporting to different regulatory bodies (e.g., ISBE, IBHE, Council for the Accreditation of Educator Preparation [CAEP], individual institutional requirements, etc.). All stakeholders must build the capacity to report

and analyze information in ways that improve school leadership preparation and development. The state should also regularly assess the data burden on credentialing program partnerships to ensure that the data collected are necessary and useful.
3. *Partnerships and Training*: Illinois should provide statewide regional partnerships for the distribution of leadership preparation resources to all school districts in Illinois, providing school districts and institutions of higher education (IHEs) with mechanisms for the recruitment, selection, and support of principal mentors and leadership coaches to ensure the continuous enhancement of leadership capacity in Illinois. These partnerships should define opportunities for residency training and extended authentic field experiences for principal candidates within districts to include those recruited as principals, assistant principals, and teacher leaders.
4. *Network Supports*: Consistent with the most recent research on "Networked Improvement Communities" (Bryk et al. 2015), Illinois should establish a statewide *community of professional practice*, with intentionally expanding connections and resources, to support ongoing professional learning in IHEs, districts, and other stakeholders committed to effective educational leadership preparation and practice.

Today, two years after the ISLAC Final Report was submitted, there are clear signs of progress in Illinois and clear signs that some of the ISLAC recommendations have yet to be initiated. It is likely that the strength of Illinois implementation of PA 096-0903 lies in the local partnerships between school districts and universities that the law has catalyzed.

Bibliography

An Act Concerning Education, Illinois Public Act 096-0903 (passed June 1, 2010).

Anderson, Erin, and A. Reynolds. *A Policymaker's Guide: Research-based Policy for Principal Preparation Program Approval and Licensure*. Charlottesville, VA: The University Council of Educational Administration, 2015.

Bryk, Anthony S., Louis M. Gomez, Alicia Grunow, and Paul G. LeMahieu. *Learning to Improve: How America's Schools Can Get Better*. Cambridge, MA: Harvard Education Press, 2015.

Commission on School Leader Preparation in Illinois Colleges and Universities. *Blueprint for Change: Illinois Board of Higher Education report of the Commission for School Leader Preparation*. Springfield, IL: Illinois Board of Higher Education, 2006.

Illinois School Leader Task Force. *Illinois School Leader Task Force Report to the Illinois General Assembly*. Springfield, IL: Illinois State Board of Education and Illinois Board of Higher Education, 2008.

Klostermann, Brenda K., Amber Stitziel Pareja, Holly Hart, Bradford R. White, and Michelle Hanh Huynh. *Restructuring Principal Preparation in Illinois: Perspectives on Implementation Successes, Challenges, and Future Outlook*. IERC 2015–3. Edwardsville, IL: Illinois Education Research Council, 2015.

Manna, Paul. *Developing Excellent School Principals to Advance Teaching and Learning: Considerations for State Policy*. New York: The Wallace Foundation, 2015.

Assembling the Right Team for Implementing a Continuously Improving Principal Preparation Program: Lessons Learned at the University of Illinois at Chicago

Shelby Cosner

A central vision has anchored our work within the Urban Education Leadership program at the University of Illinois at Chicago: preparing principals who can consistently, as the rule and not the exception, transform historically underserved urban schools. Not surprisingly, such a vision necessitates a continuous improvement orientation and ongoing improvement work. However, we also recognized the importance of reconceptualizing and re-engineering our program team if we were to make progress on these fronts. Over the last decade, we have transformed our EdD program team, and I present three key lessons learned from this work.

Diversify Roles

Historically, university-based principal preparation programs have assembled teams that are either primarily or exclusively populated by tenure-line faculty. Although our program began similarly, it has dramatically transformed over the years. What are the various roles now evidenced within our team? A core group of tenure-line faculty who teach the bulk of our classes. These individuals are also active researchers engaged in generating new knowledge to ensure that cutting-edge findings are immediately disseminated to students. We also have several clinical faculty members. Importantly, over several years external funders played a key role in helping us secure university funding for these positions. Over the last decade through external funds, we have also sustained a small team of three to four full-time leadership coaches—all former principals with considerable expertise in transforming schools and with leadership coaching. Although clinical faculty and coaches teach a small number of courses in the program, their primary work is embedded in the clinical portion of the program. Both clinical faculty and coaches serve in leadership coaching roles with our principal candidates during a yearlong, full-time resident principal experience and in the first two years following the residency as candidates transition to principal and assistant principal roles. Through a combination of university and external funds, we have also assembled a small team of researchers and school/student assessment and data analysts. These individuals play a key role in our continuous program improvement through such work as data collection and analysis and the design of tools and materials for various program uses. We also have a person in a nonfaculty, designated administrative role who oversees such things as student recruitment, enrollment management, and liaison work with our district partner.

Hire for Both Expertise and Critical Orientations/Dispositions

We look for multiple attributes in addition to expertise in our selection of new team members (yes, even in the hiring of tenure-line faculty). Given our commitment to continuous program improvement, we must hire individuals who are also oriented to achieve both individual and collective/team goals. Continuous improvement necessitates the use of a wide assortment of "collaboration routines" that engage various members of the team for various purposes and at various points in time. Therefore, we hire individuals who are predisposed to collaborate. We make this explicit in our position vacancies and throughout our interview processes and we reinforce these orientations and dispositions in our ongoing work and interactions.

Distribute Program Leadership

We quickly learned the importance of distributing program leadership across an assortment of individuals and of rapidly adjusting our leadership configurations at various points in time as particular needs have emerged. It is common for as many as five team members, among our group of roughly fifteen, to be leading one or more areas of program work at a given time. The multifaceted and complex nature of our work, both daily and in relation to continuous improvement, necessitates such an approach.

Will the New Redesigned Programs Lead to a Principal Shortage?

Lenford C. Sutton

In the aftermath of Illinois legislative changes for principal licensure, the Department of Educational Administration and Foundations (EAF) at Illinois State University allocated a significant amount of time managing public perceptions and discerning fact from fiction as to the newly adopted requirements; with special attention to speculation about forecasted school principal shortages. First, Illinois statute preempted personnel who never taught while holding a teaching license from eligibility for admission to programs and acquisition of the new principal endorsement. Second, the law required candidates to (1) hold a valid, current Illinois teaching certificate; (2) be interviewed by no fewer than two of the program's full-time faculty members; (3) pass the Illinois Test of Basic Skills; (4) complete an on-site written response to a scenario presented by the interviewers; and (5) discuss the contents of their portfolio with a professor(s) during a face-to-face interview.

Two of the most daunting requirements under the new program requirements were portfolio development and the yearlong internship. The portfolio required candidates to provide evidence of (1) support for all students achieving high standards of learning; (2) data-driven instruction producing two years of student growth in the last five years; (3) significant leadership roles in past positions; (4) strong oral and written communication skills; (5) analytic abilities to collect and analyze data; (6) demonstrated respect for family and community; (7) strong interpersonal skills; and (8) understanding of curriculum and instructional practices. The yearlong internship was indeed the source of most trepidation for internal and external stakeholders to the EAF Department. Public commentary and tales enunciated that principal licensure candidates would be unwilling to leave their current employment to complete this process.

Our first order of business was to fully explain the parameters and expectation of the internship and more importantly debunk rumors that candidates would have to leave their current jobs to complete the internships. EAF Principal Intern Supervisor Dr. Mary K. Scharf facilitated several discussions about competencies and expectations with the first cohort of applicants admitted in the fall of 2014.

Second, we met with and engaged our regional partners in conversations about succession planning to identify, coach, mentor, and develop internal or external future leaders to transition into positions as current leaders move toward retirements. This process was particularly helpful in addressing public commentary about impending school principal shortages and reframing the question to focus on the university's ability to supply candidates ready to meet the actual forecasted demand of school principals needed in the next five to seven years.

Third, the EAF Department adopted just-in-time admissions, training, mentoring, and completion. More widely known as lean manufacturing in corporate settings, this method was applied to ensure adequate inventories of students ready to assume school leadership roles based on organizational need only. Accordingly, the department did not focus solely on enrollment, but also on the actual hiring of candidates in leadership roles in our partner school districts and beyond. As a result, 32 percent of the twenty-nine students admitted during the first three years of implementing the principal preparation redesign have secured appointments to administrative roles with local school districts and beyond.

Summarily, amid rumors of principal shortages, the EAF Department remained committed to developing candidates aware of their own strengths, weaknesses, values, and how they may impact learning communities. Also, we remained engaged in succession planning with our regional partners and readied candidates to assume leadership roles as needed.

New (Better) Alliances and Greater Equity through Regional Partnership Hubs

Darlene Ruscitti, Angie Zarvell, Mark Jontry, and Jill Reis

Current Illinois leadership professional development structures (education associations, universities, Regional Offices of Education, etc.) are generally characterized as working in silos, each entity with its own agenda, policies, cost structures, and in some cases, territory. The result of such a splintered approach is a disjointedness, overlapping of efforts, a lack of communication, and under/overutilization of resources. Such structures have also been originally designed with the primary focus on supporting teachers. As a result, increasing attention to the importance of school leadership has spurred professional development for school leaders serving as an add-on service rather than something customized and designed specifically for principals and assistant principals.

ISBE and IBHE jointly convened the 2014 Illinois School Leadership Advisory Council for the purpose of developing a five-year strategic plan to support and sustain the pipeline of high-quality principals across the state. One specific recommendation by ISLAC was to "Determine geographic boundaries for school districts to access regional or neighborhood partnership 'hubs' to optimize and equalize resources for training and supporting principals throughout the state, including opportunities for principal candidates to access high-quality experiences during their internship." At the core of this recommendation was the challenge presented by higher education faculty on limited access for principal candidates across the state to early childhood, English Language Learners, and students with disabilities, if the partnering schools or districts do not have services for these student populations.

Also unique to these hubs was the intended focus not only on developing relationships and partnerships between principals and the community partners, but also on the talent development process of building principals' knowledge and skills on how to leverage community resources to support kids and families. While these are issues that have been specifically addressed regarding principal preparation, the scope of this work has implications for the continuum of support for school leaders. The ISLAC report also recommended the need for a coordinated office or entity that could regularly track supply and demand data and outcome trends among principal preparation programs.

Through a planning grant from the Stone Foundation, a thirty-three-member Advisory Committee met for a year and identified three key strategies based on survey findings and a review of the research and national models of best practices. Through this, a "hub model" was conceptualized including a mission statement, key strategies with indicators, and the recruitment of four "pilot ready" sites. Three strategies were identified to serve as the key focus of the hubs:

Strategy One: Broaden community and school supports for aspiring and practicing principals around whole child development. The whole child approach to education requires the engagement of the entire community to ensure that each child is healthy, safe, engaged, supported, and challenged. Through the hubs, aspiring and practicing principals will be connected with community partners to bring needed supports/services into the school.

Strategy Two: Provide professional development and supports for principal preparation programs and school districts on how to develop leaders who can build and support culturally responsive practices. Cultural competency occurs when the school community respects and values diversity in theory and practice; and teaching and learning are made relevant and accessible to students of various cultures, races, and ethnicities. The hubs would broker connections for aspiring and practicing principals to existing supports and services on building culturally competent practices that support academic and behavioral success, ensure access to full range of school services and activities for all students, and engage students and their families in the school community.

Strategy Three: Develop regional/local talent management strategies tied to supply/demand and succession planning, including a focus on a diverse educator pipeline. Enacting regional/local talent management strategies will ensure that districts and universities recruit and support school leaders that are the right fit for their schools and communities.

Through external funding (grants from the US Department of Education and the Stone Foundation), the "hub" concept was piloted at four Regional Offices of Education (ROE) in Illinois: ROE #19, ROE #17, ROE #1, and ROE #28. Although other organizations and entities were considered to pilot this model, ROEs seemed the most naturally suited to expand their organizational capacity to accommodate this work. While most ROEs already have well-established systems of supports for teachers, there is a void statewide for supports for school leaders. Through the hub concept, it is an expectation that the work in the ROEs (although coordinated by the ROE) will also occur hand in hand with other organizational partners, including universities, districts, community members, and other professional development providers. Leadership (LEAD) Coordinators were hired in summer 2018 at the selected four ROEs and are providing the opportunity to explore how ROEs can expand their portfolio of support to educators to customize and coordinate services/supports for school leaders within the hub.

Although the work of the "hubs" is just beginning, they are working with the end in mind. The initial concept originated in ISLAC, but now that it was put into action offers the promise of a new and better day in Illinois for leadership professional development and support. If history is a teacher, then the collaboration and innovative thinking exhibited by ISLAC partners bodes well for a positive outcome.

8 Designing a Continuous Improvement Process to Monitor Program Effectiveness for Illinois Principal Preparation Programs

Joseph Pacha, Lisa Hood, and Kristine Servais

This chapter describes how a Continuous Improvement Process (CIP) grant, funded by the McCormick Foundation of Chicago, supported methodologies to improve implementation of the new rules governing the preparation of principals in the state of Illinois for selected principal preparation programs. This chapter will address the following questions: (1) How did the new Illinois principal preparation requirements inform the Continuous Improvement Process grant from the McCormick Foundation? (2) What was accomplished by four preparation programs in the 18-month grant period as they worked to improve their programs and develop a continuous cycle of improvement process? (3) What can others learn from this work, including the use of the tools developed through the grant?

The McCormick Foundation funded the Evaluation Capacity Building Project to provide coaching support and technical assistance to selected principal preparation programs to build the program stakeholders' evaluation capacity. As such, stakeholders received coaching about building a program evaluation process that systematically collects data for the purposes of monitoring program cohesion and effectiveness. Furthermore, the evaluation process was also tasked with monitoring program fidelity to its initial state agency–approved design, and to make additional program changes based on the results of the data analysis. Each participating program was encouraged to begin the journey of continuous improvement by documenting program policies and practices, identifying the most relevant data to be collected and analyzed, and understanding what processes were driving the goals, expectations, and outcomes of the program (particularly those required by the new rules and legislation).

Program Selection for the Continuous Improvement Process Grant

The Center for the Study of Education Policy (CSEP) at Illinois State University (ISU) put out a request for proposals (RFP) from Illinois principal preparation programs that had been approved the Illinois State Educator

Preparation and Licensure Board (ISEPLB) under the new principal preparation program requirements. Proposals were sought from those that wished to participate in a principal preparation program capacity-building project focused on program continuous improvement and evaluation.

In an era of increased attention to outcomes and the use of data to guide improvement for principal preparation programs (Williams 2015), this project garnered much interest among policymakers and education stakeholders. Rather than a one-size fits all approach; however, this project involved technical assistance from trained evaluation coaches to the selected university and district partners to build capacity within principal preparation programs specifically tailored to meet the needs and design of each program (Huffman, Thomas, and Lawrenz 2008). Although there is not a standard approach to continuous improvement processes for principal preparation programs, this work was conducted in order to develop a general Continuous Improvement Process Framework or a set of models for preparation programs to follow.

The grant project included the following objectives:

- Implementation of a program theory evaluation (PTE) model to identify how policies, practices, and routines have changed as a result of the process of redesigning as well as the identification of goals, assumptions, values, and beliefs that underlie program design and implementation that define how the faculty members believe the program is supposed to work and be effective (Chen 2014; Donaldson 2007; Weiss 1998);
- Creation of a continuous improvement evaluation plan of principal preparation programs (Orr, Young, and Rorrer 2013);
- Alignment of current data and the creation of needed data sources to continuously inform the evaluation planning process (Funnell 2004);
- Provide coaching, technical assistance, and tools to inform the evaluation process, including meeting facilitation, timeline planning, data analysis, and assistance in the change process to move to a continuous improvement evaluation planning process.

CSEP staff and the evaluation coaches were not conducting a program evaluation of the principal preparation programs that choose to participate in the project. At the time of the grant, the redesigned preparation programs in Illinois were too early in their new programs to undergo an evaluation. However, it was not too early to capitalize on the early implementation and focus on the programs' ability to enhance efforts to track the quality and effectiveness of their programs and develop a comprehensive continuous improvement process that could serve as a local and national model (McNall and Foster-Fishman 2007; Orr, Young, and Rorrer 2013; Patton 2008; Sonnichsen 2000; Wholey 1983). In addition, it was believe that the project's findings could inform the Illinois State

Board of Education (ISBE) as to what types of data could be used in the future to monitor program quality and effectiveness.

Illinois principal preparation programs that were interested in participating in the Evaluation Capacity Building Project submitted a proposal to CSEP. The following principal preparation programs responded to the RFP and participated in the project: Loyola University of Chicago, North Central College, Southern Illinois University Edwardsville, and during the last six months of the grant, Western Illinois University. Each program agreed to participate by providing or agreeing to the following:

- Commitment from the department chair and/or the dean that the project would be a priority for the department and that it would devote staff time and attention as was necessary to perform all requirements effectively and efficiently (this may include technology, materials, meeting space, etc.);
- Provide a full copy of the program application that was submitted and approved by the ISEPLB (including a copy of any memorandum of understanding [MOU] from a partnering school/district) and any comments received from the Illinois Principal Preparation Program Review Panel;
- Commitment that program indicators would be shared with the evaluation coaching team when working in partnership with program staff for evaluation and improvement purposes associated with the project;
- Aggregated background summaries of faculty and district partners (per the requirement of the principal preparation design) that would participate in the design and implementation of the capacity building and continuous program improvement process.

The Evaluation Capacity Building Process for Continuous Improvement Work

The continuous improvement process for this project utilized a foundation built on concepts of Evaluation Capacity Building (ECB). "ECB is the intentional work to continuously create and sustain overall organizational processes that make quality evaluation and its uses routine" (Baizerman, Compton, and Stockdill 2002, 109). At the time of this project, the Illinois principal preparation programs had just completed the redesign process and had begun implementation of the new programs. This was an opportune time to provide support to program stakeholders (e.g., faculty and staff) to develop a program evaluation process and incorporate it into their oversight efforts. First, the data collected in this process would be used in annual reports due to state accrediting agencies. Second, program stakeholders (e.g., faculty and their program partners) could use the data to monitor the extent to which the redesigned program was being implemented as planned and make data-informed modifications as needed. Informed by a model of the ECB process outlined by Preskill and Boyle (2008), the evaluation coaches began by convening the peer group of program stakeholders in group meetings to share principles of program evaluation, such as the benefits to the program, sample evaluation designs, methods, and uses of evaluation data for program improvements. This series of learning activities was designed to promote program stakeholders' motivations to engage in the ECB process and to begin their evaluation learning journey. From there, the evaluation coaches began working with the individual programs to discuss program characteristics such as faculty evaluation expertise and motivations to participate in a continuous improvement process. They also explored the impact of program contexts such as the preparation program content and delivery mechanisms, university resources, and characteristics of the school districts the preparation program served. The coaches and program stakeholders discussed program characteristics by identifying existing motivations that would promote the use of the continuous improvement in the preparation program (e.g., complying with requirements), and program stakeholder skill sets to carry out the improvement process (e.g., data collection and analysis skills). The coaches and stakeholders also discussed possible barriers to the program's continuous improvement (e.g., resistance to evaluation, lack of resources, lack of evaluation experience/skills). After these initial conversations, the project's evaluation coaches met as a team and devised a strategy to engage the program stakeholders in the ECB process. Those strategies and the results of this process are presented in the following sections.

Beginning the Work with a Self-Assessment

In evaluation, a program theory or "theory of change" is integral to capturing a vision of what is needed to bring about desired outcomes for participants (Funnell and Rogers 2011; Haeffele, Hood, and Feldman 2011). At the onset of this project, it was important to first capture baseline data from each program. As such, each program was asked initially to complete a self-evaluation of their program to provide a "baseline" of where the program was in relation to where it wanted to be in the implementation of the new state program requirements (Fetterman et al. 1996).

In order to help programs to provide information in a common and practical format, self-assessment tools, the Illinois Principal Preparation Program Self-Assessment Review Tool, and the corresponding Self-Assessment Review Rubric, were created. The self-assessment was a total review of the program's principal preparation offerings; that is, it required each program to review and identify measures or benchmarks for nearly every component that was necessary to be approved under the new Illinois rules and legislation. Programs took time to reflect and meet with faculty, district partners, or others involved in the redesign process.

This was not an easy or quickly completed task. Programs that put forth their best efforts at this first task of self-assessment seemed to reap the most rewards from the project. They began crucial discussions involving the review of new courses, coaching, or other aspects of their program that they felt could be improved based on early implementation feedback. Additionally, program faculty and coaches moved more quickly into discussions about the subject of missing data needed to understand or evaluate whether or not those aspects of the program were truly effective or not.

The evaluation coaches used the self-assessment tool as a springboard for early discussions with the program teams. This provided a safe place to start talking about and discussing each team's program and improvement process, and allowed teams to take the lead as to the topics they wanted to discuss. Teams were asked to identify areas of strength, aspects of the program that they were proud of, and consider additions or modifications to those areas still in need of development.

Those discussions yielded interesting views as each team had new aspects of their program that had been added to address the new rules and regulations. One example was Loyola University, which created coaching positions within their principal preparation program that provided a leadership coach for each of their new program candidates throughout the program, not just during the internship. Another example was the district partnerships that Southern Illinois University Edwardsville (SIUE) sought out for their new program. No prior partnerships had existed, and SIUE worked hard to attain several area school districts as partners for its new program requirements.

The self-assessment tool was the beginning of many fruitful conversations for the teams at each university/college program. It was a vehicle to bring the programs' faculty members together to review their status, to discuss what they liked and did not like, and to decide what data they needed to determine methods for improvement and maintenance in each of the four major components of the principal preparation program: (1) admissions, (2) courses and coursework, (3) the internship, and (4) program graduates' performance in the field. Once each of the programs started looking at their work and their programs as a whole, they continued to "peel back the onion," so to speak, leading to deeper and more substantive conversations about their programmatic components.

Logic Modeling

In addition to the needs assessment, the project team had each of the preparation programs work on logic modeling, to serve "as a form of project map, to illustrate the project's theory of change and make explicit the relationships among the project's resources and activities and its products and outcomes" (Frechtling 2007; Funnell and Rogers 2011; Haeffele, Hood, and Feldman 2011). The staff at CSEP developed a sample logic model that was given to the preparation programs to guide their work (see Table 8.1). Early discussions between the university/college teams and the evaluation coaches focused on the following questions: What exactly is this continuous improvement process work? What does it look like? How will we know if we are on the right track? It was evident that a "roadmap" or process diagram was needed for the teams to use not as a strict guide but merely a starting point that could be used or adapted for use.

Table 8.1 Logic Model—Principal Preparation Program Continuous Improvement and Review Process

INPUTS: (What to invest)	OUTPUTS:		OUTCOMES—IMPACT		
Faculty Time Money Research Materials Technology Partners	Activities: *(What we do)* Review Principal Preparation Programs (Quality Program Assessments and Feedback) Support university personnel in their continuous improvement processes (Process Improvements)	Participation: *(Who we reach)* Principal Preparation Program Faculty members and ISBE University Partners, Faculty, and ISBE	Short Term: *(What the short-term results are)* Improved candidate selection Improved courses and programs Improved Internship Improved graduates of programs	Medium Term: *(What the medium-term results are)* Candidates prepared through quality coursework Candidates ready to perform Internship assessments successfully Candidates prepared to lead schools in improving learning for all students	Long Term: *(What the ultimate impacts are)* Improved learning for ALL students Improved teacher practices Improved school leadership Improved school culture and climate

(Continued)

EVALUATION: 1. Focus—2. Collect Data—3. Analyze and Interpret—4. Report—Repeat the Cycle

Table 8.1 (Continued)

1. Focus:	2. Collect Data:	3. Analyze the results:	4. Report:
1. Program Requirements 2. Internship Requirements 3. Internship Assessments 4. Coursework Requirements 5. Staffing Requirements 6. Candidate Selection	1. Data Collected for Program Improvement 2. Analysis of the Program Improvement Data 3. Program Changes Based on Data Analysis 4. Summative Internship Assessment Data: (Number of candidates; listing of each and all assessments with the scoring of each candidate on the assessment and number of times each candidate needed to complete the assessment successfully; length of the internship for each candidate) 5. Listing of Courses and Course Syllabi 6. Number of candidates and Faculty (FTE) 7. Number of Candidate Applications 8. Number of Candidates Selected 9. Number of Candidate Completers 10. Graduate's School Data Analysis over time	1. Analysis and planning for program improvement based on data 1, 2, & 3 (short-term analysis) 2. Analysis and implementation for improvement for internship and candidate success based on data 4, 5, 6, 7, 8 and 9 (medium-term analysis) 3. Analysis and planning for improvements based on data 10 (long-term analysis)	1. Program Improvement Plan 2. Internship Improvement Plan 3. Candidate Selection Improvement Plan 4. Coursework and Staffing Improvement Plan

Designing a Continuous Improvement Process 219

The logic model created by CSEP staff (Table 8.1) was used as a roadmap by participating programs. It was created as an attempt to diagram for programs the significant items that affect their programs, including inputs, outputs, outcomes and impacts, and evaluation. However, some of the teams expressed an interest in focusing more on the micro perspective (i.e., the specific component parts of the preparation program) rather than the macro (whole program overall). Since the logic model did not resonate with team members as originally thought, its use was limited in early continuous improvement discussions. The logic model was a "big picture" look at the work, whereas teams wanted to get very granular with specific program components. In response, the evaluation coaches retooled the logic model by pairing it with the Principal Preparation Program Continuous Improvement Progress (PPP CIP) Diagram (Figure 8.1).

The PPP CIP Diagram helped the preparation program faculty focus on each of the component parts and the flow of information that would impact the continuous improvement of each. Robust discussions took place regarding various metrics that could be collected and explored to indicate the effectiveness in each of the component parts illustrated in the diagram.

The PPP CIP Diagram was combined with the Logic Model, and seemed to work best in describing what continuous improvement involves for the teams. The four-step continuous improvement process is based upon the quality improvement work done by Walter Shewhart and W. Edward

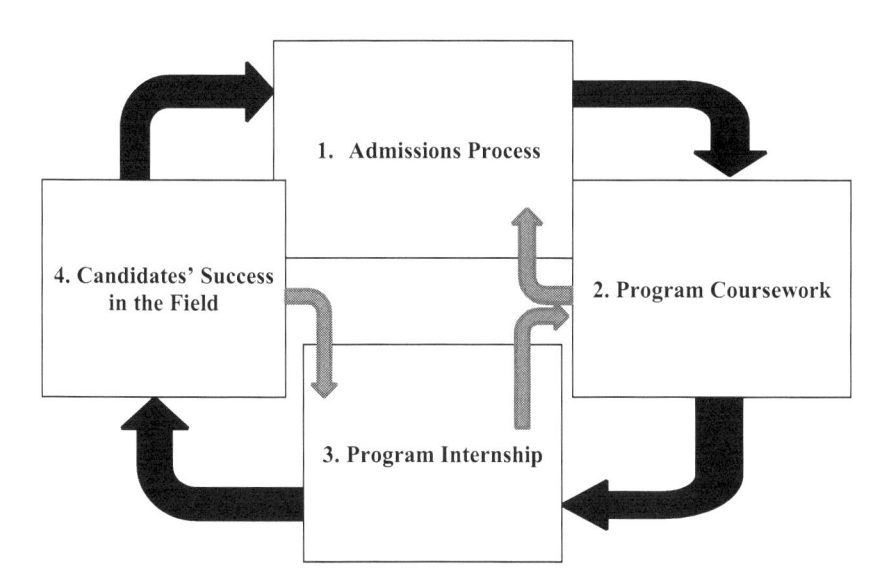

Figure 8.1 Principal Preparation Program Continuous Improvement Process (PPP CIP) Diagram

Deming (Shewhart 1939), pioneers of the quality movement in this country. The Deming Cycle is based on four steps: Plan, Do, Study, and Act to improve any program process (Shewhart 1939). Each of the four steps has been added to and modified since their inception but the basic philosophy remains the same: any process can be improved if the use of the quality improvement cycle is applied and followed using appropriate and significant data for understanding how a process is working and what needs to be improved to make it better.

The PPP CIP Diagram consisting of four simple component processes with feedback loops of data for each component, described and outlined what was to be done within each of the project phases of delivery. Below is an expansion of Figure 8.1 that describes in more detail how it interfaces with the Logic Model and Deming Cycle.

Short-Term—Preparation Program Admissions Process (#1)

- *Plan*—create the recruitment processes; admissions processes; initiation processes; etc. for this first step of the program;
- *Do*—collect data to understand how each of these processes is working;
- *Study*—the data from each of the processes for improvement;
- *Act*—based on the data, make changes to the processes, and work until they become internalized.

Medium-Term—Preparation Program Coursework Processes (#2):

- *Plan*—create/rewrite program coursework; align coursework to standards; align assessments of each course to the standards and to the internship assessments; prepare and implement training for multiple faculty who teach the same courses for continuity of programming and assessments;
- *Do*—collect data from each course's assessments to understand how each course is contributing to the candidates' knowledge and skills to attain the course assessments in preparation for the internship;
- *Study*—the data from each of the course's for course improvement and alignment to the standards and internship assessments;
- *Act*—based on the data, make changes to the courses, alignments, and work to internalize the changes.

Medium-Term—Preparation Program Internship Process (#3)

- *Plan*—create/rewrite internship assessments and assignments; align assessments to standards; prepare and implement training for candidates, mentor principals, and faculty supervisors for continuity of programming and assessments;

- *Do*—collect data from each internship assessment to understand how each candidate is demonstrating knowledge and skills from the coursework; ability to meet the standards of the internship; and, ability to perform as a principal in the field. Collect data on mentor supervisors and mentor principals to inform these processes;
- *Study*—the data from each of the internship assessments to understand the preparation of candidates to be able to meet the internship standards and be prepared to perform in the field as a principal;
- *Act*—based on the data, make changes to courses, alignments, assessments, internship processes, and work to internalize the changes.

Long-Term—Preparation Program Candidates' Successes in the Field (#4)

- *Plan*—create the processes to track successful candidates as they begin work in the field;
- *Do*—collect data to understand how the successful candidates are providing for successful student achievement in the schools they are leading;
- *Study*—the data from each of the candidates working the field for improvement or admissions, coursework, and internship processes;
- *Act*—based on the data, make changes to the processes and until they become internalized.

The Logic Model and Deming Cycle gave teams a visual depiction of what the work was and a simplistic manner in which to attack the component parts. This model seemed to give teams the assurance that the work could be done—albeit not easily—and that they had the capacity to do the work.

A Breakthrough—The Leadership Program Data Collection Process Matrix Tool

The leadership program teams tended to focus on the improvement of the program by looking at the present challenges they were encountering, rather than looking at the bigger picture, and what the team hoped to accomplish with their new preparation programs. The coaches worked to keep teams focused on the total program, and to especially focus on data and data collection methods for all four major components of their programs, in order to be able to understand and evaluate how each component was functioning. It was after one of these discussions that a breakthrough occurred.

The North Central College (NCC) team put together a matrix entitled the Leadership Program Data Collection Matrix. The matrix contained four columns: (1) Program Data Points; (2) Type of Data; (3) Purpose of the Data; (4) Storage of the Data (see Table 8.2). NCC faculty presented this document to the coaches during a coaching session midway through the grant period. It was simple and clear yet a very comprehensive document that displayed every type of data the program was collecting and the purpose for which the data was being collected in each of the four major components of the continuous improvement processes for the program.

As shown in Table 8.2 component one, Program Admissions Points, included data from the candidates' admission into the program, a dispositions inventory, completion of teacher evaluation modules, and the Illinois State Exam for Principal Endorsement. In component two, fieldwork formative assessments from coursework (medium-term outcomes), the program looked at data from fieldwork in courses, formative assessments from courses, and alignment of coursework to the standards and other requirements. The third component, assessments from internship (medium-term outcomes), included data from the internship for the three required state assessment, data from the internship requirements (using SREB competencies), data demonstrating competency of the ISLLC Standards, and other program requirements that yielded data during

Table 8.2 Leadership Program Data Collection Matrix

COMPONENT 1				
PROGRAM ADMISSION DATA POINTS:	Type of Data	Purpose of Data	Storage of Data	How to Use the Data? What areas does it inform?
Admission into Leadership Program				
Dispositions Inventory				
Completion of Teacher Evaluation Modules *Prior to Internship				
Illinois State Exam for Principal Endorsement *Prior to Completion of the Internship				
COMPONENT 2				
FIELDWORK FORMATIVE ASSESSMENTS FROM COURSEWORK	Type of Data	Purpose of Data	Storage of Data	How to Use the Data? What areas does it inform?
Standards Projects:	Field Assignment:	Identify Standards:		

Table 8.2 (Continued)

COMPONENT 3				
ASSESSMENTS FROM INTERNSHIP	Type of Data	Purpose of Data	Storage of Data	How to Use the Data? What areas does it inform?

Assessment #1

Assessment #2

Assessment #3

Assessment #4

Assessment #5

Assessment #6

Assessment #7

INTERNSHIP STATE SUMMATIVE ASSESSMENTS:	Type of Data	Purpose of Data	Storage of Data	How to Use the Data? What areas does it inform?

State Assessment #1

- Part 1.1
- Part 1.2
- Part 1.3
- Part 1.4

State Assessment #2

- Part 2.1
- Part 2.2
- Part 2.3

State Assessment #3

- Part 3.1
- Part 3.2
- Part 3.3

Other Assessments:

OTHER PROGRAM DATA REQUIREMENTS:	Type of Data	Purpose of Data	Storage of Data	How to Use the Data? What areas does it inform?

Capstone Assessment

Dispositions Inventory

(Continued)

Table 8.2 (Continued)

COMPONENT 4				
POST-PROGRAM: FOLLOW-UP WITH CANDIDATE'S FIRST POSITION	Type of Data	Purpose of Data	Storage of Data	How to Use the Data? What areas does it inform?
School Achievement Data				
School demographic data				
School 5 Essentials Survey data				
Other data				

the internship. The fourth component, post-program, included follow-up with candidate's first position (long-term outcomes), post-program follow-up with candidates (such as the candidates' school achievement data), school demographic data, and culture and climate data. This identification process was enlightening, while also somewhat daunting, since it demonstrated the amount of data being collected, but it also begged this critical question: How was the data being used?

It was during this discussion that a fifth column was added to the matrix—How to Use the Data and What Areas Does the Data Inform? The addition of this column brought the data collection and analysis through a full improvement cycle loop. The discussion of the matrix and its new fifth column opened the door to even more ideas about data, whether more data was needed for understanding certain components, and additional data use to inform the program of as to how it was achieving its outcomes. The matrix became the focal point of discussions for several coaching sessions as the NCC team gave permission for the coaches to disseminate the matrix format to other programs involved in the grant, so they could also benefit from its use.

Final Stages of the Grant—Documentation and Continued Growth

It became apparent to all during these discussions that significant documentation of the program was occurring in the final stages of the grant, and all of its components, as well as any changes and updates, needed to be well maintained and frequently discussed among faculty in the program. Although this was not necessarily a new concept, the process needed to be done often and it needed oversight on nearly a daily basis by someone (or teams of people) within the program. Interestingly, several of the teams had embarked on the four-step continuous improvement cycle of Plan/Do/Study/Act without even knowing that they were doing it.

Through the use of the continuous improvement cycle, teams made improvements to processes, courses, and assessments. These changes then became the center of further discussions to see if indeed the changes were effective or not. Coaches continued to ask teams to "document"—that is write down in some fashion—what it was they were doing and what was being changed. One coach was fond of saying, "What if none of you are here tomorrow, who will know what wonderful work you have done and be able to use it in the future for the betterment of the program and its candidates?"

Documentation of work completed by programs is a tedious and thankless job, and one that is not often completed or even attempted. Because of this challenge, many organizations continue to do the same work over and over again and keep asking the question, "Didn't we do this differently at some time in the past?" Without documentation and purposeful communication, organizations fail to use good data to make decisions and do not learn from the past. The organizations involved in this grant began to understand the power of data, effective documentation, and purposeful discussion and communication.

Lessons Learned

Engagement in the continuous improvement process allowed each program to learn something unique about their program, and each had a different focus than the others. A brief synopsis of each program's findings is discussed below.

The grant coaches would agree that North Central College (NCC) made the most progress and achieved most of its goals during the project. This success is due in large part to the fact that it is a small program; therefore, meetings and discussions between the two primary faculty members and the chair were more easily achieved than at the larger universities where multiple faculty members needed to be gathered. Those faculty were also open to change and appreciated the purpose of data collection to improve the overall program. Additionally, NCC was also one of the first programs to be reviewed and to achieve new program approval from the state.

Having completed the approval process early allowed the NCC program to begin their new program sooner than most other programs; thus, when they joined the project, they candidates from their first cohort were just about to start the internship phase of the program. Therefore, they had candidates that had already completed several components of the four phase preparation program, could go back and review what had been done, and look at data for improvement purposes or decide what additional data collection was necessary in order to improve the process. Some of the other programs were just starting with coursework.

The need for more data also spurred NCC to begin the documentation of all their improvement efforts. This need, in turn, led to the internal development of the Leadership Program Data Collection Matrix. This tool was perhaps the "breakthrough" for the NCC team (as well as a source of help to the other teams) as it resulted in many discussions and insights into areas that could be addressed, and data collection points that would help inform the program of its candidates' progress. Two significant tools also came out of this work: (1) the program's Educational Leadership Program Manual and (2) the Educational Leadership Program Internship Manual. Within the two publications, the program was able to clearly document their entire program and could easily retrieve information as needed. These also became invaluable communication tools for candidates and partners.

Loyola University of Chicago also made some great strides during their participation in the project. Meeting discussions with grant coaches, and the team's work outside those meetings, provided much-needed documentation and data necessary for making program improvements. A significant part of their new program was the addition of individual coaches for each of their candidates from the beginning of the program through the internship. Loyola coaches had prior experience as administrators and teachers, and were specifically trained in helping the candidates achieve success during the program. The coaches were especially helpful for candidates as they worked through the new internship requirements.

Southern Illinois University at Edwardsville (SIUE) began working with the project as two new faculty members came on board to help with the implementation of the newly redesigned program. Further, the program was facing stringent university budget restrictions which presented additional challenges to overcome in trying to implement the state's new program requirements successfully. The SIUE program, after completion of their Leadership Program Data Collection Matrix, settled on a path of improvement that included all department faculty members in curriculum meetings, following a professional learning community protocol called a *Tuning Protocol* from the Coalition of Essential Schools. The curriculum meetings, using the tuning protocol, included: (1) a brief five-minute introduction to the meeting; (2) a 15-minute presentation (usually a faculty member sharing their program course content and assessments); (3) five minutes of clarifying questions; and (4) 15-minutes of examination of student work samples. Team leaders provided many examples of how this protocol helped the department make significant changes where there was discovered overlap of content and/or lack of content coverage. These significant "safe" conversations allowed faculty to discuss program requirements and to look at ways to improve the program for candidates.

Western Illinois University (WIU) joined the grant significantly later than the other programs due to the timing of their program application and approval from the state. This delay motivated them to achieve even more in a shorter amount of time since they saw themselves as "behind the others and needing to catch up." WIU made significant progress through meetings with faculty and discussions with coaches in areas of data and assessment documentation, internship process clarification and internship assessments and data. They also benefited from lessons learned by programs that started the project earlier. Through work utilizing the Data Collection Matrix, clarification of coursework content was also made. Finally, WIU's work with their local school partner, Quincy Public Schools, added significantly to the internship implementation and assessment outcomes.

All in all, each program engaged in an internal reflection about their programs. By looking at the admissions process data, programs learned what was helping them make good candidate selections and what areas of the admissions process needed additional improvement. By utilizing the Leadership Program Data Collection Matrix, programs were able to see how coursework either did, or did not, align to the new program standards requirements, and if all content was addressed, if certain content was lacking, or where there were overlaps in the coursework (intentional or unintentional). Additionally, nearly all programs made some coursework assessment and data collection changes based on the discussions at faculty meetings as a result of the project. Every program made a concerted effort to not only document their program and program processes, but to also set up methods for continuous updating of data and documentation so that everyone knew what changes had been made for program improvement and why those changes were deemed necessary. Finally, nearly every program found a new methodology for program improvement that had not been in place before their participation in the project and worked to keep those changes in place, conducting the work for continuous program improvement.

Conclusion

Even though the project ended, it would be of great interest to revisit these programs to determine if the continuous improvement and learning cycles implemented at each college/university continues and what, if any, additional strides have been made to improve the processes to prepare the best principals for the children of the state of Illinois. Additional questions to be answered would be:

- Has the continuous improvement processes and learning continued? Why or why not?
- If not, what could have been done to help cement the methodologies into place to help keep the programs on track? What seemed to be the downfall of the programs not keeping the processes in place and working?

- What could implementers of the original Continuous Improvement Process Project have done better, added to, taken away from, or strengthened during the implementation of the grant?

External funding is not necessarily needed for principal preparation programs to engage in deep internal review. However, two components were identified as the most beneficial from this project. One, the program stakeholders who participated in this continuous improvement process grant suggested that bringing peer universities together into a network developed a community of practice among themselves. Furthermore, and second, stakeholders recognized the value of the external coaches for building the evaluation capacity of faculty and their partners. Although the continual improvement process posed significant challenges, and often vulnerability for these programs, the future improvement of programs in Illinois rests on the commitment of all faculty members to sustain rigor and quality in the preparation of school principals.

Bibliography

Baizerman, Michael, Donald W. Compton, and Stacy Heuftle Stockdill. "New Directions for ECS." *New Directions for Evaluation*, no. 93 (2002): 109–119.

Chen, Huey T. *Practical Program Evaluation: Theory-driven Evaluation and the Integrated Evaluation Perspective*. Thousand Oaks, CA: Sage Publications, 2014.

Donaldson, Stewart I. *Program Theory-driven Evaluation Science: Strategies and Applications*. New York: Taylor & Francis Group, LLC, 2007.

Fetterman, David, Shakeh J. Kaftarian, and Abraham Wandersman. *Empowerment Evaluation: Knowledge and Tools for Self-assessment, Evaluation Capacity Building, and Accountability*. Thousand Oaks, CA: Sage Publications, 1996.

Frechtling, Joy A. *Logic Modeling Methods in Program Evaluation*. San Francisco: Jossey-Bass, 2007.

Funnell, Sue C. "Developing and Using a Program Theory Matrix for Program Evaluation and Performance Monitoring." *New Directions for Evaluation*, no. 87 (2004): 91–101.

Funnell, Sue C., and Patricia J. Rogers. *Purposeful Program Theory: Effective Use of Theories of Change and Logic Models*. Hoboken, NJ: John Wiley & Sons, 2011.

Haeffele, L., L. Hood, and B. Feldman. "Evaluation Capacity Building in a School-University Partnership Grant Program." *Planning and Changing* 42, no. 1 (2011): 87–100.

Huffman, Douglas, Kelli Thomas, and Frances Lawrenz. "A Collaborative Immersion Approach to Evaluation Capacity Building." *American Journal of Evaluation* 29, no. 3 (2008): 358–368.

McNall, Miles, and Pennie G. Foster-Fishman. "Methods of Rapid Evaluation, Assessment, and Appraisal." *American Journal of Evaluation* 28, no. 2 (2007): 151–168.

Orr, Margaret Terry, Michelle D. Young, and Andrea K. Rorrer. *Developing Evaluation Evidence: A Formative and Summative Evaluation Planner for Educational Leadership Preparation Programs*. Center for the Evaluation of Educational Leadership Preparation and Practice: University Council of Education Administration and Utah Educational Policy Center, 2013, www.ucea.org/wp-content/uploads/2014/08/Developing-Evaluation-Evidence-2013.pdf

Patton, Michael Quinn. *Utilization-focused Evaluation*. Thousand Oaks, CA: Sage Publications, 2008.

Preskill, H., and S. Boyle. "A Multidisciplinary Model of Evaluation Capacity Building." *American Journal of Evaluation* 29, no. 4 (2008): 443–459. doi.org/10.1177/1098214008324182.

Shewhart, W. *Statistical Method from the Viewpoint of Quality Control*. Washington, DC: Graduate School of the Department of Agriculture. Reprint 1986. New York: Dover, 1939.

Sonnichsen, Richard C. *High Impact Internal Evaluation*. Thousand Oaks, CA: Sage Publications, 2000.

Weiss, Carol H. *Methods for Studying Programs and Policies*. Upper Saddle River: Prentice Hall, 1998.

Wholey, Joseph S. *Evaluation and Effective Public Management*. Boston: Little, Brown, 1983.

Williams, Sheneka M. "The Future of Principal Preparation and Principal Evaluation: Reflections of the Current Policy Context for School Leaders." *Journal of Research on Leadership Education* 10, no. 3 (2015): 222–225.

Vignette

Instituting a Continuous Improvement Model at the Program Level: Another Version of Groundhog Day?

Kathy Black

The constant attention that universities gave to principal preparation programs after the Illinois state-mandated redesign requirements came out, including its internship and related classes, began to feel a bit like the movie *Groundhog Day*. Meetings on-site, at our interns' schools, and at IL-PART regional meetings all involved continual discussion of the internship requirements with constituents suggesting ideas for implementation and conversations that resulted in tweaking, tweaking, and more tweaking of implementation procedures. In the beginning, there was much ambiguity in how to best implement the internship experience and components were discussed until we reached consensus on high-quality content and fieldwork that interns needed to experience.

In the movie *Groundhog Day*, each sequence began the same way, but each day "Phil" changed his responses, trying to improve his situation. Some days were unproductive; crashing and burning. Other days became more productive, and the project he was involved in was distinctly different from his first version. Similarly, the IL-PART partner meetings with universities and districts focused on how each had modified/enhanced components of their program to meet the spirit of the new principal preparation regulations and institutions benefitted from taking ideas from each other and problem-solving together. During some collaborations, we reached resolve on implementation issues and on others additional discussions and processing were needed to reach an agreement. Partnership teams noted that this collaboration was most important to promote growth and continual improvement within the individual programs. Quality reigned through the by-product of a 232-page toolkit with samples of forms, assessments, and documents that represented several years of work from forty-nine contributors.

The development of the most valuable collaborative product was facilitated by retired Illinois State University faculty member, Joe Pacha, resulting in a Principal Preparation Program Pre- and Post-Assessment, which became known as the 5 Ps. Partners worked laboriously on it, revising and tweaking the content, field testing and revising again. The final product would allow principal preparation programs to measure candidate growth in areas linked to the Illinois Performance Standards for School Leaders. Because of the collaborative efforts, a much richer and effective tool emerged.

For the North Central College principal prep program, the sharing of sample rubrics, products, and ideas in collaborative settings, resulted in improved assessment tools and processes, bringing increased rigor and relevance to our program. These improvements could not have happened without faculty willingness to receive feedback from others and to continually evaluate candidate performance to make changes to improve the program. Candidates hired in principal and assistant principal roles reported our program prepared them to be effective leaders and that "the rigor of the assignments and collaborative group work have given me the skills I need to be successful in this role, serving students, families, and teachers. Every day has been an adventure and a challenge, but one that I feel completely prepared to take on!"

The *Groundhog Day* experience was worth it!

9 Statewide Collaborations for Improvement
Lessons Learned from the State of Illinois

Michelle D. Young and Marcy A. Reedy

In the early 2000s, the state of Illinois identified a critical issue: the lack of quality in educational leadership. Illinois and fifteen other states worked with The Wallace Foundation to strengthen educational leadership throughout state education systems (Wallace 2002). This initiative, State Action for Educational Leadership Preparation (SAELP), however, was merely Illinois' first step in a nearly two-decade journey to support a cohesive leadership system. Over that time, stakeholders in Illinois have engaged in extensive policy advocacy, formation, revision, and implementation through which the state has intentionally improved and supported high-quality principal preparation programs.

The Illinois story is unique in many ways. Unlike the other fourteen states identified and funded by The Wallace Foundation, Illinois consistently focused on supporting quality leadership. The efforts in many other states have been more sporadic, punctuating their state education work with a focus on leadership (Phillips 2013; Young 2013). Furthermore, the Illinois story is one of collaboration, engaging multiple stakeholder groups in meaningful ways. In contrast, many of the efforts in other states during this same time period were more directive. Finally, the Illinois story is a story of success.

The Illinois story provides insight into how statewide efforts can lead to positive change. The process followed in Illinois has led to the adoption of licensure and preparation program approval policies that foster an environment in which high-quality leadership preparation can thrive and low-quality leadership preparation will not be tolerated. Reports from schools and districts indicate that recent graduates of these more rigorous preparation programs are highly recruited (Applegate and Holt 2016). Not only have these initiatives resulted in higher quality programming throughout the state, but they have been tied to promising school outcomes. Lessons can be drawn from the Illinois experience, particularly with regard to how statewide initiatives can support quality leadership preparation and practice. This chapter will highlight some of the most important lessons. This begins with an overview of the context for improvement, and then the delineation of the key steps that Illinois took to create a foundation for statewide collaboration. Subsequently highlighted are key policy and program changes, changes that have already had significant implications for the quality of leadership in the state.

The Context for Improvement

In broad terms, school leadership has not traditionally occupied a prominent place on state policy agendas. According to Dr. Paul Manna in a 2015 report by The Wallace Foundation, "Although nobody would deny that school principals are important, the principal's role has received consistently less attention relative to other topics on state education policy agendas. State policymakers give much more attention to teachers and teacher-related issues than principals" (7). Nonetheless, educational leadership and leadership preparation have not been completely neglected.

Over the last two decades, awareness has grown around the importance of educational leadership, and increased attention has focused on leadership preparation. The research base greatly expanded offering more detailed knowledge about the importance of school leadership (Leithwood and Jantzi 2000; Robinson, Lloyd, and Rowe 2008) and what makes for effective principal preparation (Young et al. 2009). This work has provided important insight into what leadership practices are most impactful for school improvement and student learning, as well as what key program attributes are indicative of an effective program. The latter include a well-defined, leadership-for-learning focus; coherence; challenging and reflective content; student-centered instructional practices; competent faculty; positive student relationships; a cohort structure; supportive organizational structures; and substantive and lengthy internships (Darling-Hammond et al. 2007; Jackson and Kelley 2002; Young et al. 2009).

As the research developed, university preparation providers responded to internal and external criticisms to seek improvements in their preparation programs (Young, and Petersen 2002). Furthermore, increased attention to school leadership has manifested at multiple levels, including federal and state governments, as well as private foundations. The early 2000s bore witness to multiple state and national task forces focused on leadership preparation and an increase in the number of individual scholars who examined the nature of leadership and university-based leadership preparation programs.

Among initiatives by private foundations, The Wallace Foundation has been a leader for the field. The Wallace Foundation's SAELP initiative, for example, was considered the cornerstone of its Leader's Count initiative, a multi-year, $150 million investment. The initiative leveraged state-district collaboration focused on developing policies and practices that strengthen quality leadership and the ability of leaders to support student learning (Wallace 2002). SAELP states like Illinois were expected to develop or enhance requirements for licensing and preparation; provide incentives for leadership recruitment; and support creative and effective working conditions and governance structures. The Wallace Foundation has maintained its focus on leadership, supporting basic research, policy work and professional development. Its most recent initiative, the University Principal Preparation Program Initiative, is a $47 million commitment to improve how aspiring principals are trained. State departments of education and districts are considered critical partners in this initiative.

At the state level, a variety of approaches have been taken to improve leadership preparation and practice. In a few states, attention to school leadership has been accompanied by state-led efforts to specifically address quality of preparation. These efforts have taken a variety of forms, including "the review, revision, sun setting, and/or closure of educational leadership programs, often on a statewide basis" (Young 2013, 249). A 2013 special issue of the *Journal of Research on Leadership Education* documented five state efforts to improve leadership preparation (Phillips 2013). The efforts had several key similarities: (1) each of the states required all university preparation programs to review and redesign regardless of the quality; (2) all but one state (i.e., Florida) began in a collaborative manner; (3) each of the processes started with a program assessment; (4) the processes emphasized developing university-district partners; and (5) the initiatives focused on increasing the amount and intensity of field experiences (Young 2013).

Activity at the federal level has been less robust. The US Department of Education has funded leadership development initiatives, spurring important, though limited, activity when given inadequate funding. Recently, however, the federal Every Student Succeeds Act, authorized in December of 2015, offered a renewed focus on school leadership and recognizes the impact of leaders on school improvement and effective instruction (Young, Winn, and Reedy 2017). The law provides states and districts new opportunities to fund school leadership and explicitly acknowledges leadership as a legitimate target of educational-improvement activities.

Many education leadership faculty members have capitalized on research and development work in the field to redesign the content and delivery of their preparation programs (Young et al. 2009). The state of Illinois has played a leading role in this effort. Indeed, significant attention throughout the state has been focused on understanding and fostering high leverage policy and best practice in leadership preparation.

Establishing a Firm Foundation

The Illinois story has had multiple chapters and has had its fair share of challenges. Like many of the issues confronting our nation over the years, the challenges of educational leadership are complex and interconnected. Key to the success of any effort to meaningfully change, the preparation of school and school-system leaders is a commitment among educational leadership stakeholders to find common ground and work interdependently toward the realization of jointly developed goals (Young, and Petersen 2002). Leaders in Illinois understood this, and they took steps to develop a firm and collaborative foundation based on five key ideas: (1) persons must have the authority to make change; (2) key stakeholders must be included from the very beginning; (3) stakeholders must be authentically engaged; (4) evidence must be used; and (5) additional resources must be sought.

One of the first steps taken was to identify the entity that would convene the effort. It was essential that this entity not only have the authority to make changes but also operate with the intention of making needed changes. With support from SAELP, the legislature passed a joint resolution that enabled the Illinois State Board of Education (ISBE) and the Illinois Board of Higher Education to convene a School Leadership Task Force (Illinois General Assembly 2007). The Task Force was charged with recommending a set of strategic steps to implement improvements in school leadership preparation in the state.

A second important step was the identification of key stakeholders. The joint resolution specified some of these key groups including principals, Chicago Public School principals, educational leadership faculty, private college and university education deans, public university education deans, teachers, superintendents, school board members, the state Board of Education, and the Board of Higher Education. The task force represented a diverse array of viewpoints and experiences, which significantly enriched its work. Furthermore, the expansive engagement ensured the initiative was broadly supported.

Third, the task force ensured that members had adequate time to discuss, define, and build consensus on the problem they were seeking to address. Furthermore, the contributions of the various stakeholders ensured the development of recommendations that broadly represented the values of the education community in Illinois. Building ownership and buy-in through collaboration were critical to the success of the Illinois School Leadership Task Force, just as it has been critical to the success of redesign initiatives in other states (Young 2013). "Only through collaboration can we establish a clear and common agenda, and only through interdependent efforts can we achieve our common goal—the development of competent, compassionate, and pedagogically oriented leaders committed to the successful education of all children" (Young and Petersen 2002, 13). Through their authentic engagement, task force members understood why change was needed, how it would be implemented, and their role in realizing the task force's goals.

A fourth critical step was anchoring the goals, discussions, and anticipated outcomes of the task force to evidence. The task force used a variety of data to understand the problem, to guide conversations and work at critical points of disagreement, and to track whether and how they were moving toward their goals. Research was also used in this way. Data and research grounded all stakeholders in a common mission, vision, and terminology, which greatly supported the program redesign policy efforts. Data and research were also used to communicate with external audiences, both to help them understand the nature of the problem as well as to demonstrate that what they were doing mattered.

Finally, task force leaders worked to attract additional resources to support the work. As they developed more momentum and visibility for their work, attracting funding became somewhat easier. The School Leadership Task Force received funding from The Wallace Foundation, the Illinois Board of Higher Education (IBHE), a CSEP grant, and the McCormick Foundation. These resources were essential to moving the work beyond the initial investment of time and money.

Leveraging Candidate and Program Requirements and the Program Approval Process

What was accomplished in Illinois was just as powerful as how they worked together as a state. The task force provided substantive guidance for the state using the five strategies delineated above and leveraging the growing body of research on school leadership and leadership preparation. In their report to the legislature, the task force made three key recommendations to improve the preparation of principals, including:

1. Develop a specific principal endorsement separate from the general supervisory certificate;
2. Develop new criteria for approving principal preparation programs;
3. Establish a new licensure exam for principals.

The work of the task force and their recommendations led to the development of a state policy environment that supported quality leadership preparation. Subsequently, the state adopted research-informed policies regarding the eligibility for certification and licensure. The state mandated that preparation programs adopt specific program features and increased the rigor of the state program approval process.

Certification and Licensure

Candidate licensure and certification is an essential policy lever for controlling candidate quality, yet policy concerning principal licensure varies across states. According to the UCEA Policymakers Guide, there are seven high leverage criteria that states can use, including teaching experience, a master's degree in educational leadership, completion of an accredited certification program, completion of a licensure assessment that is aligned to standards, completion of a portfolio review, renewal distinguishes between types of licensure, and renewal requires continuing education (Anderson and Reynolds 2015).

Illinois meets four of the seven criteria identified by UCEA. As a result of the task force work, Illinois requires a targeted PK-12 Principal Endorsement designed specifically to prepare principals capable of addressing the challenges faced by today's schools. To gain this endorsement, candidates must have at least four years of teaching experience. Teaching experience is considered essential to the work of educational leadership, given that leaders are the lead learners and teachers. Knowledge and experience with quality teaching are needed to be a strong instructional leader (Young et al. 2009).

Illinois also requires the completion of an accredited preparation program and that program graduates pass an eight-hour exam administered by the state, prior to being awarded a PK-12 Principal Endorsement. Participation in a standards-aligned and research-informed program is essential to leadership success, and licensure that is anchored to preparation in essential leadership skills and knowledge should be standard practice. Licensure is intended to ensure that candidates have the knowledge and skills to lead. Instead of assessing these competencies using a generic exam such as the School Leadership Licensure Assessment (SLLA), the state of Illinois uses an exam that reflects state standards and expectations. Specifically, Illinois requires a competency-based assessment of candidate performance aligned to the Interstate School Leadership Licensure Consortium (ISLLC) Standards (CCSSO 2016), the Southern Regional Education Board (SREB) thirteen critical success factors, and thirty-six leadership tasks (SREB 2005).

Program Criteria

Research accumulated over the last two decades has enhanced our understanding of the features and characteristics of leadership preparation that positively influences leadership practice (Young et al. 2009). Not only does leadership preparation and development shape an aspiring leader's identity, assumptions, and aspirations, but it also builds the knowledge, experiences, and skills needed for successful practice. Task force members capitalized on research and development work in the field to identify key preparation program requirements. For example, the state required that programs change the way they selected candidates for program admission. Now selection involves, at a minimum, two phases. The first phase involves the submission of a candidate portfolio that includes evidence of positive impact on student growth, previous leadership experiences, and exemplary interpersonal skills. Subsequently, candidates participate in face-to-face interviews with program faculty.

A 2006 report from the Illinois Board of Higher Education, *School Leader Preparation: A Blueprint for Change*, argued:

> The primary client of school leader preparation programs is the individual who seeks to be admitted and to complete the program rather than the school districts and the students the graduates will serve. This inevitably results in preparation programs that almost exclusively emphasize the priorities of the leadership candidate, making the needs of school districts, schools, and children secondary. Individuals seek admission to preparation programs for a variety of reasons, including those unrelated to improving student achievement.
>
> (26)

The Illinois School Leadership Task Force understood the importance of anchoring the goals of preparation to the impact of school leadership on student learning. They were also informed by research on leadership preparation that indicated that learning is advanced through university-district partnerships that tailor preparation to the needs of the districts, more closely aligning theory to practice, and use internships that provide candidates with the opportunity to practice in core leadership responsibilities (Anderson et al. 2017). As a result, the state adopted a requirement that formal partnerships be established between principal preparation programs and districts that require faculty to collaborate with school district officials in the design, delivery, and continuous improvement of the principal preparation programs.

Three other requirements are strongly aligned to and dependent upon having strong university-district partnerships. First, the state mandates a yearlong, performance-based internship designed to provide the candidates with authentic leadership experiences intended to increase their proficiency in areas shown to improve student learning. Second, the state mandated collaborative supervision and support of candidates by a faculty supervisor and a mentor principal. Third, the state established minimum qualifications and training requirements for mentor principals and faculty supervisors, including at least two years of experience as a successful school principal and/or superintendent, as evidenced by positive student growth data, and successfully completing state-mandated training and assessments on the new teacher evaluation system.

State Program Approval

Since the introduction of the ISLLC standards in 1996, a number of states have adopted program review and redesign initiatives that involved alignment to state or national leadership standards and the adoption of specific program features, such as expanded field experience requirements

(Baker, Orr, and Young 2007). Although most agree that state program approval is a strong policy lever for initiating program change, few agree that the strategy is always used well and to promising ends (Young et al. 2013). In discussing several cases of state-mandated program redesign, Young (2013) noted:

> In each of the cases, state departments of education required all university-based educational leadership preparation programs to review and redesign their programs regardless of the quality or specific focus of the various programs. Thus, a highly selective program focused on urban leadership with strong partnerships among and endorsements from the field was asked to undergo the same process as a program that offered generic preparation to any student who enrolled in the program.
>
> (249)

Although Illinois did mandate significant changes to preparation programs, Illinois was successful where many other states were not. Illinois' program redesign and approval were informed and fostered by a broad-based and widely supported effort to improve leadership preparation and practice. The idea for a new targeted PK-12 Principal Endorsement designed specifically to prepare principals capable of addressing the challenges faced by today's schools came directly from stakeholders. To ensure that all programs aligned their practice to this new requirement, programs leading to a General Administrative (Type 75) certificate were terminated. Once providers had designed the new leadership programs targeted to prepare PK-12 Principals, they submitted their program redesign to the state for review and approval.

Conclusion

Looking across the states that have engaged in program improvement efforts, one can place states on several continua from orderly to chaotic, from strong communication to weak communication, from collaborative to authoritative, and from effective to ineffective (Phillips 2013). Illinois would be strongly represented on each continua. The Illinois experience, and program improvement results thus far, is evidence that program change can happen on a statewide basis by working in a sustained, collaborative, and comprehensive manner.

According to David Cohen and Jal Mehta (2017), education policy reforms that succeed have several characteristics in common. First, they address problems of substance that have persisted over time. Second, in working to address the root cause of the original problem, they reveal and define new, and often related, challenges. Third, they align their work and the development of solutions with the values of stakeholders.

Fourth, they respond to pressures for change with thoughtful and appropriate recommendations for change. Fifth, and finally, they profile innovative practice and accessible tools to support the implementation of the change. As discussed above, the Illinois State Leadership Task Force incorporated each of these practices into its work.

While it is impossible to identify a single formula for preparing principals that can be universally applied, understanding the practices promoting success in the Illinois experience can provide valuable lessons for future efforts. The lessons to be drawn from the Illinois experiences are of two types: how they approached their work as well as the substance of their work. With regard to the former, the Illinois State Leadership Task Force experience indicates that to be successful: (1) you must have the authority to make change; (2) you must include key stakeholders from the very beginning; (3) you must authentically engage stakeholders; (4) you must use evidence; and (5) you must seek additional resources. The substance of their work, then, reveals the importance of using the state's authority to foster effective practice. Task force members used data and research to identify both what policy levers to use as well as the nature of helpful policy change. Furthermore, task force members advocated for flexibility to ensure that if a policy mandate didn't work or had unintended consequences, it could be modified. Finally, task force members operated as a true professional learning community where data and research-informed practice and authentic communication and collaboration created an environment of trust where all stakeholders felt committed and valued.

The Achilles' heel of many state initiatives is a failure to collaborate authentically. Educational leadership preparation must meet the needs of our current and future school children. All educators and educational stakeholders have this common goal. However, if we are to realize the goal of ensuring the educational excellence and equity for all children, we must first recognize that our work is interdependent. This work will require that stakeholders come together as they did in Illinois, seek mutual and comprehensive understanding of the problems we face and the contexts in which they exist, build shared goals, and work together to realize them (Young, Petersen, and Short 2002).

Bibliography

Applegate, James and Janet Holt. *School Leadership Matters: Illinois Leading Reforms in Principal Preparation*. Washington, D.C.: Education Commission of the States, 2016.

Anderson, Erin, and Amy Reynolds. *A Policymaker's Guide: Research-based Policy for Principal Preparation Program Approval and Licensure*. Charlottesville, VA: The University Council for Educational Administration, 2015.

Anderson, Erin, Kathleen Winn, Michelle Young, Cori Groth, Susan Korach, Diana Pounder, and Andrea Rorrer. "Examining University Leadership Preparation: An

Analysis of Program Attributes and Practices." *Journal of Research on Leadership Education* (2017): 1–23. https://doi.org/10.1177/1942775117735873.

Baker, Bruce, Margaret Orr, and Michelle Young. "Academic Drift, Institutional Production, and Professional Distribution of Graduate Degrees in Educational Leadership." *Educational Administration Quarterly* 43 (2007): 279–318. https://doi.org/10.1177/0013161X07303320.

Cohen, David, and Jal Mehta. "Why Reforms Sometimes Succeed: Understanding the Conditions that Produce Reforms that Last." *American Educational Research Journal* 54, no. 4 (2017): 644–690.

Council of Chief State School Officers (CCSSO). *Interstate School Leadership Licensure Consortium (ISLLC) Standards*. Washington, D.C.: CCSSO, 2016.

Darling-Hammond, Linda, Michelle LaPointe, Debra Meyerson, and Margaret Orr. *Preparing School Leaders for a Changing World: Lessons from Exemplary Leadership Development Programs, Vol. 6*. Stanford, CA: Stanford Educational Leadership Institute, 2007.

Illinois General Assembly. "Senate Joint Resolution, SJR0056." 2007, www.ilga.gov/legislation/fulltext.as DocName=&SessionId=51&GA=95&DocTypeId=SJR&DocNum=56&GAID=9&LegID=33582&SpecSess=&Session

Jackson, Barbara L., and Carolyn Kelley. "Exceptional and Innovative Programs in Educational Leadership." *Educational Administration Quarterly* 38, no. 2 (2002): 192–212.

Leithwood, Kenneth, and Doris Jantzi. "The Effects of Transformational Leadership on Organizational Conditions and Student Engagement." *Journal of Educational Administration* 38, no. 2 (2000): 112–129.

Manna, Paul. *Developing Excellent School Principals to Advance Teaching and Learning: Considerations for State Policy*. New York: The Wallace Foundation, 2015.

Phillips, Joy C. "State-Mandated Principal Preparation Program Redesign: Impetus for Reform or Invitation to Chaos?." *Journal of Research on Leadership Education* 8, no. 2 (2013): 139–151.

Robinson, Viviane, Claire Lloyd, and Kenneth Rowe. "The Impact of Leadership on Student Outcomes: An Analysis of the Differential Effects of Leadership Types." *Educational Administration Quarterly* 44 (2008): 635–674.

Southern Regional Education Board (SREB). *The Principal Internship: How Can We Get It Right?* Atlanta, GA: SREB, 2005.

Wallace Foundation. *Wallace Launches Major State-District Initiative to Strengthen School Leadership*, 2002, www.wallacefoundation.org/news-and-media/press-releases/pages/1-8-02-districtstate.aspx

Young, Michelle. "Is State-Mandated Redesign an Effective and Sustainable Solution?" *Journal of Research on Leadership Education* 8, no 2 (2013): 247–254.

Young, Michelle, Gary Crow, Joseph Murphy, and Robin Ogawa. *The Handbook of Research on the Education of School Leaders*. New York: Routledge, 2009.

Young, Michelle, and George Petersen. "Enabling Substantive Reform in the Preparation of School Leaders." *Education Leadership Review* 3, no. 1 (2002): 1–15.

Young, Michelle, George Petersen, and Paula Short. "The Complexity of Substantive Reform: A Call for Interdependence Among Key Stakeholders." *Educational Administration Quarterly* 38, no. 2 (2002): 137–175.

Young, Michelle, Pamela Tucker, Hanne Mawhinney, Cynthia Reed, Erin Anderson, Gary Crow, Donald Hackmann, Carolyn Kelley, Margaret Orr, Alexandra Pavlakis, Amy Reynolds, and Rod Whiteman. *Leveraging What Works in Preparing Educational Leaders*. New York: The Wallace Foundation, 2013.

Young, Michelle, Kathleen Winn, and Marcy Reedy. "The Every Student Succeeds Act: Strengthening the Focus on Educational Leadership." *Educational Administration Quarterly* 53, no. 5 (2017): 705–726.

Vignette

Principal Preparation Reform in Illinois: Lessons for Greece

Angeliki Lazaridou

After receiving a Fulbright Foundation scholarship in 2013 to study the new principal preparation program in Illinois, I had the opportunity to work under the guidance of Dr. Linda Lyman at Illinois State University (ISU). Through this experience, I immersed myself in the context, practices, procedures, and preparation of school principals in Illinois, including ISU's program. Due to coming from a different cultural background, this experience broadened and enriched my perspectives on how to approach policy change at the state level, leading to successful implementation. The lessons learned not only impacted my career and my work in revamping a program in Greece but could also benefit others initiating a similar change in another state or country.

The research conducted during my four-month involvement at ISU resulted in two publications (Lazaridou 2015; Lazaridou 2017) in which I used contemporary theories of change, leadership, and complexity to interpret the information I collected from multiple sources. I concluded that effecting changes in Illinois' principal preparation program involved a complex, dynamic process that was grounded deeply in a wide distribution of control and leadership as well as the development of interconnected relationships among all interested stakeholders that supported free-flow communications between and among the participants and their constituencies.

Indeed, the success of the whole initiative was the result of the many networks and complex interactions that allowed for new knowledge to develop through nonhierarchical and multi-level structures. What took place in the State of Illinois was a massive *adaptive* change that did not just alter principal preparation programs across the state but *redefined* the notion of school leadership. Moreover, my data confirmed that adaptive change, such as the one that took place at ISU, is not without its costs. Because of its transformative nature, adaptive change challenges people to adjust their values, beliefs, and philosophical systems, to redefine aspects of their identity, to take losses, and to experience uncertainty. All these things occurred during the implementation of the new principal preparation programs in Illinois. Yet, despite all the challenges and resistance, the change was successful in the end because it was seen to serve a higher moral goal: *the betterment of children's learning* in Illinois.

At my home university, I have taught and supervised students for the last ten years in the Educational Administration and Leadership (EAL) program. My research and study of the Illinois principal preparation redesign efforts equipped me with valuable theoretical knowledge about how to approach change, as well as some practical tools for revamping our program.

Recently, the Greek Ministry of Education issued a directive to restructure all graduate programs across the country to conform to principles of social justice, equity, and inclusiveness. In addition to integrating the theoretical knowledge I gained from my research in Illinois into my teaching, I have introduced new courses based on the redesigned principal preparation program curriculum at ISU. One example is the course Introduction to Neuroscience for Principals and Teachers, which is currently being taught in our program at the University of Thessaly.

The ideas for this course came from Linda Lyman's (2016) recent edited book, *Brain Science for Principals: What School Leaders Need to Know*. Our graduate program is the first to teach such a course to future educational leaders in Greece, and to enable this I initiated a translation of the book into Greek. This edition will be published in the fall of 2019. Additionally, I have introduced an in-service mentoring program for teachers and school principals. The program is at the pilot stage, being implemented in one school district. The feedback we have received from teachers and principals are positive, and we hope to expand this venture to other school districts in the near future.

Finally, my immersion in the implementation of the new principal preparation program in Illinois, has taught me that having a clear vision of a better education system is indispensable. Making that vision a reality is an extraordinary challenge that can bear fruit only if funneled through a clear moral purpose, which is the glue that will hold a system together when it courts the disequilibrium that inevitably goes with initiatives to change.

Bibliography

Lazaridou, Angeliki. "Reinventing Principal Preparation in Illinois: A Case Study of Policy Change in a Complex Organization." In *Multidimensional Perspectives on Principal Leadership Effectiveness*, edited by Kadir Beycioglu and Petros Pashiardis, 18–38. Hershey, PA: IGI Global, 2015.

Lazaridou, Angeliki. "Reinventing a University Principal Preparation Programme: Complexity, Change, and Leadership." *International Journal of Leadership in Education* (2017): 1–16.

Lyman, Linda L., ed. *Brain Science for Principals: What School Leaders Need to Know*. New York: Rowman & Littlefield, 2016.

Contributors

Editors

Alicia Haller, PhD, serves as a Co-director of three projects that have been awarded over $21 million in grants from the US Department of Education: IL-PART (School Leadership Program); Partners to Lead (Education Innovation and Research); and TEAM Lead (Supporting Effective Educator Development). An educator with previous experience working in K-12, higher education, and educational philanthropy, she began her career as a teacher and principal in Milwaukee. Prior to partnering with the Center for the Study of Education Policy at Illinois State University and the DuPage Regional Office of Education, she headed the Chicago Public Schools Office of Principal Preparation and Development under then CEO Arne Duncan. She has a strong background in education and policy, having formerly staffed initiatives for the Illinois State Board of Education and the Illinois Board of Higher Education involving improvements to regulations governing principal preparation and development. She received MEd in Instructional Leadership from the University of Illinois at Chicago, a CAS in Human Development and Psychology from Harvard University, and a PhD in Cultural and Educational Policy from Loyola University.

Lisa Hood, PhD, is Senior Policy Analyst and Researcher in the Center for the Study of Education Policy (CSEP) at Illinois State University. In this role, she has administered over $15 million in grants to research and develop policies, practices, and resources for school leaders and teachers to create seamless birth to Grade 12 education systems at the state and local levels. Currently, she is a co-principal investigator on a $12.5 million US Department of Education TEAM Lead (Supporting Effective Educator Development) grant. She also directs projects funded by the McCormick Foundation that focus on developing leaders who understand how to effectively lead early childhood programs and classrooms. She administers a project funded by the Illinois State Board of Education, the B-3 Continuity Project, that provides alignment supports to participating districts and programs in the Illinois Preschool Development Grant program. In the past, she was instrumental in redesigning Illinois state policies related to the preparation of early childhood teachers, principals, and superintendents and continues to support these policies through the work of state policy groups and in the development of resources and supports. She earned a BA in Psychology, an MEd and PhD in Educational Psychology with a concentration in Research Methods and Program Evaluation from the University of Illinois, Urbana-Champaign.

Erika Hunt, PhD, is Senior Policy Analyst and Researcher in the Center for the Study of Education Policy at Illinois State University. She brings experience in state policy as a former staff member for Governor Jim Edgar. She serves on several state task forces, including the Governor's P-20 Education Council and co-chairs the P-20 Council Committee on Teacher and Leadership Effectiveness, which has worked on initiatives around building a diverse educator pipeline, teacher and principal preparation accountability measures, and teacher leadership. She currently co-directs three federal grants including a $12.5 million US Department of Education TEAM Lead (Supporting Effective Educator Development) grant, a $4 million Partners to Lead (Education Innovation and Research) grant, and a $4.6 million US Department of Education IL-PART (School Leadership Program) grant. She also directed a $6 million Wallace Foundation statewide school leadership grant that resulted in key state policy changes, including the redesign of all principal preparation programs under new program requirements. In addition to this work, she is a small business owner of an early childhood center serving over 450 children and forty staff members. She received her BA in English at Illinois College, her MA in Higher Education Administration from Illinois State University, and her PhD in Education Policy at the University of Illinois at Urbana-Champaign.

Maureen Kincaid, EdD, Professor of Education at North Central College, served as the Department of Education chairperson from 2007 to 2016. Since 1998, she has taught courses in elementary literacy, classroom management, social studies methods and children's literature as well as the first-year experience courses. In her tenure as department chairperson, she led the department in the implementation of the edTPA and taught student teaching seminars designed to support candidates through the edTPA process. She has also been actively involved in implementation issues with the redesigned principal preparation program at the state level, participating in the Illinois Principal Preparation Implementation Review Project (I-PREP), the Illinois School Leadership Advisory Council (ISLAC), and as a team member on the Illinois Partnerships Advancing Rigorous Training (IL-PART) Project, a five-year program funded by the US Department of Education.

Editorial Assistance

Jonnell Baskett is the gifted coordinator for School District 186 in Springfield, Illinois. She has served as a teacher, school improvement coach, principal, and district coordinator. A lifelong Illinois resident, she participated in The Wallace Foundation pilot next-generation principal preparation partnership between Illinois State University and School District 186 to receive her MS in Education Administration. She is currently a PhD candidate in Education Administration at Illinois State University, where her research focuses on equity in education.

Chapter and Vignette Contributors

Jim Applegate, PhD, is Visiting Professor in the Center for the Study of Education Policy at Illinois State University and previously served as the State Higher Education Officer for the State of Illinois as well as Senior Vice President and head of grant-making for the Lumina Foundation. He has devoted his career in higher education leadership to dramatically expanding opportunity for college access and success, especially for underserved and adult students.

Debra Baron, PhD, an independent researcher and public policy consultant, has chronicled efforts in Illinois to redesign principal preparation programs. She has also studied early childhood educator preparation reform efforts and school district use of 5 Essentials Survey data to drive school improvement in Illinois.

Kathy Black, EdD, is a retired administrator who served as an assistant superintendent and principal in the public schools. Currently she is an Assistant Professor and the coordinator of the master's programs in Education at North Central College.

Ben Boer is the former Deputy Director of Advance Illinois. He is now an independent consultant working on policy and school improvement efforts.

Pamela Bonsu was a qualitative analyst for the evaluation of the Illinois Partnerships Advancing Rigorous Training (IL-PART) project. As a researcher at American Institutes for Research (AIR), she brought her experience in qualitative research to mixed method evaluations and technical assistance projects in topics that included college and career readiness, early childhood education, educator performance, and principal preparation. She earned a master's degree in Public Health from Columbia University and currently works as a research associate at Oregon Health and Science University.

Michael Boyle, PhD, is the director of the Andrew M. Greeley Center for Catholic Education at the School of Education at Loyola University Chicago. His research interests include developing leadership for faith-based schools and addressing the needs of students with disability in Catholic school settings. He has worked in education in a variety of settings and roles. As a school psychologist at both the high school and elementary levels, he worked with students across a broad range of areas of exceptionality. He has also served as a special education administrator in several public school districts. Additionally, he served as principal in a Catholic elementary school.

Alexandra Broin is a writer, educator, and advocate who currently serves as policy and advocacy director at New Leaders, where she engages partners and school leaders in policy development, advocacy, and communications. She previously worked for the Obama Administration at the US Department of Education and as a middle school language arts and social studies teacher in Denver, Colorado.

Melissa Brown-Sims is Senior Researcher and Project Director at the American Institutes for Research (AIR) with more than twelve years of experience in successfully seeking funding and managing multiple, concurrent, and multi-year projects on such topics as school leadership, district-level transformation initiatives and needs assessments, teacher preparation, teacher evaluation, teacher mentoring and induction, college enrollment, and alternatives routes to certification programs. She earned a master's degree in Social Science from the University of Chicago.

Matthew Clifford, PhD, is Principal Researcher at the American Institutes for Research (AIR). He directs research studies on school-level leadership as it is distributed among staff and manifest in principals, particularly studies of leadership preparation and professional learning; develops products to support school leadership for use by principals and their supervisors; and consults with states and districts on school leadership pipeline policy issues. He is a former secondary teacher and administrator.

Shelby Cosner, PhD, is Professor in the Department of Educational Policy Studies at the University of Illinois at Chicago (UIC). She is also the Director of UIC's Center for Urban Education Leadership. She is an expert is leadership for school improvement, the preparation and development of educational leaders, and leadership preparation program improvement.

Mark Daniel, PhD, is the 12th Superintendent of McLean County Unit 5, taking on the position in July 2014. An educator for twenty-nine years, he was previously superintendent of Dowagiac Union Schools in southwest Michigan. Prior to that, he was principal at Leo Junior/Senior High School in Indiana for twelve years. He also spent three years as assistant principal at the high-achieving, nationally recognized school, where previously taught math and business for many years in addition to coaching football, basketball, baseball, track and golf. He earned his bachelor's degree from the University of Toledo, his master's degree from Indiana University, and his doctorate from Indiana State University in Educational Administration.

Jean Desravines serves as CEO of New Leaders, a national nonprofit organization dedicated to ensuring high academic achievement for all children, especially students in poverty and students of color, by developing transformational school leaders and advancing school leadership policy. As CEO, he has grown the organization to support over three thousand educational leaders in twenty cities and regions and over one hundred charter schools across the country.

Norman D. Durflinger, EdD, is an award-winning leader of K-12 education in Illinois, and the former director of the Center for the Study of Education Policy (CSEP) at Illinois State University. He has served in both teacher and leadership roles in K-12 schools, retiring as a school superintendent, spending most of his career in Morton, Illinois. He is a recognized expert on education finance and has advised the Illinois State Superintendent, Illinois State Board of Education, and numerous school districts on financial issues leading grassroots efforts to pass state laws to strengthen educational leadership.

Judy Erwin is a former Illinois State Representative and Chair of the Higher Education Committee. She also served as the executive director of the Illinois Board of Higher Education from 2005to 2010.

Gail Fahey, PhD, is a retired public school administrator currently working for the DuPage Regional Office of Education (ROE) as the LEAD Grants Project Coordinator.

Michaela Fray currently serves as the Regional Office of Education #1 LEAD Coordinator, serving districts and schools throughout six counties across west central Illinois. Previously, she has served as a teacher, principal, grant coordinator, and district office administrator. Michaela, a lifelong educator, is currently a doctoral student at Western Illinois University in Educational Leadership. She is passionate about school leadership, adult learning, and rural school education.

Carol Frericks currently serves as the Director for Student Services PreK-12 in Quincy School District # 172. As a lifelong educator, her experiences include serving as a superintendent, principal, and district literacy coordinator/coach as well as teaching students as a college professor, secondary science teacher, elementary teacher, special education teacher, literacy interventionist, and Reading Recovery teacher.

Jackie Gran serves as the Chief Policy and Evaluation Officer for New Leaders, where she oversees the organization's efforts to evaluate and learn from programmatic work, inform federal and state school leadership policy, and build a community of leaders through alumni engagement. Previously, Jackie has served at the U.S Department of Education; as a legislative aide to Senator Edward M. Kennedy on the Senate Health, Education, Labor, and Pensions Committee; and as a middle school teacher in New York City.

Cornelia Grumman is the Education Program Director at the Robert R. McCormick Foundation. Prior to joining McCormick, Grumman was the director of policy and strategic communications at the Urban Education Institute at the University of Chicago. Grumman also spent five years with the Ounce of Prevention Fund as the founding executive director of the First Five Years Fund, spearheading the start-up of an influential campaign designed to secure greater federal investments in high-quality early education. With a journalism career spanning more than twenty years, Grumman held reporting duties with the *News & Observer* (Raleigh) and the *Chicago Tribune*, where in 2003 she was awarded the Pulitzer Prize in Editorial Writing for her editorials on capital punishment.

Lynne Haeffele, PhD, directs the Center for the Study of Education Policy (CSEP) at Illinois State University, where she provides research, program evaluation, and policy analysis expertise across a variety of funded projects. She has also been a high school science teacher and teacher educator, and has served as chief deputy superintendent for the Illinois State Board of Education and education policy director for the former Illinois Lieutenant Governor Sheila Simon.

Dean Halverson, PhD, has extensive experience working in PreK-12 education and is a faculty member in the educational leadership program at Western Illinois University.

Herschel Hannah, EdD, is a thirty-year educator who believes in the power of public education to transform lives. He has served students and staff as a classroom teacher, principal, and a cabinet-level administrator.

Holly Hart, PhD, is Survey Director at the University of Chicago Consortium on School Research. She is a mixed-methods researcher with a background in psychology and adult development. As a senior research associate, she has conducted a number of studies focused on teachers and principals throughout their careers.

Cindy Helmers, former assistant superintendent for the Bloomington School District, has spent thirty-five years actively involved with data analysis, assessment and professional development with the vision "If we can measure it; we can improve it." She has conducted a substantial amount of statistical research and evaluation while serving as a classroom teacher, principal, and cabinet-level administrator.

Zipporah K. Hightower, EdD, is a proud graduate and former teacher and principal of Chicago Public Schools. In her current role as Executive Director of Principal Quality with CPS, she takes pride in creating opportunities for aspiring and current principals to expand and grow their leadership.

Janet K. Holt, PhD, is former executive director of the Illinois Education Research Council at Southern Illinois University Edwardsville.

Patricia Huizar served as the Illinois Partnerships Advancing Rigorous Training (IL-PART) Coordinator and LEAD Coordinator/Coach for the Team LEAD Project. She worked for the Archdiocese of Chicago for twelve years, six years as a teacher and six as an administrator. Huizar previously worked with partner universities, Diocesan Offices of Education, and CCSE staff to assist in creating systems to address the expanding needs of Catholic schools. She holds a BA in Spanish, a BS in Biology, and an MEd from Loyola University Chicago as well as an MA in School Administration from Dominican University.

Brad K. Hutchison is the Coordinator of P-12 principal preparation programs in the Education Administration and Foundations Department at Illinois State University. He also serves as the Vice President of the Illinois Council for Professors for Education Administration (ICPEA) and serves on the Board of Directors for the Illinois School for Advanced Leadership (ISAL), also acting as an ISAL coach for practicing superintendents. He is the former superintendent of Olympia CUSD 16 School District and served in multiple education roles spanning from teacher, coach, counselor, assistant principal, principal, director of curriculum and technology, and assistant superintendent over his long career in education.

Michelle Hanh Huynh is Research Specialist at the University of Chicago Consortium on School Research.

Janice Jackson, EdD, is a former student, teacher, principal, network chief, and chief education officer, and now serves as CEO of the third largest school district in the country: the Chicago Public Schools. She is a forward-thinking educator who is focused on improving excellence, equity, and access in all CPS schools. Her efforts, along with those of Chicago's dedicated teachers and principals, have propelled CPS students to record-breaking academic gains and have caused education experts across the country to regard Chicago as a national leader in the field of urban education.

Mark Jontry has served as the Regional Superintendent of Schools for DeWitt, Livingston, Logan, and McLean Counties since 2008 and currently serves as the President of the Illinois Association of Regional Superintendent of Schools. He earned his BA in History Education at Eureka College in 1994 and his master's in Educational Administration from Illinois State University in 2001.

Adam Kennedy, PhD, is Associate Professor of Early Childhood Special Education in the School of Education at Loyola University Chicago. He oversees the field-based Early Childhood Special Education program and develops the community partnerships upon which this program rests. His research focuses on field-based B-5 educator preparation, as well as investigating the development of teachers' perceptions of cultural responsiveness and authentic approaches to assessment and intervention with infants, toddlers, and preschoolers with special needs.

Kathleen King is Assistant Professor of Education at North Central College, focusing on the graduate Educational Leadership and Teacher Leader programs. She has served as a teacher, curriculum director, assistant principal, principal, and district technology director in K-12 schools, including a school recognized as a national service-learning leader school.

Brenda K. Klostermann, PhD, is Associate Director and Assistant Research Professor at the Illinois Education Research Council at Southern Illinois University Edwardsville.

Christopher Koch, PhD, was appointed as President of the Council for the Accreditation of Educator Preparation (CAEP) in October 2015. He previously served as Illinois State Superintendent of Education from 2006 to 2015 and in a variety of administrative capacities at the Illinois Education agency since 1994. Koch served on the board of the Council of Chief State School Officers (CCSSO), including as president from 2010 to 2011. In addition, he was selected by the Council to serve on the presidential transition team in 2008.

Angeliki Lazaridou is Assistant Professor of Educational Administration and Leadership at the School of Humanities and Social Sciences, University of Thessaly, Greece, and a Fulbright Scholar at Illinois State University (2013). Her main research interests are principalship, school leadership, values and ethics, and women in leadership positions.

Dan Montgomery began his career as a English high school teacher and is currently the President of the Illinois Federation of Teachers and also serves as a Vice President of the American Federation of Teachers (AFL-CIO), where he serves on the Executive Committee with President Randi Weingarten. He is a vice president of the Illinois AFL-CIO; a member of the Illinois Educational Funding Advisory Board and serves on the boards of directors of the Albert Shanker Institute, the Center for Tax and Budget Accountability, and Chicago's Theater Oobleck. He served seven years as a director of the National Board for Professional Teaching Standards and is a trustee of the Lincoln Academy of Illinois. He received his BA in English summa cum laude from the University of Michigan and holds an MSEd from Northwestern University.

Diane Morrison, EdD, most recently served on the faculty of Loyola University Chicago, Department of Education and was executive director of the Center for School Evaluation, Intervention and Training, now serving as a consultant for numerous school districts and cooperatives across Illinois. She received her Bachelor of Arts in Education from Ohio State University, her Master of Arts in School Psychology from Illinois State University, and her Doctorate of Education from Loyola University Chicago.

Joseph Pacha, EdD, is a former high school principal and superintendent in Iowa with thirty-five years of experience in K-12 education. Using his experience and expertise as a teacher and school administrator, he joined the faculty of Illinois State University to help in the preparation of school administrators and became involved in the reforming of principal preparation programs in the state of Illinois.

Amber Stitziel Pareja, PhD, is a former senior research analyst at the University of Chicago Consortium on School Research and currently serves as the Executive Director of Institutional Research at Illinois Mathematics and Science Academy.

Marcy A. Reedy is a Project Director with the University Council for Educational Administration (UCEA). She specializes in educational policy and coordinates UCEA's policy and advocacy work. She is currently coordinating a comprehensive review of state ESSA plans, with a specific focus on the use of Title II funds for educational leadership development initiatives.

Elliot Regenstein is a Chicago-based partner with Foresight Law + Policy, whose work focuses on education policy. He has been a member of the Illinois Early Learning Council since 2004 and served as its co-chair from 2004 to 2009.

Jill Reis is the current Regional Superintendent of Schools for Adams, Brown, Cass, Pike, Morgan, and Scott Counties. She began work at the Regional Office of Education in 2010 as the assistant regional superintendent and became the regional superintendent in 2015.

Dianne Renn, PhD, is Associate Professor in Educational Administration and Foundations at Illinois State University and has served as an evaluator for several statewide projects funded by the Illinois State Board of Education and the Illinois Board of Higher Education. She previously taught in urban public schools and the teacher education program at Alverno College in Milwaukee.

Darlene Ruscitti, EdD, is the Regional Superintendent of Schools for DuPage County, Illinois, and the first woman to be elected to this position. Her experience includes myriad appointments to education and business committees, numerous awards for educational excellence, and under her leadership, the DuPage ROE has secured millions of dollars in grants to provide critical educational programs to schools.

Diane Rutledge, PhD, is the former superintendent of Springfield Public Schools District 186 and executive director of the Large Unit District Association (LUDA). She is currently a partner with District Leadership Solutions (DLS) and continues her work in support of leadership development.

Mary Kay Scharf, EdD, served as a principal and administrator for twenty-nine years. She currently provides leadership coaching to area principals and supervises principal interns through Illinois State University.

Kristine Servais, EdD, is a former teacher and principal, Associate Professor at North Central College, and most recently, a leadership coach of Lifeline for Courageous Leadership, LLC. She was at the forefront for leadership change in Illinois as a participant in the Illinois School Leader Task Force, the Illinois Partnerships Advancing Rigorous Training (IL-PART) Project, the Leadership to Integrate Learning (LINC) project. Servais has published numerous articles and several books on leadership, *The Courage to Lead: Choosing the Road Less Traveled* and *The Courage to Grow: Leading with Intentionality*. She has done widespread presentations in Illinois and at national conferences and continues to be an advocate for learning and growth for all leaders, including herself.

Sara R. Slaughter is currently the Executive Director of the W. Clement & Jessie V. Stone Foundation, which funds early childhood education, and education and youth development in five major urban areas. She has over thirteen years of experience in philanthropy. Prior to joining the Stone Foundation, she served for ten years as the director of the Education Program at the Robert R. McCormick Foundation, focused on building a system of quality early care and education for Illinois children from birth to third grade. In addition to her philanthropic experience, Slaughter's career spans the fields of law and government.

Audrey Soglin is the Executive Director of the Illinois Education Association (IEA), the statewide teachers' union that represents 135,000 education employees. She started her career as a teacher in Evanston, Illinois, and taught there for twenty-five years. Prior to her current position, Soglin was the director of the Center for Educational Innovation for IEA and the executive director of the Consortium for Educational Change, a not-for-profit organization associated with IEA, focused on collaboratively improving student learning and achievement.

Robin Steans currently serves as Board Chair of the Steans Family Foundation, where she helps guide education and community development grantmaking in the North Lawndale and North Chicago communities. A former teacher and longtime Chicago public school parent, Steans has spent nearly thirty years working to improve school programs and policies. Most recently, Robin served as executive director of Advance Illinois, a bipartisan, nonprofit education policy and advocacy organization working to ensure every child in Illinois has access to quality schools.

Lenford C. Sutton, PhD, is Professor and Chair of the Department of Educational Administration and Foundations at Illinois State University, where he has held an academic appointment for the last four years. The results of his research have been published in a variety of journals, including *Educational Considerations, International Journal of Education Reform*, and the *Journal of Education Finance*.

Steve Tozer, PhD, is Professor Emeritus in the Educational Policy Studies Department at University of Illinois at Chicago. Prior to retiring in 2018 after thirty-six years on faculty at the university, he was founding coordinator of the UIC EdD Program in Urban Education Leadership and founding director of the UIC Center for Urban Education Leadership.

Carol Webb, EdD, is a faculty member in the educational leadership program at Western Illinois University with extensive experience working in PreK-12 education.

Joyce Weiner is Policy Manager at Ounce of Prevention Fund, where her advocacy efforts have focused on expanding teacher preparation and professional development opportunities for teachers and administrators supporting Illinois' youngest birth-to-eight learners.

Bradford R. White is the Director of Research and Evaluation at Southern Illinois University Edwardsville's East Saint Louis Center. In his previous role with the Illinois Education Research Council, his research focused on school reform and human resource management in education.

Lora Wolff, PhD, has extensive experience working in PreK-12 education and is a faculty member in the educational leadership program at Western Illinois University.

Michelle D. Young, PhD, is Professor of Leadership at the University of Virginia. Young works with universities, practitioners and state and national leaders to improve the preparation and practice of educational leaders and to develop a dynamic base of knowledge on excellence in educational leadership. Her work is published in the *Educational Researcher*, the *American Educational Research Journal, Educational Administration Quarterly*, and the *Journal of Educational Administration*, among other journals. She is the editor of the *Handbook of Research on the Education of School Leaders*. Her work has significantly increased the focus of education research on leadership preparation and brought that research to bear on the work of policymakers. Young is currently chairing the revision of national educational leadership preparation standards and serves as the president of the National Policy Board for Educational Administration.

Angie Zarvell is the current Regional Superintendent of Schools for Bureau, Henry, and Stark Counties. She began work at the Regional Office of Education in 2002, became assistant regional superintendent in 2004, and regional superintendent in 2011.

Index

Note: Page numbers in *italics* indicate a figure and page numbers in **bold** indicate a table on the corresponding page.

Administration and Supervision (Ad/Su), program redesign by 147, 149
Advance Illinois 76, 99–101, 202
advocacy coalition 51
Advocacy Coalition Framework (ACF) 21, 28–33, 48–50; absence of another forum 40–42; deep core beliefs 32, 33; diagram of *30*; external disruption(s) 35–36; external events *30*, 31, 52–53; external pressure 45–46; forums to discuss principal preparation **41**; funding of 42–43; involvement of actors with legislative or regulatory authority 47–48; levers of policy change 42; long term coalition opportunity structures *30*, 53; open forum 46; policy brokers 43–44; policy concepts of 50–53; policy-oriented learning across 36–40; policy subsystem 28–29, *30*; policy subsystem in Illinois 33–34; relatively stable parameters *30*, 31; research 44–45; significant internal event(s) within policy subsystem *30*, 34–35
advocacy organizations, influence of 99–101
Advocates for Children in New Jersey 89
American Educator (journal) 63
American Federation of Teachers (AFT) 63
American Institutes for Research (AIR) 156, 157, 158
American Recovery and Reinvestment Act (ARRA) 99
Ashby, Diane 58

Bell Elementary School (Chicago) 100
Bennett, William 63
Black, Kathy 167–169, 173–174, 229–230
Blinn, Maggie 55
Bloomington Public Schools, Illinois State University and 150, 165–167
Blueprint for Change (IBHE) 65–66, 67, 69, 70, 72, 88, 200, 203
Boer, Ben 99–101
Boyle, Michael 179–183
Brain Science for Principals (Lyman) 242
Broin, Alexandra 55–57, 84–86

Cairney, Paul 50–53
California 89, 91, 94
Campaign for College Opportunity 89
candidate selection and placement, engaging district leaders in 163–165
Career and Technical Education (CTE) teacher 172–173
Catholic Principal Preparation Program (CPPP) 181–182
Catholic schools, preparing leaders of 179–183
Center for the Study of Education Policy (CSEP) 5, 26, 29, 36, 38, 39, 44, 50, 64, 71, 92, 102, 121n2, 125–128, 212–214; *see also* Illinois State University (ISU)

Chicago Leadership Collaborative (CLC) 79–80, 140
Chicago Office of Catholic Schools (OCS) 140
Chicago Principals and Administrators Association (CPAA) 64, 67, 101
Chicago Public Schools (CPS) 10, 27; Chicago Principals and Administrators Association (CPAA) and 67; joint resolution 234; New Leaders and CPS partnership 67–68; partnerships 140; principal eligibility standards 64; story of 79–80; University of Illinois at Chicago (UIC) and 68–70, 80–83; "worst school system in America" 63
Chicago School Reform Panel 63
Chou, Vicki 81
Coalition of Essential Schools: Tuning Protocol 226
Cohen, David 238
Commission on School Leader Preparation in Illinois Colleges and Universities 6–7, 44, 88
Commission on School Leadership 24
competency-based assessment 155–156, 173–174
Consortium on Chicago School Research 74, 77
continuous improvement: applying processes to policy 199–204; certification and licensure 235–236; context for 232–233; distributing program leadership 206; hiring aims 206; lessons learned at University of Illinois at Chicago 205–206; model at program level 229–230; principal preparation implementation 195–196; program cohesion and 203; program criteria 236–237; resolving tensions between comprehensiveness and specialization 197–198; state program approval 237–238
Continuous Improvement Process (CIP) grant 212; beginning work with self-assessment 215–216; diagram of Principal Preparation Program (PPP) *219*; documentation and continued growth 224–225; Evaluation Capacity Building (ECB) for 214–215; final stages of 224–225; further questions for 227–228; Leadership Program Data Collection Matrix 221–222, 224; lessons learned in 225–227; logic model **217–218**; logic modeling 216–221; long-term PPP candidate successes in field 221, **224**; medium-term PPP coursework processes 220, **222**; medium-term PPP internship process 220–221, **223**; objectives of 213; program selection for 212–214; short-term PPP admissions process 220, **222**
Cosner, Shelby 205–206
Council for the Accreditation of Educator Preparation (CAEP) 134
Creating Leaderful Organizations (Raelin) 131
credibility, policy entrepreneur 91, 92
Critical Success Factors for Principals (SREB) 105, **107–110**, 112, 115, 117
curriculum, principal preparation implementation 192, *193*

Danforth Foundation 63
Daniel, Mark 176–178
Danielson framework 24
Deming, W. Edwards 219
Deming Cycle 220–221, 225
Demuzio, Deana 10, 47
Department of Principal Quality (DPQ) 79, 80
Desravines, Jean 84–86
diffusion of innovation theory 125; *see also* policy network(s)
district leaders: candidate selection and placement 163–165; leadership and mentoring 169–170; program coursework and voice 165–167
district-university partnerships: Bloomington Public Schools and Illinois State University 150, 165–167; comprehensive principal preparation in 176–178; principal preparation 150–151; program implementation 188–189, *190*, 196; Quincy Public Schools and Western Illinois University and 150, 169–170; value for program implementation 158; *see also* Illinois Partnerships Advancing Rigorous Training (IL-PART) Project

Index

Duncan, Arne 24, 81, 99
DuPage Regional Office of Education (DuPage ROE) 151, 175–176
Durflinger, Norman D. 102–104
dynamism strategy 91

Early Childhood Special Education (ECSE): faculty engaging in principal preparation redesign 147–148; program implementation 192, *194*
Eason-Watkins, Barbara 81
East Aurora School District, North Central College (NCC) and 150, 183n1
Educating School Leaders (Levine) 35, 62
Education Administrative, and Foundations (EAF) Department 163–165, 207–208
Educational Administration and Leadership (EAL) program 242
Education Commission of the States (ECS) 90, 94
Education Law Center 89
Education Leadership (journal) 72
Elementary and Secondary Educational Act 64
Elmore, Richard 63
Emanuel, Rahm 79
English Language Learners (ELLs) 8, 12, 59, 118, 125–126, 128, 138, 154, 160, 209; program implementation 192, *194*, 197
Enlightenment 51
entrepreneurs: policy 90–92; *see also* policy entrepreneur(s)
Erwin, Judy 23, 24–26
Evaluation Capacity Building (ECB) Project 212, 214–215
Every Student Succeeds Act (2015) 60, 233

Fahey, Gail 175–176
faith-based schools, preparing leaders of 179–183
forum, definition 40–41
Frank E. Newman Award in Policy Innovation 77, 94, 200
Fray, Michaela 170–173
Frericks, Carol 170–173
Fulbright Foundation 241

Gates Foundation 59
Geringer, Jeff 166
Gran, Jackie 55–57
Greece 241–242
Greek Ministry of Education 242
Greeley Center for Catholic Education (GCCE), Loyola University Chicago (LUC) 150, 180–181
Groundhog Day (movie) 229–230
Grumman, Cornelia 26–27

Haller, Alicia 104–106, 118
Halverson, Dean 169–170
Hannah, Herschel 165–167
Helmers, Cindy 165–167
Hightower, Zipporah K. 79–80
Hood, Lisa 104–106, 118, 118–121
Huizar, Patricia 179–183
Hunt, Erika 104–106, 118
Hutchison, Brad K. 163–165

Illinois: certification and licensure in 235–236; context for improvement in 232–233; lessons for Greece 241–242; lessons learned from state of 231, 235–238; principal preparation policy changes (2000–2015) 15, 19–21; principal preparation timeline **16–18**; Professional Standards for Education Leadership (PSEL) 106, **107–117**; program criteria 236–237; reforming principal preparation 92; school leader preparation reform 99–101; state program approval 237–238; story of 231–232, 233–235; supply and demand of administrative positions 103; *see also* policy entrepreneur(s)
Illinois Administrative Code 155
Illinois Association of School Administrators 40
Illinois Association of School Boards (IASB) 48
Illinois Board of Higher Education (IBHE) 5, 7–10, 23, 46, 70, 201; actors with authority 47–48; crosswalk of standards and internship requirements **107–117**; preparing school leaders 24–26; principal endorsement **14**; principal preparation timeline **16–18**; trust and 93–94

Illinois Business Roundtable 101
Illinois Community College Board (ICCB) 9, 70
Illinois Council of Professors of Educational Administration (ICPEA) 13, 40
Illinois Department of Children and Family Services 9
Illinois Department of Human Services 9
Illinois Education Association (IEA) 24, 59
Illinois Education Research Council 40, 77
Illinois Federation of Teachers (IFT) 59
Illinois General Assembly (ILGA) 21, 25, 34, 35, 42; passing legislation 99–100; rules process 100–101
Illinois Governor's Council on Educator Quality 70
Illinois New Principal Mentoring Program (INPMP) 175
Illinois Partnerships Advancing Rigorous Training (IL-PART) Project 150; collaborative supervision and support 156; competency-based assessment 155–156, 173–174; data collection activities 157; district-university partnerships 150–151, 165; graduate hires by position 160; lessons learned 161–162; PEL administrative endorsement achievement 161; perceptions of internship experience 158–160; postgraduate pursuits 160; program outcomes 156–157; selective candidate admissions criteria 151–153; thinking creatively about internship 170–173; value of district-university partnerships for program implementation 158; yearlong performance-based internship 153–155
Illinois Performance Evaluation Reform Act 46
Illinois Principals Association 23, 40, 202
Illinois Professional Educator License Administrative Endorsement 157
Illinois Public Act 096–0903 (2010) 10, 15, 25, 32, 49, 76–77, 88, 118, 125, 127, 200–201, 204; collaborative supervision and support 156; forums to discuss 41; selective candidate admissions 151
Illinois Public Act 096–0861 (Performance Evaluation Reform Act) 36
Illinois Public Act 098–0872 (2014) 21
Illinois School Board Association, principal preparation timeline 17
Illinois School Board of Education (ISBE): crosswalk of standards and internship requirements 107–117; supply and demand of administrative positions 103
Illinois School Code 11, 31, 70, 141
Illinois School Leader Redesign Committees 8–10
Illinois School Leader Redesign Teams 41
Illinois School Leadership Advisory Council (ISLAC) 27, 101, 175, 198, 199–204, 209, 211
Illinois School Leadership Task Force 234, 235
Illinois School Leader Task Force 7–9, 23, 34, 40, 41, 47–48, 71–74; chair of 49; composition of 71; internship discussions 105; principal preparation timeline 16, 17; recommendations of 75–76
Illinois Standards Achievement Test (ISAT) 27
Illinois State Action for Education Leadership Project (IL-SAELP) 5, 10, 14, 35, 36, 38–39, 41, 64, 88; New Leaders 55, 84; open forum 46
Illinois State Board of Education (ISBE) 7–13, 15, 23, 46, 70, 201; actors with authority 47–48; database 49; Educator Licensure Information System 161; preparing school leaders 25–26; principal preparation timeline 16–18; trust and 93–94
Illinois State Educator Preparation and Licensure Board (ISEPLB) 15, 212–213, 214; principal endorsement 14
Illinois State Exam for Principal Endorsement 222

260 Index

Illinois State University (ISU) 57–58, 121n2, 150; Bloomington Public Schools and 165–167; candidate portfolios 153; candidate selection and placement 163–165; case in policy network 129–130; Center for the Study of Education Policy (CSEP) at 5, 26, 29, 36, 38, 39, 44, 50, 64, 71, 92, 102, 121n2, 125–128, 212–214; Educational Administration and Foundation (EAF) 207–208; *Leading Learning for Stages of Mind* 140; postgraduate pursuits 160; principal preparation program 241–242; Principal Preparation Program (PPP) at 176–178; role of policy network 129–130, 132, 134–135, 137–142, 144; Springfield School District 186 and 64, 66; *see also* Continuous Improvement Process (CIP) grant; policy network(s)
Illinois Task Force for School Leadership 99, 239
implementation *see* program implementation
Individualized Education Program (IEP) 59, 125, 155
innovation: decision process 138; definition 126; diffusion of theory 125; *see also* policy network(s)
Institutions of Higher Education (IHEs) 81–82, 157–159, 204
internship(s): creative thinking about 170–173; competency-based requirements 104–106; ISU's Principal Preparation Program (PPP) 178; perceptions of experience 158–160; policy changes to principal **107–117**; principals' thinking and new requirements 167–169; status of certification attainment by type *161*; yearlong performance-based 153–155
Interstate New Teacher Assessment and Support Consortium (INTASC) 63–64
Interstate School Leadership Licensure Consortium (ISLLC) 64; faith-based schools 179–183; principal preparation standards **107–117**; standards 11, 19
Irvin, April 55

Jackson, Janice 79–80, 83
Joint Committee on Administrative Rules (JCAR) 12–13, **18**, 100–101
Jontry, Mark 208–211
Journal of Research on Leadership Education (journal) 233

Kennedy, Adam 147–149
Koch, Christopher 23–24, 70

Large Unit District Association (LUDA) 76, 87, 101, 119, 121n2
LAUNCH model 67, 68
Lazaridou, Angeliki 241–242
Leadership to Integrate the Learning Continuum (LINC) 26, 39, **41**, 46, 135, 145n1; Advisory Group 9
Leahy, Jason 23
Learning Forward standards 155
Leithwood, Ken 63
Levine, Arthur 5, 6, 24, 62, 64–65
Levine Report 5, 7, 44
Lockenvitz, Jeff 166
Loyola University Chicago (LUC) 150; case in policy network 130; collaboration with Early Childhood Special Education (ECSE) faculty 147–148; collaboration with school psychology faculty 148–149; continuous improvement process 226; Evaluation Capacity Building Project 214; Greeley Center for Catholic Education (GCCE) 150, 180–181; in policy network 130, 132, 134–135, 137–138, 140–142, 144–145; principal preparation EdD program 147–149; self-assessment 216; *see also* Illinois Partnerships Advancing Rigorous Training (IL-PART) Project; policy network(s)
Lyman, Linda 241, 242

McCormick Foundation 9, 26–27, 38, 42, 125, 188, 202, 212, 235
Manna, Paul 77, 232
Mayborn, Frank W. 105
Mehta, Jal 238
Montgomery, Dan 59–60
Morrison, Diane 147–149
Multi-tiered Systems of Support (MTSS) 149
Murphy, Joe 11, 105

National Assessment of Educational Progress (NAEP) 65, 72
National Council for Accreditation of Teacher Education (NCATE) 7, 44, 134
National Louis University 67
National Standards and Benchmarks for Effective Catholic Elementary and Secondary Schools (NSBECS) 179–183
Nation at Risk, A (National Commission on Excellence in Education) 62, 63
network(s) *see* policy network(s)
New Jersey, 89, 91, 97
New Leaders 10, 55–57, 64, 77, 83; Chicago Public Schools and 67–68; continuous improvement of 86; internship experience of 85; model for principal preparation program reform 84–86; recruiting in selection process 84–85; school district partnerships with 86
No Child Left Behind (NCLB) 31, 35, 36, 45, 64, 73
North Central College (NCC) 150; candidate portfolios 153; case in policy network 130–131; changing thinking with internships 167–169; continuous improvement process 225, 225–226, 230; East Aurora School District and 150, 183n1; Evaluation Capacity Building Project 214; *Leadership for the Twenty-First Century* 140; Leadership Program Data Collection Matrix 221–224, **222–224**, 226; in policy network 130–131, 132–137, 139–142, 144; postgraduate pursuits 160; *see also* policy network(s)

Office of Network Support 80
Ounce of Prevention Fund 101

Pacha, Joe 230
Parent Teacher Association 119
partnerships: alliances and equity through 208–211; strategies of 209–210; training and 204; *see also* Illinois Partnerships Advancing Rigorous Training (IL-PART) Project

Performance Evaluation Reform Act (PERA) 36
policy broker(s) 29, 36, 42, 45; Advocacy Coalition Framework (ACF) 43–44; policy subsystem *30*; sovereign and 51
policy change over a decade or more 51
policy entrepreneur(s) 90–92; collaboration for collective impact 94–96; communication by 95; coordinating role of 95; credibility 91, 92; development of common agenda 94; networking and advocacy by 92–93; shared measurement by 94; trust in 93–94
policy feedback process 128
policy learning 51
policy network(s): coherence of resulting programs 140–141; emphasis on field experience 141–142; essential elements of change 133–136; faculty adjustments 142–144; Illinois State University (ISU) 129–130, 132, 134–135, 137–142, 144; implementation process 131–133; literature review 127–128; Loyola University Chicago (LUC) in 130–132, 134–135, 137–138, 140–142, 144–145; methods 129; network supports 204; North Central College (NCC) in 130–131, 132–137, 139–142, 144; partnership focus 138–140; process completion time 136–138; redesign team composition 131–133; sample baseline and case profiles 129–131; value of, to members of 144–145; Western Illinois University (WIU) in 131, 132–135, 137, 139–144
policy transfer (local to state): Chicago Public Schools (CPS) and Chicago Principals and Administrators Association (CPAA) 67; conditions for change 63–64; CPS and New Leaders partnership 67–68; CPS and University of Illinois at Chicago (UIC) 68–70; from blueprint to policy change (2007–2012) 70–74; policy change *vs* "change at scale" 76–78; program diversity and scalability

74–76; Springfield District 186/ISU partnership 66; turning point for Illinois (2005–2006) 64–66
PreK-20 Commission on School Leadership Preparation 65
principal(s): importance as leaders in early childhood 60–61; supply and demand of administrative positions **103**
Principal Endorsement: approval process for **14**; new PK-12 programs 59–60; Type 75 certificates 102–104
principal preparation: aligning redesign of, to superintendent and teacher leadership programs 118–120; distributing program leadership 206; district-university partnerships providing comprehensive 176–178; diversity roles in improving program 205–206; hiring for expertise and orientation 206; implementation of programs 187–188, 196–198; integrating early childhood content into 126; ISLLC standards (2008) **107–108, 112, 115–117**; LEAD districts for 87–88; logic model for continuous improvement program 216–217, **217–218**, 219–221; networking and advocacy 92–93; New Leaders as model for reform of 84–86; outside faculty redesigning courses 147–149; policy change process 4–15; policy changes in Illinois (2000–2015) 15, 19–21; research of 3–4; standards for **107–117**; statewide teacher unions 59–60; timeline for Illinois **16–18**; *see also* Illinois Partnerships Advancing Rigorous Training (IL-PART) Project; policy entrepreneur(s); program implementation
Principal Preparation Program Review Board (PPPRB) 13
Principal Preparation Program Review Panel (PPPRP) **14**, 15
Principal Preparation Steering Committee (PPSC) 12, 13
Principal Story, The (PBS program) 99
Professional Standards for Education Leaders (PSEL) 106, **107–117**

Program Advisory Council (PAC) 139
program implementation 187–188; candidates filling vacancies 196; continuous improvement 195, 195–196, 197–198; curriculum 192, *193*; data and methods 188; findings 188–196; implications of 196–198; instructional leadership *193*, 197; mentoring and internships 192, 195; organizational management *193*, 197; partnerships in 188–189, *190*, 196; recruitment and enrollment 189, *191*; special student populations 192, *194*

quality, school leadership programs **6**
quality assurance 203–204
Quality Counts 72
Quincy Public Schools (QPS): principal internship experiences with Western Illinois University (WIU) 170–173; WIU and 150, 169–170, 227
Quinn, Pat 10, 21, 100

Race to the Top (RTTT) 24, 35–36, 46, 99
Raelin, Joseph 131
Reading Recovery teacher 172
Regenstein, Elliot 60–61
Regional Offices of Education (ROEs): alliances and equity through 208–211; DuPage ROE 151, 175–176
Reis, Jill 208–211
Renn, Dianne 118–121
Robert R. McCormick Foundation *see* McCormick Foundation
Ruscitti, Darlene 208–211
Rutledge, Diane 57–58, 87–88, 199–204

Sabatier, Paul, 28
scaling policies *see* policy transfer (local to state)
Scaling Up Success (Dede et al) 62, 77
Scharf, Mary K. 165–167, 207
School Leader Preparation: A Blueprint for Change **16**, 24, 35, 70, 200, 237
School Leadership Licensure Assessment (SLLA) 236

School Leadership Program (SLP) 150, 165; nine-point template for judging quality of **6**
school psychology faculty, principal preparation redesign 148–149
self-assessment tools 6, 215–216
Shewhart, Walter 219
Slaughter, Sara R. 26–27
Smith, Mike 10, 47
Soglin, Audrey 24, 59–60
Southern Illinois University Edwardsville (SIUE): continuous improvement 226; Evaluation Capacity Building (ECB) Project 214; Leadership Program Data Collection Matrix 226; self-assessment of 216; *Tuning Protocol* 226
Southern Regional Education Board (SREB) 11, 19, 174, 176, 200, 236; assessment 155; *13 Critical Success Factors for Principals* 105, **107–110, 112, 115, 117**
special education students, program implementation 192, *194*
Springfield School District 186 64, 66, 72; LEAD district for change 87–88
Stake, Robert 129
State Action for Educational Leadership Preparation (SAELP) **41,** 231–232, 234
State Educator Preparation and Licensure Board (SEPLB) 12–13, 48
state policy changes: collaboration for collective impact 94–96; credibility 92; entrepreneur for 90–92; influencing, with data and messaging 102–104; networking and advocacy for 92–93; reform 89; trust and 93–94
Steans, Robin 99–101
Stone Foundation 27, 209, 210
subsystems 51
Superintendent Advisory Group 118
Superintendent Preparation Program Standards 119–120
Sutton, Lenford C. 207–208

Teachers College at Columbia University 5
Tozer, Steve 23, 27, 71, 80–83, 199–204

Tuning Protocol, Coalition of Essential Schools 226
Type 75 programs 99–100; enrollment 189; general administrative endorsement 59, 81, 102; grandfathered holders of old certificates 49; licenses prior to reform 121n1; number of certificates *vs* vacancies **103**; old system of 167; pool of certificate holders 196, 198; qualifying for 68; reviewing for school success 198; termination of 13, 15, 104, 238

universities *see* policy network(s)
University Council for Educational Administration (UCEA) 77, 200, 235–236
University of Illinois at Champaign-Urbana 101
University of Illinois at Chicago (UIC) 23, 27, 101; Chicago Public Schools (CPS) and 68–70, 80–83; continuous improvement of principal preparation program 205–206; impact of program 83; program design 81–82; story of 80–83
University of Washington 63
University Principal Preparation Program Initiative 233
Urban Education Leadership 82, 205; Ed.D program 68
Urban School Leadership 121n2
US Department of Education 24, 35, 150, 165, 183n1, 210, 233

Vanderbilt University 11, 105
Voices for Illinois Children 101

Wallace Foundation 5, 33, 38, 42, 57, 64, 66, 78, 83, 87, 188, 200, 202, 231, 232–233
Washington, Harold 63
W. Clement and Jessie V. Stone Foundation 27, 209, 210
Webb, Carol 169–170
Weiner, Joyce 60–61
Western Illinois University (WIU) 150; case in policy network 131; continuous improvement process 226, 226–227; Evaluation Capacity Building Project 214; *Leading*

the Core Curriculum 141; in policy network 131, 132–135, 137, 139–144; postgraduate pursuits 160; principal internship experiences with Quincy Public Schools (QPS) 170–173; QPS and 150, 169–170; *see also* policy network(s)

What Matters Most (National Commission on Teaching and America's Future) 63

Wolff, Lora 169–170

Yin, Robert 129

Zarvell, Angie 208–211